THE MEGALITHS OF
NORTHERN EUROPE

The north European megaliths are among the most enduring structures built in prehistory; they are imbued with symbolic meanings which embody physical and conceptual ideas about the nature of the world inhabited by the first northern farmers. *The Megaliths of Northern Europe* provides a much needed up-to-date synthesis of the material available on these monuments, incorporating the results of recent research in Holland, Germany, Denmark and Sweden. This research has brought to light new data on the construction of the megaliths and their role in the cultural landscape, and Magdalena Midgley offers a fascinating interpretation of the symbolism of megalithic tombs within the context of early farming communities. This wealth of new evidence suggests the northern European megaliths were important foci in the wider north-west European context.

The construction of dolmens and passage graves, using huge glacial boulders, demanded both great communal effort and considerable skill. In addition to this technical expertise the master builders also made use of their esoteric knowledge of rituals. This was expressed in the use of exotic building materials and special architectural features, and in the placement of tombs within the natural and cultural landscapes, creating new metaphors and images.

Fully illustrated, this book will be of interest to both undergraduate and postgraduate students of archaeology, prehistoric anthropology and European prehistory, as well as architects who study ancient architecture and social anthropologists who study modern megaliths.

Magdalena S. Midgley is a Senior Lecturer in Archaeology at the University of Edinburgh. Her teaching and research interests are mainly in the European Neolithic. They include early farming communities, monumentality, burial traditions and ceremonial sites. She is also interested in antiquarianism, megalithic representations in art, archaeological theory and the history of archaeology as a discipline.

THE MEGALITHS OF NORTHERN EUROPE

Magdalena S. Midgley

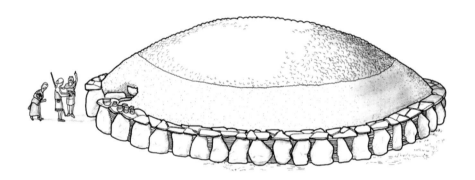

 **Routledge**
Taylor & Francis Group

LONDON AND NEW YORK

First published 2008 by Routledge
2 Park Square, Milton Park, Abingdon, Oxon OX14 4RN

Simultaneously published in the USA and Canada
by Routledge
270 Madison Avenue, New York, NY 10016

Routledge is an imprint of the Taylor & Francis Group, an informa business

© 2008 Magdalena S. Midgley

Typeset in Times New Roman by
Bookcraft Ltd, Stroud
Printed and bound in Great Britain by
CPI Antony Rowe, Chippenham, Wiltshire

British Library Cataloguing in Publication Data
A catalogue record for this book is available from the British Library

Library of Congress Cataloging in Publication Data
A catalogue record for this book has been requested

ISBN 10: 0–415–35180–4 (hbk)
ISBN 10: 0–203–69855–X (ebk)
ISBN 13: 978–0–415–35180–5 (hbk)
ISBN 13: 978–0–203–69855–6 (ebk)

CONTENTS

List of illustrations   vii
Acknowledgements   xii
Preface   xiii

1   Cultural and ceremonial background to the
    north European megaliths   1

    The TRB culture 1
    Before the stones 11

2   Megaliths in thought and space   23

    Preliminary theoretical considerations 23
    Distribution and location of megaliths
      in the landscape 28

3   To build a megalith   43

    General considerations 43
    The dolmens 56
    Passage graves 73
    Principles of chamber construction 82
    Conclusions 107

4   Body and soul   108

    Burial within megaliths – general considerations 108
    Grave goods in dolmens and passage graves 134
    Dressing and adorning the dead 143
    Interpretation of burials 145
    Votive deposits in front of megalithic tombs 148

5   Architects of stone and symbols   155

     Symbolic use of raw materials 155
     Concepts of duality in the megaliths 161
     Megaliths and the wider north European
     *   ceremonial landscape 167*

6   The wider European megalithic context   178

     Megaliths in north-western Europe 178
     Conclusions 193

     Bibliography   201
     Index   218

ILLUSTRATIONS

While every effort has been made to trace copyright holders and obtain permission, this has not been possible in all cases. Any omissions brought to our attention will be remedied in future editions. Diagrams have been redrawn with the kind permission of the copyright holders.

Votive offering ceremony at a passage grave
(Source: adapted from Hansen 1993)   Frontispiece

1.1   Distribution of the TRB culture
      (Source: adapted from Midgley 1992)   3
1.2   Typical examples of TRB material culture
      (Source: adapted from Jażdżewski 1981)   7
1.3   Plan of the Flintbek LA 3 long barrow
      (Source: adapted from Zich 1993)   15

2.1   The 'inner skeleton' of the Luttra passage grave, Falbygden,
      Sweden   26
2.2   Distribution of dolmens in northern Europe
      (Source: adapted from Midgley 1992)   29
2.3   Distribution of passage graves in northern Europe
      (Source: adapted from Midgley 1992)   30
2.4   Distribution of megalithic tombs on the Falbygden plateau
      (Source: adapted from Axelsson *et al.* 2003)   33
2.5   Passage graves at Karleby on the Falbygden plateau, with the
      Ålleberg mountain in the background   34
2.6   Plough marks under the chamber discovered in the process of
      restoration at Maanehøj passage grave on south Zealand   41

3.1   Großer Karlstein megalithic chamber, Osnabrück, Lower Saxony   46
3.2   J. J. Assendorp by the glacial boulder at Karlstein, near
      Neu-Wulmstorf, Lower Saxony   47
3.3   *Spejder Stenen* glacial boulder at Halskov Vænge on the island
      of Falster   47

3.4 Capstone employed to its limits at the passage grave of
Soderstorf, Lower Saxony 48
3.5 Dolmen at Poskær Stenhus on the Djursland peninsula,
Jutland 50
3.6 (a) Dolmen (Naschendorf 2) at Everstorfer Forst, Mecklenburg;
(b) Passage grave at Grønnehøj on western Zealand 52
3.7 Plan of the passage grave in a double stone setting at Thuine in
Emsland (Source: adapted from Schlicht 1979) 53
3.8 Passage grave at Thuine in Emsland 53
3.9 Massive façades at (a) Visbeker Braut and (b) Visbeker
Bräutigam, near Wildeshausen, Lower Saxony
(Ute Bartelt kindly provides the scale in both pictures) 54
3.10 Grønjægers Høj long dolmen on the island of Møn 55
3.11 Reconstruction of Kong Svends Høj passage grave on the island
of Lolland (Source: adapted from Dehn *et al.* 1995) 56
3.12 (a) Reconstructed long dolmen mound at Munkwolstrup,
Schleswig; (b) Long dolmen no. 1 at Mankmoos, Mecklenburg 57
3.13 Christoph Steinmann at one of the guard stones at the great
dolmen of Nobbin on the island of Rügen 58
3.14 (a) Plan of the passage grave (Naschendorf 4), Everstorfer
Forst, Mecklenburg (Source: information from Schuldt 1972);
(b) Western façade at Everstorfer Forst, Mecklenburg 59
3.15 Simple dolmen chambers: (a) Everstorfer Forst (Naschendorf
no. 1), Mecklenburg; (b) Kläden, Lüneburger Heide; (c) and (d)
Two dolmen chambers from the Stokkebjerg Skov long dolmen,
north-west Zealand 60–1
3.16 Plans of dolmen chambers
(Source: information from Aner 1963) 62
3.17 Accessible dolmens: (a) Mürow, near Prenzlau, Brandenburg;
(b) Everstorfer Forst (Naschendorf no. 2), Mecklenburg;
(c) Munkwolstrup, Schleswig; (d) Poppostein, Schleswig 64–5
3.18 South Scandinavian dolmens: (a) Toftebjerg, north-west
Zealand; (b) Torben Dehn at Poskær Stenhus on the Djursland
peninsula; (c) Svend Hansen at Bakkebølle, south Zealand;
(d) Hofterup, south-west Scania 66–7
3.19 Megalithic centre at Tustrup, Jutland: (a) SE dolmen prior to
placement of the capstone; (b) SE dolmen after recent
reconstruction with a capstone placed on top; (c) NW dolmen
without capstone; (d) cult house 68–9
3.20 Dolmen at Haga, Island of Orust, Bohuslän 70
3.21 The entrance arrangements at the great dolmen of Lancken
Granitz 4, seen from inside the chamber, island of Rügen 71
3.22 Dolmen from Utersum, island of Föhr
(Source: adapted from Kersten and La Baume 1958) 72

3.23 Two passage graves from the island of Zealand, showing the position of the passage in relation to the chamber (Source: adapted from A. P. Madsen 1896)   74

3.24 Reconstructed plan of the chamber at König Surbold, on the Hümmling, Lower Saxony (Source: adapted from Laux 1989)   75

3.25 Passage graves with longitudinally arranged capstones: (a) Heidenopfertisch, near Wildeshausen, Lower Saxony; (b) Stöckheim, Altmark   76

3.26 Passage grave D at Sieben Steinhäuser, near Fallingbostel, Lower Saxony (Source: adapted from Schirnig 1982)   77

3.27 (a) Rectangular passage grave at Hjelm, island of Møn; (b) The so-called 'foot-shaped' passage grave at Sparresminde, island of Møn (Source: adapted from A. P. Madsen 1896)   78

3.28 Plan of the axe-shaped chamber at Kong Svends Høj, island of Lolland (Source: adapted from Dehn *et al.* 1995)   79

3.29 Twin passage grave of Klekkendehøj as drawn *c.* 1880, island of Møn (Source: adapted from A. P. Madsen 1896)   80

3.30 Distribution of twin passage graves in Denmark (Source: adapted from Dehn and Hansen 2000)   81

3.31 Two separate chambers covered by a single mound at Snæbum, north Jutland (Source: adapted from A. P. Madsen 1900)   82

3.32 Bi-chambered type of passage grave from Suldrup, north Jutland (Source: adapted from A. P. Madsen 1900)   83

3.33 Tony Axelsson at Karleby 4 passage grave, Falbygden   84

3.34 Principles of chamber construction (Source: adapted from Dehn and Hansen 2000)   85

3.35 Chambers displaying the arrangement of orthostats inclined inwards at the top: (a) Sprove dolmen, island of Møn; (b) Röra dolmen, island of Orust; (c) Troldstuerne passage grave, south chamber looking towards the right from the entrance, north-west Zealand; (d) Knudshoved passage grave looking towards the left from the entrance, south Zealand   86–7

3.36 Passage graves displaying examples of boulders placed on narrower ends: (a) Sparresminde, island of Møn; (b) Ubby Dysselod, north-west Zealand   88

3.37 Dry-stone walling in Danish passage graves: (a) Knudshoved, south Zealand; (b) Sparresminde, island of Møn   90

3.38 Schematic mound stratigraphy at the passage grave of Jordehøj, island of Møn (Source: adapted from Dehn *et al.* 2000)   91

3.39 Unconventional construction of a mound at Birkehøj, north-west Zealand (Source: adapted from Dehn *et al.* 2004)   93

3.40 Examples of intermediary layer construction in South Scandinavian passage graves: (a) Torbjörn Ahlström at Gillhög, Scania; (b) Nissehøj; (c) Maglehøj; (d) Rævehøj (all on Zealand)   96–7

3.41 Elevations of the northern chamber at Troldstuerne passage
grave on north-west Zealand, showing construction of
intermediary layer: (a) entrance wall, (b) back wall
(Source: adapted from Dehn *et al.* 2000) 98

3.42 Post holes in association with megalithic chambers:
(a) Tannenhausen, (b) Tinaarloo, (c) Noordlaren
(Source: adapted from Bakker 1992) 100

3.43 Passages at Danish passage graves: (a) Knudshoved, south
Zealand; (b) Kong Askers Høj, island of Møn 102

3.44 Reconstructed dolmen chamber at Munkwolstrup with burnt
flint covering the chamber floor, Schleswig 103

3.45 Floor partitioning at the great dolmen of Lancken Granitz 2,
island of Rügen (Source: adapted from Schuldt 1972) 106

3.46 Partitioning and floor slabs arrangement at the passage grave of
Gnewitz 2, Mecklenburg (Source: adapted from Schuldt 1972) 107

4.1 Idealised version of Lindgren's drawing of the passage grave at
Onskulle, Sweden, as popularised in megalithic literature
(Source: adapted from Masset 1997) 111

4.2 Early Danish dolmens: (a) section and plan of the Ølstykke
dolmen, north-east Zealand; (b) plan of the Kellerød dolmen,
west Zealand (Source: adapted from P. O. Nielsen 1984) 112

4.3 Human remains in the Grøfte dolmen, south-west Zealand:
(a) Chamber A, (b) Chamber B
(Source: adapted from Ebbesen 1990) 114

4.4 The disarticulated burial in the closed dolmen at Hjortegårdene,
north Zealand (Source: adapted from A. P. Madsen 1896) 116

4.5 Burials in *Urdolmen* in Mecklenburg: (a) Everstorfer Forst
(Naschendorf 1); (b) Friedrichsruhe
(Source: adapted from Schuldt 1972) 118

4.6 Burials in the great dolmen at Liepen, Mecklenburg
(Source: adapted from Schuldt 1972) 119

4.7 Disarticulated remains in the chamber of the passage grave
no. 2 at Nebel, island of Amrum
(Source: adapted from Kersten and La Baume 1958) 121

4.8 Human remains piled inside the passage grave at Uggerslev,
island of Fyn (Source: adapted from A. P. Madsen 1896) 122

4.9 Raklev's plan of his excavation at the passage grave of
Kinderballe (the two levels apparently represent excavation
layers rather than two separate horizons), island of Langeland
(Source: adapted from Dehn *et al.* 2000) 123

4.10 Disposition of human remains in Chamber B at Sieben
Steinhäuser, near Fallingbostel, Lower Saxony
(Source: adapted from Jacob-Friesen 1925) 125

4.11 Disposition of human remains in the passage grave at Liepen 1,
Mecklenburg (Source: adapted from Schuldt 1972)   126

4.12 Arrangement of niches within the Falbygden passage graves:
(a) Hjelmar's Cairn, (b) Rössberga
(Source: adapted from Persson and Sjögren 2001)   130

4.13 Collapsed skeleton of a female aged 40–50 years, discovered
just inside the entrance to the chamber at Frälsegården,
Falbygden (Photograph by Tony Axelsson, reproduced here
with his kind permission)   131

4.14 Plan and sequence of burials in the passage grave at
Landbogården, Falbygden
(Source: adapted from Persson and Sjögren 2001)   132

4.15 Burial and accompanying grave goods from the long dolmen at
Bogø, south Zealand
(Source: adapted from A. P. Madsen 1896)   136

4.16 Burials and grave goods at the passage graves of Oldendorf,
Lower Saxony: (a) chamber II, (b) chamber IV
(Source: adapted from Laux 1980)   138

5.1 Maglehøj passage grave, east Zealand, with birch bark
surviving *in situ* between the dry-stone walling slabs   160

5.2 Ground plan of the twin passage grave at Troldstuerne: the two
chambers are mirror images of each other, rotated along the
main axis which runs through the common orthostat, north-west
Zealand (Source: adapted from Dehn *et al.* 2000)   164

5.3 Ground plans of passage graves at (a) Ubby Dysselod and
(b) Grønnehøj; (c) superimposition of both plans
(Source: information from Dehn and Hansen 2007)   164

6.1 The small chamber of the first phase at Prissé-la-Charrière long
mound, Deux-Sèvres   182

6.2 Bougon long tumulus F, Deux-Sèvres: (a) passage grave F0 at
the south end of the monument, (b) chamberless long mound F1
extending north from F0   183

6.3 Passage grave at La Table des Marchands with a broken menhir
for its capstone, Locmariaquer (Photograph by Serge Cassen,
reproduced here with his kind permission)   184

6.4 The massive chamber at Bagneaux, near Saumur,
Maine-et-Loire (Photograph: S. J. Midgley)   186

6.5 Position of burials in chamber I at La Hoguette
(Fontenay-le-Marmion), Calvados, displaying spatial
arrangements according to sex
(Source: adapted from Chambon 2003b)   190

6.6 Position of burials in chamber C at Condé-sur-Ifs, Calvados
(Source: adapted from Chambon 2003b)   191

ACKNOWLEDGEMENTS

It would not have been possible for me to conduct the necessary research and to complete this book without the involvement of many people. I therefore acknowledge their advice, intellectual stimulus and encouragement, hospitality and help with preparing this work. I am especially grateful to those who took time to travel with me through the countryside and who imparted their knowledge and understanding of the megaliths they know so well. In particular I wish to pass on my thanks to the following: Torbjörn Ahlström, Jan Joost Assendorp, Tony Axelsson, Jan Albert Bakker, Ute Bartelt, Serge Cassen, Torben Dehn, Barbara Fritsch, Svend Hansen, Sönke Hartz, Henning Haßmann, Kristian Kristiansen, Lars Larsson, Torsten Madsen, Johannes Müller, Paul Otto Nielsen, Chris Scarre, Karl-Göran Sjögren, Christoph Steinmann, Jørgen Westphal and Bernd Zich. I also learned a lot from discussing the megalithic issues with Ewald Schuldt and Jürgen Hoika in the past but, alas, they are no longer with us today.

Two individuals deserve particular thanks: Dr Catriona Pickard helped with many tasks involved in preparing this book, including illustrations; and my husband Stephen, as always, helped to improve my English. I thank them both heartily.

The research for this book was carried out partly during the sabbatical period agreed by the University of Edinburgh. I also acknowledge with thanks the financial assistance of the University of Edinburgh Development Trust Research Fund and the Munro Trust.

PREFACE

The megaliths represent the most tangible remains of the Neolithic period in northern Europe. Unlike the contemporary settlements, fields, enclosures and workshops, which have all but disappeared, the megaliths are dramatic and enticing structures with a particularly powerful presence in the flat north European landscape. They have featured in medieval documents and chronicles, as well as in popular fairytales and stories about giants. Later they inspired some of the finest works of art within the northern Romantic tradition, exemplified by such fine paintings as *Hünengrab im Schnee* (1807) by Caspar David Friedrich or *Hünengrab im Winter* (1824/1825) by Christian Dahl. It is hardly surprising that antiquarians, as well as nineteenth- and twentieth-century archaeologists, were attracted to these monuments; indeed they continue to hold our attention today.

The idea for this book arose rather informally. In October 2002 I attended an international conference on European megaliths. It was held in the wonderful museum devoted to megaliths at Bougon, France, with my brief being to talk about the megaliths on the north European plain. Later on that day I was engaged in conversation with a Danish colleague who quite casually remarked that, in contrast to many books on the French megaliths which we were both avidly purchasing at the conference bookstall, there was not really an up-to-date synthesis on those found in northern Europe.

Over the subsequent months, as I was preparing my conference paper for publication, this casual exchange began to develop into a much firmer idea. My Danish colleague may well have regretted that remark, as ultimately he became my principal source of information and advice on the Danish megaliths, answering numerous queries, seeking out obscure publications, and driving me around the wonderful Danish countryside from one megalith to the next. I am hopeful that we still remain friends!

Megaliths have always held a great fascination for me and are the most exciting sites I have ever visited in the field. Indeed, one of my earliest archaeological visits was to that 'Mecca' of European megaliths at Carnac in Brittany. That was long before I knew enough about them to appreciate what I saw, but I remedied this in the summer of 2007 during a whole week of tramping around these fabulous sites, this time with a rather better idea of what I was exploring.

Although I have written briefly about megaliths in my book on the TRB culture (Midgley 1992, Chapter 9), the research for the current work was a very different proposition. While I knew it was impossible for me to see each and every site in northern Europe, in the course of researching for this book I have been privileged to visit many extraordinary places, and have benefited greatly from the knowledge and experience of many colleagues who share my interest in these magnificent monuments. Unlike Christopher Tilley, I did not mind when it was raining; after all, one can always find refuge inside the megalith, provided the capstones are still in place.

One idea which, as a result of my fieldwork, impressed itself very firmly on my mind is that megaliths are dramatic, three-dimensional structures and that two-dimensional plans, while important from the point of view of study, do not do them justice. Indeed, one cannot teach megaliths without taking students to see them! It is for this reason that I have included many pictures of the sites I visited to give the reader ample visual images.

The megaliths are but one element in the complex web of cultural and symbolic manifestations on the north European plain and in southern Scandinavia. To consider them on their own would have meant presenting them in abstract. For this reason, Chapter 1 sets the background in terms of the archaeological culture (the TRB) and the emergence of monumentality in the form of the long barrows which preceded the construction of megaliths in all regions of northern Europe. The sheer number of sites, either still in existence or on record, as well as the geographical size of the area under consideration, make it very difficult to interpret the manner in which megaliths were placed in the landscape but, in Chapter 2, I offer some general principles which may have influenced the different ways by which locations were chosen. Being a firm believer in traditional fieldwork and excavation, I discuss in Chapter 3 the form and the construction of individual sites, to highlight similarities as well as differences in megalithic architecture. Indeed it is through traditional fieldwork that new discoveries are made and thus that interesting ideas on the symbolism of megalithic architecture can be discussed; I explore these ideas in Chapter 5.

Reflecting upon the wider function of the megaliths within Neolithic society, it is imperative that we do not lose sight of the fact that they were used for burial and, in Chapter 4, I offer some interpretations of the various burial practices for which the megaliths provide ample evidence. The ultimate significance of megaliths within the early farming communities is not unique to northern Europe and, for this reason, Chapter 6 presents the wider north-west European background. While some of my conclusions relate specifically to the megaliths in northern Europe, it is hoped that others may be of relevance to the problems of megalithic research in other areas where megalithic tombs were built.

1

CULTURAL AND CEREMONIAL BACKGROUND TO THE NORTH EUROPEAN MEGALITHS

Before the advent of agriculture, northern Europe was a land of hunter-gatherers. The process of transition here, from hunting-gathering to farming, was part of a much wider development that was taking place over the vast area of north-western Europe. Through their agricultural practices, the farmers altered the natural landscape in which they lived: forests were cut to create land suitable for crop fields, meadow pastures and settlements, and natural resources were transformed into economically and socially beneficial goods. Their most powerful and lasting legacy, however, was achieved not so much through agricultural practices but rather through the creation of a rich ceremonial landscape – a theatrical setting for social interaction and for expression, through rituals on a scale never encountered before, of the cosmological principles that shaped their vision of the universe in which they lived.

The most enduring testimony of that distant world view is offered by the megalithic tombs which, in the earlier part of the fourth millennium BC, the northern farmers built across the land in their thousands. It is these tombs, set within the context of the wider ceremonial landscape, that are the subject of this work. However, megaliths in northern Europe began to be built only after the first farming communities were fully established across the area. Even more importantly, they emerged on the scene after the early farmers had already developed a taste for expressing some of their ideas about the world through other ceremonial structures, namely the long barrows. These, although not built of such enduring materials, created architecture which was monumental not only in size but also in its conception, and thus they prepared the way for the subsequent feats in stone. By way of setting the appropriate scene this chapter therefore discusses, however briefly, first the culture and then the earliest monumental creations of the north European farmers.

The TRB culture

The megalithic tombs in northern Europe were created by communities which, in the archaeological literature, are known under the name of the TRB culture (from the German name *Trichterrandbecher* for one of the most characteristic vessel forms of the period, the funnel-necked beaker). The adoption of farming economy in northern Europe began, along the southern fringes of the north European plain, some time during the middle of the fifth millennium BC. At least half a millennium separated these first indigenous attempts and the final appearance of farming in southern Scandinavia. In its final extent, the distribution of the TRB culture was vast – from the Netherlands in the west to south-eastern Poland in the east, and from Bohemia and Moravia in the south to southern Scandinavia in the north – and several regional groups are recognised, which differ slightly from one another in details of material culture as well as chronology (Figure 1.1).

The idea of large-scale colonisation by central European Danubian farmers migrating from the south is no longer supported, and it is generally assumed that hunter-gatherers themselves adopted agriculture, although this does not exclude the movement of individuals as well as smaller communities. While the considerable degree of continuity with the preceding period is important, nevertheless many aspects of everyday life were given a new content and symbolism, not just in terms of novel economy but also, significantly, in the transformations within cultural, social and ideological spheres. In order to illustrate some of these phenomena, we may briefly consider aspects of settlement, economy and industrial developments, all of which demonstrate the originality and profundity of this historically momentous process.

The chronology of the TRB culture

The relative chronology of the TRB culture is based primarily upon the analysis of ceramic styles and is well established in all regions (see Midgley 1992, Chapter 4, for a detailed discussion of typo-chronology). The difficulties in establishing the absolute chronology result from the small number of radiocarbon dates, especially those in the transitional and early stages of the culture, as well as from the complexities of calibration.

In absolute terms the emergence of the TRB culture in its core area, which stretches from Kujavia in Poland to Lower Saxony in Germany, is dated to 4500/4400 BC, and it took at least half a millennium to manifest itself in southern Scandinavia. Dates from the area of Schleswig-Holstein suggest the presence of the TRB from about 4200–4100 BC onwards, and in Scandinavia a little later, from about 4000–3900 BC. The end of the TRB culture, some time between 2900 and 2700 BC, was as complex a process as its emergence. Within the broad north European context, the TRB culture was succeeded by the new cultural complex of the Corded Ware, although the situation is complicated in regional terms by the presence of smaller cultural groups such as the Globular Amphora culture on the north European plain and the Pitted Ware culture in southern Scandinavia.

Within this overall chronological framework the burials in flat graves and in monumental long barrows belong to the earliest horizon, beginning around 4400 BC on the north European plain and from about 3900 BC in Scandinavia; they continue in use until the end of the EN (Early Neolithic in the Scandinavian nomenclature), with

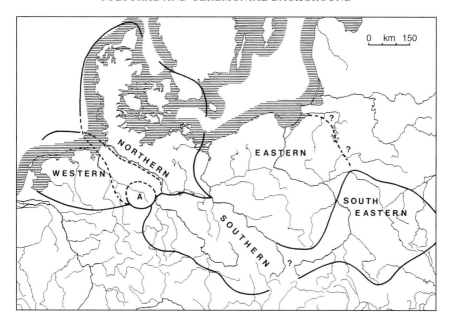

Figure 1.1 Distribution of the TRB culture

flat graves being in use throughout the entire TRB culture. The earliest dolmens contain pottery belonging to the EN II (the earliest dated dolmen is from Rastorf in Schleswig-Holstein, *c.* 3700/3500 BC) and the youngest materials belong to the MN I/MN II ceramic horizon. None of the passage graves contain materials older than MN I, and they continued to be built throughout MN II. Although there is some indication that the passage graves in the Falbygden area of central Sweden might have been built as early as 3500 BC (Persson and Sjögren 1996) the traditional view places most passage graves somewhat later, at around 3300 BC.

TRB settlement and land use

The early farmers in northern Europe chose to settle upon light soils, placing their settlements in undulating landscapes which were interspersed with boggy and marshy areas and stretches of open water. This choice of topography underlined the significance of the dry higher landscape and the low-lying wetter ground; it offered ecological diversity in which the forest, meadow and arable land created conditions suitable for early agriculture but also facilitated the traditional exploitation of wild resources.

Once fully established, the economy of the TRB culture was based on mixed farming, although these resources may have been taken up at varying rates and in accordance with regional climatic and ecological conditions. Cereals of various types (wheats and barley), leguminous plants such as peas and beans, and flax are

3

known from all regions of the TRB culture, although barley seems to have been particularly suited to the cooler climatic conditions of southern Scandinavia. Domesticated animals – cattle, pigs, sheep and goats – were an important source of food in the form of meat and dairy produce, and of raw materials, providing hides, wool and bone for tool manufacture. In the case of oxen, pulling power was becoming economically important, and undoubtedly their ownership also enhanced the social position of individuals and small communities.

Traditional exploitation of wild resources – hunting of game, fishing and fowling – continued alongside agricultural activities throughout the TRB, with farmers making good use of the hunting and fishing stations established along lakes, rivers and coasts during the Late Mesolithic. The lake belt across the north European plain provided a favourable environment for fowling and freshwater fishing, and the forests were abundant in deer, bison, wild boar and a range of smaller animals. Forests and river meadows also provided seasonal edible plants and fungi, as well as various wild fruits which, although rarely attested in the archaeological record, must have been gathered to provide medicines and add nourishment to the daily diet.

In the coastal regions, on the Baltic and along the North Sea, seals, migratory birds and deep-sea fish continued to be caught, and the Mesolithic shell-middens demonstrate that marine shellfish – oysters, cockles and periwinkles – were still collected as important nutritional supplements. Bones of wild animals provided suitable raw materials for manufacture of tools, and the continued, if somewhat diminished, importance of wild animal teeth, boars' tusks and fish vertebrae in the crafting of ornaments suggests that hunting was still an important social pursuit, providing opportunities for gaining prestige and experience outside the ordinary quotidian sphere.

Against the background of the solidity and permanence of the megalithic chambers, the archaeological record with respect to the actual settlement sites is ambiguous. Early TRB settlements generally appear small and of relatively short-lived duration, although this view may to some extent be influenced by the excavation strategies, especially at sites only partially preserved under later monuments such as the Neolithic or Bronze Age mounds. Such seems to have been the case at Sarnowo in Kujavia, where small rectangular houses have been found preserved under the long mounds, although the settlement does seem to have shifted to a higher and drier location by the time the cemetery was being constructed. Similar finds are known from Denmark, for example light buildings found underneath the mounds of Mosegården in Jutland or Lindebjerg on Zealand.

However, recent rescue excavations in western Sweden suggest that we may have underestimated the scale of some of the early sites. At Saxtorp 23, in western Scania, an area of 15,000 m^2 was settled, with clear division of space for dwellings, wells, industrial pits and even burials; while at Dagstorp, another site nearby, there were at least two long houses (of the so-called Mossby type, after a settlement on the south coast of Scania).

Indeed this type of house, long with rounded gable ends and central roof-bearing posts, is now commonly identified on the EN Scandinavian sites and may well represent a characteristic form of early TRB dwelling in this region. Such structures are known from the early phase at Limensgård on the island of Bornholm – the settling of which must have posed a considerable challenge to the early farmers – at Mossby itself and at Dagstorp in Scania, Slottsmöllan and Hästhagen in Halland, and Ornehus on east Zealand. They vary in length from 12 to 18 m and are usually between 5 and 6 m wide. The sites also contain, scattered in between the houses, large numbers of pits full of domestic debris, suggesting that many activities may have taken place outside the actual dwellings. Similar oval houses are known from Lower Saxony, at Wittenwater and Engter (P. O. Nielsen 2004; Andersson 2004; Malmer 2002).

The later TRB settlements display a somewhat different character. Although house structures continue to be elusive, some of the sites can be quite large; thus settlement traces at Spodsbjerg on Langeland covered 300,000 m^2, and at Bronocice in southern Poland the settlement spread out over an area 500,000 m^2 in size. Indeed, in the later TRB some of the earlier ceremonial enclosures, such as Sarup, Siggersted, Hygind and Bundsø, became places of permanent or at least long-term settlement, with rich occupational traces.

The island of Bornholm continued to be occupied during the later TRB, and long houses up to 22 m in length are known from Limensgård and Grødbygård. They appear to have been sturdier than the EN houses, with foundation trenches on at least three sides. The overlap of many of the Grødbygård houses suggests that perhaps only two or three buildings were contemporary (P. O. Nielsen 1999). Further evidence from this island comes from Vasagård and Rispebjerg (Kaul et al. 2002). Vasagård became a large settlement, twice the size of the original EN causewayed enclosure, protected by a double timber palisade. Although there was a large amount of typical domestic debris, certain structures – for instance circular features defined by post holes – as well as the character of some deposits (burnt flint) suggest that cults and rituals continued here alongside quotidian activities. Rispebjerg appears to have been an even more complex site, with at least 14 palisades, the outermost enclosing an area six hectares in size.

That palisaded settlements were quite common in the later TRB is also demonstrated by a number of other Scandinavian sites, for example at Sigersted and Spodsbjerg in Denmark, and Dösjebro near Malmö in Scania (P. O. Nielsen 2004; Svensson 2004). Palisaded sites may suggest a need for a degree of protection, especially in areas where other cultural groups (such as the early Corded Ware) may have been engaged in economic and social competition. The ultimate burning of the palisade at the Dösjebro settlement – a site strategically placed at the confluence of two rivers – although it post-dates the TRB occupation, may be indicative of socially unstable times.

Although houses continue to be elusive on some of these large settlements, once again the Scanian evidence provides some indications of the layout of settlement sites. Thus during the MN period at Dagstorp one rectangular and four trapezoidal houses (some divided into individual rooms) were built side by side, clearly in simultaneous use. Other structures, identified through post holes in between the houses, could represent workshops in small huts or protected by temporary windbreaks, as they contained large amounts of flint and pottery (Andersson 2004, 169).

The 1938–40 excavations at the TRB settlement of Hunte 1, on the Dümmer lake in Lower Saxony, are well known in literature, and this evidence is currently in the process of re-evaluation. Owing to the waterlogged conditions there was excellent preservation of structures and finds, and ultimately substantial information on the construction and use of middle TRB settlements will be available (Kossian 2003).

The settlement, close to the banks of the river Hunte, was first inhabited around 3300–3200 BC, with renewed activity towards the end of the TRB, after 2900 BC. The area in the vicinity of the Dümmer lake and the marshlands around it were clearly inhabited long before the Hunte 1 settlement was established, as the discovery of trackways at Campemoor, to the south-west of the lake, clearly demonstrates (Metzler 2003). The crossing of this peatland must have been of considerable importance, as wooden trackways were being laid there from about 4800 BC, possibly in relation to seasonal hunting and fishing; one of the tracks across the moor was built around 2900 BC, when the Hunte 1 site was certainly in occupation.

The settlement was surrounded by a timber palisade and altogether about two dozen buildings, arranged in several rows, have been recorded, although it is not clear how many structures belong to the initial phase. Domestic activities, within and outside the houses, were represented by remains of hearths and undisturbed flint-knapping residues, suggesting local tool manufacture; the survival of tools and jewellery made of organic materials is particularly important, extending the range of everyday objects made of wood, bone and antler.

The Hunte houses were constructed of pointed ash tree trunks, with a diameter of about 8–20 cm, driven into the ground. Repeated repairs and renovations of plank floors, observed during the excavation, may indicate returns after periodic abandonment of the settlement on account of the rising ground water. These dwellings – with some of the larger houses divided into separate rooms – compare well in terms of size and form with other, more sporadic house finds in Lower Saxony, notably from Flögeln near Cuxhaven and the two recently discovered houses at Pennigbüttel (Assendorp 2004b). The two slightly trapezoidal houses at Pennigbüttel were sturdy, with large timber posts driven into a foundation trench, while the Flögeln house may have been of lighter, wattle-and-daub construction fixed on a framework of several freestanding posts.

Material culture

One of the consequences of the introduction of farming into northern Europe was the development of new crafts and industries catering for the practical as well as the social needs of farmers. The most important among these were mining for flint and mass production of tools, manufacture of pottery, and fashioning of trinkets, ornaments and other everyday items (Figure 1.2).

Figure 1.2 Typical examples of TRB material culture

While small implements such as knives, scrapers, sickles and even arrowheads could usually be made from abundantly available surface flint, the manufacture of axes for forest clearance and woodworking required good-quality flint that had to be quarried from primary sources. The chalky cliffs of the eastern Danish islands, as well as chalky deposits in southern Scania and northern Jutland, provided deeply placed flint deposits that were exploited by means of surface extraction as well as deep-shaft mining. Further south, the flint deposits along the Baltic Sea cliffs on the island of Rügen, as well as the primary flint sources in the Holy Cross Mountains, were among the most intensely exploited materials.

The northern flint mines and workshops, for example at Ålborg, Bjerre, Hov and Kvarnby, as well as the more southerly workshops from settlements in southern Poland which relied upon primary sources in the Holy Cross Mountains – for example at Ćmielów and Świeciechów – provide details of extraction and production processes. These activities were clearly carried out by specialists with expert knowledge of mining techniques, flint properties and tool manufacture. The flint nodules were often subject to on-the-spot quality control: one of the Kvarnby shafts had on its floor about three hundred roughly worked nodules that had been tested and rejected. Similarly abandoned axe pre-forms have also been found in workshops along eastern Danish shores.

Although workshops outside the shafts at Kvarnby show that at least some tools were finished and even hafted on the spot, elsewhere hoards of axe blanks indicate that axes normally left the mines as semi-products, to be worked elsewhere. Evidence from the southern Polish workshops also demonstrates that individual craftsmen worked different types of flint with equal ease – in this case understanding the different properties of the so-called 'chocolate', the Świeciechów and the banded Krzemionki flint varieties.

The polished flint axe is a *tour de force* of the flint industry. Experiments in axe manufacture conducted by Danish archaeologists (as well as those conducted elsewhere, for example by French researchers) show that an accomplished craftsman must have had a precise notion of what the finished product should look like, and that the production of a rough-out (the initial rough form, with only a few hammerings to give it the shape from which an axe would be made) could have been accomplished in about ten minutes. Further knapping for about two hours was needed to produce a well-proportioned axe; but the polishing, which ultimately is responsible for the aesthetics and the excellent working quality of the TRB flint axes, was a truly time-consuming and demanding process, taking from six to thirty hours of work. Moreover, as we shall consider later (Chapter 5), apart from the practicalities of making an axe – or indeed any other object – the spiritual involvement in the production of artefacts represented an equally important aspect of skilled crafting which tends to be forgotten against the background of the industrial process.

Indeed the enormous scale of these industrial activities is difficult to imagine. Not only were the various axe manufacturing centres able to satisfy the seemingly continuous demand for axes as tools, used both locally and for long-distance exchange with communities which did not have direct access to suitable raw materials, but they also produced a surplus used in a variety of votive and ceremonial contexts. Thus an essential everyday tool was also regarded as an important social resource with symbolic meaning, used in complex inter-communal exchanges and freely disposed of in waterlogged locations, at megalithic tombs and in causewayed enclosures (Chapters 4 and 5).

Ceramics are the most common of finds in all TRB culture contexts; the manufacture and use of pottery was clearly very important. The strongly decorative nature of the TRB ceramics, as well as important regional stylistic differences, mean that they feature in the archaeological literature more as an aid to the construction of elaborate typo-chronologies than as a significant element of the material culture enlightening us as to its role in the quotidian and ritual spheres of activity. In everyday life, clay vessels were naturally used for storing and cooking food. Although the late north European hunter-gatherers were keen potters, the TRB vessels were technologically vastly improved. The tempering was increased to withstand high temperatures and to prolong the lifespan of the pot as a cooking vessel, and there was a wide range of forms and decoration.

In the early TRB, bowls were generally used in the mixing and serving of food, whereas beakers may have been used largely as cooking vessels – staining on their exterior walls indicating foods that had boiled over. Later the beakers were replaced by a variety of richly decorated bowls and hanging vessels, and finally simple, virtually undecorated bucket shapes became predominant. Throughout the TRB, flat clay discs were also used in culinary activities; the term 'baking plates' could well be a reflection of their function.

Apart from household activities and possible inter-communal exchanges, from the very beginning, pottery was employed in a wide range of contexts extending well beyond the quotidian sphere. Indeed, the most expertly made and beautifully decorated vessels, such as the *Prachtbecher* or the so-called pedestalled bowls with spoons, were produced primarily for display and for use in ceremonies and rituals. Thus pots, together with other objects, were deposited in bogs and at the edges of lakes (Chapter 5). They were also disposed of at ceremonial enclosures and, as we shall discuss later (Chapter 4), played a significant role in the funerary ritual: pots accompanied the dead as grave goods and were also used in ceremonies that involved extravagant destruction of vessels, and presumably their contents, outside the megalithic tombs.

Although pottery and flint tools are the commonest components of the TRB material culture, many other crafts for which we either have the evidence or can make reasonable inferences were also practised. Crystalline rocks, for instance, were used in the manufacture of different forms of the so-called battleaxes, which are found throughout the entire distribution of the TRB culture. Whether these were standard weapons used in conflicts or whether they had a largely ceremonial and status function is difficult to determine. Malmer considers battleaxes as 'splendidly and expertly varied sculptures in stone ... with no value as tools and inefficient as weapons' (Malmer 2002, 34). However, the evidence of devastating blows to the head and other parts of the body, seen in some of the skeletons preserved in the Scandinavian bogs (Chapter 5), suggests that battle and strife were more than just a casual occurrence within TRB society, and there is no doubt that, if necessary, an implement such as a battleaxe could inflict serious damage, although bow and arrow were most probably an even more lethal weapon. On the other hand, the deposition of such items in ceremonial contexts, for example the beautifully fashioned battleaxe discovered at Sarup II (Andersen 1997, Figure 106), does suggest a largely ceremonial and prestige role for such objects.

Among other notable crafts we should also mention woodworking – not just in the context of house construction and interior furnishings, but in terms of more intricate objects. Wooden vessels, spoons and other domestic utensils must have been common, but they survive only rarely (for example at Hunte 1 or in the Scandinavian bogs). While amber, bone and (later) copper were important raw materials in the manufacture of personal jewellery and other trinkets, many ornaments would also have included wooden components. Moreover, dug-out canoes and other sailing paraphernalia undoubtedly continued the earlier Mesolithic traditions, with travel and transport of goods by water not only an efficient form of communication along the rivers and coastlines, but quite simply essential between islands. The previously noted settling of the island of Bornholm is a remarkable testimony to the navigational skills of the northern farmers, and sea travel would have constituted a very important Neolithic craft.

The demise of the TRB culture

The end of the TRB culture some time between 2900 and 2700 BC was, like its origins, a complex process. It is poorly documented in the archaeological record, and its interpretation remains largely intuitive. In global terms the TRB culture was succeeded by another pan-European phenomenon, the largely pastoral Corded Ware culture, although the situation is complicated further by the presence of other cultural components such as the Globular Amphora culture on the north European plain and the Pitted Ware culture in southern Scandinavia.

Although fanciful notions of horse-mounted eastern warriors were invoked in the past to explain the appearance of the Corded Ware culture in Europe, it now seems that a local, if regionally diversified, emergence is a more appropriate working hypothesis. There is sufficient evidence to show a degree of continuity and to demonstrate that the processes of social and economic change that led to the emergence of the Corded Ware culture can be perceived within the later TRB itself. The exploitation in the later TRB of secondary animal products, such as milk and wool, began to alter the overall role of cattle and sheep, leading to an increase in the size of herds, which in turn led to the expansion of grazing areas, and resulted in a change from a largely mixed to a predominantly pastoral economy.

Summary

While intellectual orthodoxies see the introduction of farming economy in northern Europe as leading to social and ideological change, the evidence suggests that alterations in subsistence and diet need not have been the prime mover. The archaeological record indicates that, while the proportion of domesticated foodstuffs was increasing steadily, the principal changes originated in the spheres of ideology and social relations, and that they ultimately led these communities to an entirely singular vision of themselves and their role in the world around them. This vision possessed its own energy and led to new initiatives. One such direction was the emergence of monumentality, and it is this development to which we should briefly turn now, before we can move on to consider the phenomenon of the north European megaliths.

Before the stones

The megalithic tombs that form the main subject of this work are the most enduring expression of the monumental funerary tradition in northern Europe. However, in this region at least, the megaliths represent an elaboration of an earlier tradition of monumental burial structures which relied predominantly on timber and earth – the so-called long barrows. The latter, on account of their raw material, have not fared as well as the virtually indestructible glacial erratic boulders, and thus their number is much smaller in comparison with the known megaliths. On the other hand, better field methods and reconsideration of older excavation reports have considerably increased the number of long barrows known across many areas; we can assume them to have been a widespread phenomenon.

It is these monuments, with their timber chambers, wooden façades and huge earthen mounds, that form the prelude to the emergence of the megalithic structures. Indeed, although from about 3700 BC timber was being largely abandoned in the construction of burial chambers in favour of the more durable stone, it continued to be employed – on a massive scale – in other ceremonial sites, the so-called Sarup-type (or causewayed) enclosures. Thus the interplay between timber and stone architecture continued for quite some time, and it is simply the manner in which archaeologists go about discussing and interpreting the categories of sites – long barrows, enclosures and megaliths, often as unrelated to one another – that has created the dichotomy between the timber- and stone-built monuments. It is improbable that those who used long barrows, megaliths and enclosures ever made such a distinction themselves, although they undoubtedly had views on the desirability, appropriateness and symbolism of the materials they used.

I have recently discussed the European monumental long barrow cemeteries (Midgley 2005), and the interested reader is referred to that work for details. Here we shall therefore consider only some very general aspects of these monuments, which are pertinent to our understanding of the transition from timber to stone in burial ritual in northern Europe.

Long mounds in their natural landscape

The tradition of monumental burial structures in northern Europe thus commences with massive earthen mounds piled upon timber-built chambers. In some areas these mounds form veritable cemeteries, for example in Kujavia, Little Poland, western Pomerania and parts of Lower Saxony. The argument that the Danubian villages, with their imposing long houses, provided an inspiration for the creation

11

of the long barrow cemeteries in this zone, where the northernmost enclaves of the Danubian farmers were adjacent to those of the newly emerging TRB communities, has been discussed many times and requires no repetition here (Midgley 1985, 1997a, 1997b, 2000, 2005).

However, it is significant that further north – for example in Schleswig-Holstein, Denmark or Sweden – the long barrows do not form cemeteries but tend to be found singly or in pairs. In these regions, the Danubian world would have been known at some remove, based perhaps on the surviving ancestral accounts of hunter-gatherer contact with farming peoples further south; nevertheless the idea of a mound imitating an ancient long house must have been an attractive and symbolically significant proposition to have permeated that far north.

Sometimes these long barrows form the initial core of a subsequently larger concentration of monuments, with stone chambers replacing timber ones, for example along the river Warnow in Mecklenburg, where several megalithic groups in fact have a long barrow in their midst. At Onsved Mark in north Zealand the recently investigated group of megaliths also commences with a long barrow with a timber-built chamber and a timber façade (Kaul 1988) and at Flintbek, Schleswig-Holstein, in an area of about 12 km^2, at least three long barrows represent not only the earliest mounds in the large group of prehistoric monuments but, significantly, they all contained timber- and stone-built chambers side by side (Zich 1993, n.d.a, n.d.b).

The location of long barrows in the natural and cultural landscapes is important. The deliberate choice of elevations surrounded by boggy, marshy areas, or in close proximity to water can be demonstrated everywhere from southern Poland to Denmark. The location of the Kujavian long barrows is well known (Midgley 1985, 37; 2005, 82); the barrows of the monumental cemetery at Słonowice in Little Poland converge slightly towards the west, which is the direction towards the nearby river (Tunia 2003), and a classic example is offered by the site of Barkær, on the Djursland peninsula in Jutland, where a pair of barrows was built on a hill in the sea inlet of Kolind Sund (Glob 1949; Liversage 1992, 13–16). Indeed I have argued that in some cases such elevations were seasonally cut off by flood waters from the surrounding landscape – becoming, temporarily at least, 'islands of the dead' (Midgley 2005, 82–4).

The significance of such locations should not be underestimated. They may reflect important ancestral locales, of economic and social significance to the preceding hunter-gatherers and thus imbued with special meaning for the subsequent TRB farmers. Furthermore, the proximity of water may have distinguished symbolically between the worlds of the living and the dead; such a use of natural landscapes might have ensured that the dead were retained within their appropriate locales.

Recently Bradley, drawing upon a wide range of evidence from prehistoric Europe, has emphasised once again the very close relationship between the domestic and non-domestic spheres, noting among other things the recurrent link between mortality, house structures and the agricultural cycle (Bradley 2005).

Indeed, the long barrow provides one of the most evocative examples of these relationships.

The location of these mounds upon abandoned settlements and ploughed fields is a widespread characteristic, evidenced throughout all areas where such structures are encountered. Although we have evidence that some north European hunter-gatherers were burying their dead within and in close proximity to their settlements, for example at Skateholm and Vedbæk (Albrethsen and Brinch Petersen 1977; Larsson 1988b, 1995, 2004), it is really with the construction of the first burial mounds that the relationship between houses – ancient and contemporary – and tombs acquires a new meaning. Similarly, while Mesolithic burials may have had some relation to natural resources – for example the location of the Skateholm cemeteries on a sea lagoon may, among other things, have emphasised fishing rights – within the context of the first monumental burial structures, farming activities and death are given a new symbolic and ritual dimension.

The early interpretation of one of the barrows at the Sarnowo cemetery, Kujavia, as placed upon an earlier ploughed field has been fairly controversial, but there is now a considerable body of evidence demonstrating that many long mounds were built upon cultivated fields. This is seen at barrows as far apart as southern Poland and Denmark. One of the two recently excavated barrows at Zagaj Stradowski in southern Poland has clearly been placed upon an old field (Burchard 1998, Figure 2). Thrane (1982) has studied the placement of long barrows in Denmark, unarguably establishing that many were placed upon previously cultivated fields, with plough marks surviving under the protective mantle of the mounds.

While the placement of a monument upon a ploughed field can be demonstrated practically, the interpretation of this phenomenon has been polarised in the archaeological literature between ritual ploughing prior to the creation of the monument and accidental survival of the plough furrows under the mound (Rowley-Conwy 1987; Kristiansen 1990). However, there is another way of looking at this phenomenon that may help to explain the close relationship between cultivation and the dead, and this will be explored later (Chapter 6).

A further important common feature is the foundation of the long barrows upon disused settlements, although sometimes this has contributed to false interpretations, considering the denuded long mounds as remains of long houses. Indeed, the original interpretation of the two Barkær long barrows as remains of two Danubian-style long houses was not unreasonable in the context of the then current thinking (Glob 1949), while other Danish sites, for example the two structures at Stengade, have been argued to represent house remains. However, it was precisely here in Denmark that appropriate field research methods and re-evaluation of older records helped to correct this perception and to identify many of the long barrow characteristics.

In northern Europe many barrows were located upon earlier TRB settlements, and this encompasses numerous Kujavian and western Pomeranian cemeteries, for example Sarnowo, Gaj, Leśniczówka, Łupawa, and the cemetery of Sachsenwald not far from Hamburg. Further north the individual barrows were also located upon disused settlements. Such was the case at Flintbek (barrow LA 3) where some traces of settlement, as well as ard marks, were encountered; and the location of Danish barrows on recently abandoned TRB settlements is very well documented at Lindebjerg, Mosegården, Konens Høj and Stengade, to name but the most obvious examples. Indeed, sometimes the graves are placed within the foundations of houses. At Bjørnsholm, the TRB community used the earlier Ertebølle shell-midden for establishing their own settlement and, when that was abandoned, a grave was dug into an old TRB house foundation and subsequently covered with a mound (S. H. Andersen and Johansen 1992, 54 and Figure 4), making it abundantly clear that such a placement was intentional. Indeed, a similar interpretation may be given to the location of the grave at the eastern end of Bygholm Nørremark.

Construction of the long barrows

The shape of the north European long barrows varies in outline from oval, rectangular, trapezoidal to triangular, with lengths ranging from 20 m to about 125 m; the width is rarely greater than 10 m. While ditches are rare, two main forms of delimiting barrows include either a stone kerb setting – prevalent on the north European plain – or a timber palisade set within a trench, which tends to be more common further north, in southern Scandinavia, but it is not a hard and fast rule. Thus the Flintbek long barrows were eventually delimited by a setting of kerbstones, while at the recently investigated cemetery at Słonowice in southern Poland there were massive walls in front of palisades built of timbers about 30 cm in diameter set within trenches up to 1 m in depth (Tunia 2003). The use of timber enclosing the interior of the monuments is well documented in Denmark. This may involve a continuous timber palisade, for example at Harreby, Mosegården, Bygholm Nørremark and Troelstrup (Midgley 1985, Figures 40 and 41) or be defined by a timber façade at some distance from the grave chamber, for example at Bjørnsholm, Barkær, Vedskølle, Lindebjerg and others (Kaul 1988, 64–71).

Extensions and alterations of existing mounds may well have been a more widespread feature than is normally assumed, but the recognition of this phenomenon depends partly upon survival of the evidence and partly upon the field methodology. Some of the Kujavian long barrows had been extended to accommodate additional burials (for example Sarnowo 8) and sequential construction has been documented on a number of sites in Denmark.

The manner of construction of the Barkær long barrows, in a series of rectangular segments, in itself suggests a staged activity which may have catered for different groups engaged in construction; the northern barrow was extended on at least one occasion, with the southern one being elongated twice, eventually reaching nearly 90 m in length (Liversage 1992). The Lindebjerg barrow seems to have been increased in height upon the construction of the second burial chamber (Liversage 1981). The Asnæs mound was built in at least two stages, the second extending the mound to the north (Gebauer 1990), while Bygholm Nørremark offers an excellent

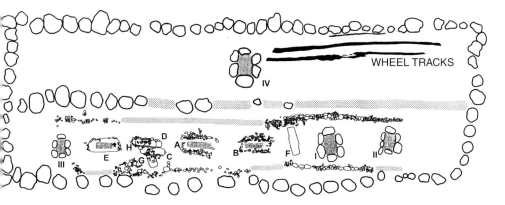

igure 1.3 Plan of the Flintbek LA 3 long barrow

example of an aggrandisement, with the original timber enclosure being replicated permanently in stone (Rønne 1979).

Bernd Zich's excavations at Flintbek provide ample evidence for the gradual growth of the long barrows. At LA 37 two extended dolmens and two earth graves (one of the latter associated with its own long timber structure) were finally set within a stone kerb 36.2 × 7.5 m, and a third dolmen was built immediately outside this kerb.

At LA 3, where timber- and stone-built chambers also stand side by side (see below) at least seven stratigraphically distinct construction phases were identified, with the barrow progressively increasing in length, acquiring a stone kerb by stage six, and finally doubling in width when the last megalithic chamber was built (Figure 1.3). From a small oval mound initially covering timber grave A, Flintbek LA 3 grew to a barrow 54 metres long and 18 metres wide (Zich 1999; B. Zich, pers. comm. 2005).

Indeed, Flintbek LA 3 is remarkable in another respect, as the final mound extension preserved stretches of parallel wheel tracks created, undoubtedly, as the building materials were brought to and from the barrow. The tracks were 6 cm wide, which corresponds to the width of Neolithic disc wheels, and they run only to the edge of the rather large foundation trench for the last dolmen chamber; clay transported from this trench has been estimated at about 6.5 cubic metres.

The reasons for such alterations may well be sought in multiple causes. The data from Flintbek suggest that the addition of new burial chambers obviously necessitated the enlargement of the mound, but clearly here the decision to build new chambers in the proximity of the older ones was a communal choice. The initial small earthen mound need not have survived for long, and most certainly would have been totally eradicated by modern agricultural activities. Thus the initial grave must have created a sacred location to which people returned over and over again – emphasising their relationship with this locality, their belonging to a particular social group, or possibly even appropriating the already existing monument for their own use.

While not all long barrows were built sequentially, we shall see later that alterations – extensions, rebuilding, construction of secondary chambers, changes to the shape and form of the mound – are characteristic not only of the long barrows but also of mounds with megalithic chambers, and such alterations may well have been a significant expression of the relationship between a community and a particular locality.

Activities around the barrows

In the case of the long barrows it is clear, from the number of interred dead, that the actual burials were few and far between, but the sites also provided a focus for activities of a commemorative nature, which may have taken place within or outside the enclosed space. At sites where such were erected, the timber and stone enclosures of the long barrows served other purposes than merely retaining the final earthen mound: they defined the sacred ceremonial ground, separating it from the zone of quotidian activities. The graves within the long barrows generally take up only a small amount of the interior, and there is ample evidence that other activities – either directly related to burial ceremonies or of a more general ritual nature – were taking place at various stages of use of the monuments.

Internal divisions in some monuments in Denmark and western Pomerania, where smaller spaces were created through low transverse stone walls or timber fences, are difficult to interpret. Such arrangements may have been important in the creation of separate spaces designed to accommodate different stages of the burial. We know very little about the actual ceremonies, from the moment of death to the final interment within a long barrow. Bodies may have been put on public display in spaces separate from those where the grave was being constructed, to enable the kin to grieve, pay final respects and perform the necessary rites, before the dead were committed to their grave; indeed, time may have been needed to build the grave, while the body was being cared for in its liminal stage within the sacred confines of the monument.

While there is little indication of the precise nature of the timber enclosures – especially the apparently massive eastern timber façades known from Denmark – I have suggested that, in some cases, they may have held decorated timber posts, in the manner of totem poles (Midgley 2005, 97). Nevertheless, it is important to note that while such a tradition of decoration is typical of the Atlantic province, where it survives for us in the form of decorated menhirs, the explicit lack of any decorative art in the north European megaliths may suggest that expressions of belonging to a specific community were carried out using different media – for example through pottery decoration rather than external carvings.

Nevertheless, the façades – decorated or not – were clearly important. They defined a ceremonial space and may have screened burial activities from the outside world, but they also provided a focus for activities taking place outside the monument. At many Danish long barrows votive deposits of pottery – mostly in the form of beakers and funnel-necked bowls – were placed against the façade, for example two vessels at Onsved Mark, one pot at the southern and two vessels at the northern barrow at Barkær, or three vessels at Storgård and Rude (Madsen 1979; Kaul 1988). As we shall see in Chapter 4, deposition of goods outside the chambers – most commonly, albeit not exclusively, centring upon the façades and shallow forecourts in front of the entrances to the megalithic tombs – was a very significant ritual activity. In some cases it involved depositions of hundreds of vessels, flint and stone tools and other items. It is important therefore to realise that this custom began prior to the construction of the stone-built chambers, commencing at the timber façades of the long barrows.

Graves and burials

Graves in the long barrows, in contrast with previous assumptions, must have been quite elaborate structures, some possibly permitting access to the interior on more than one occasion. The simplest were undoubtedly wooden coffins, for instance the so-called tree coffins encountered at Flintbek, and the rarest were cists lined with thin stone slabs such as are encountered at the Rude long barrow (Madsen 1980). There is a variety of timber-built forms, such as the tent-like chamber known as the Konens Høj type, which is commonly encountered as far south as Schleswig-Holstein; and the so-called Troelstrup grave, principally a rectangular box-like chamber built of timber planks. This latter is the most widely distributed form, but the name tends to be used mainly in southern Scandinavia.

Although we do speak of timber-built graves it seems that, while timber was indeed the primary and predominant building material, stone was always employed in some capacity or other. Thus the propping-up or securing of the timber chamber within a stone frame seems to have been the most common and is witnessed everywhere, for example at Wietrzychowice in Kujavia, Gnewitz and Rothenmoor in Mecklenburg or at numerous Danish sites. There are also versions of burial chambers which use a combination of timber and stone elements, for example stone walls and timber roof at the Skibshøj long barrow in Jutland – a chamber which was ultimately destroyed by fire (Jørgensen 1977b).

It has been known for quite some time that certain long mounds contain examples of both timber- and stone-built chambers and that the two forms were in contemporary use at the transition from Early to Middle Neolithic. Such examples are known to us from western Pomerania (for example at Łupawa 2 barrow 5, Jankowska 1999, 217, Figure 1), Schleswig-Holstein (for example at Flintbek) and Denmark (for example at Tolstrup, Troelstrup, Skibshøj, Mosegården, Bygholm Nørremark and Lindebjerg); doubtless this was the case in other regions and the lack of information is related to poor preservation and, equally, to methods of excavation, where visible chambers provided a focus for investigation at the expense of other parts of the barrow.

The close morphological relationship between timber- and stone-built chambers is very clearly expressed in the westerly grave in the southern barrow at Barkær, which seems to be a stone replica of the neighbouring timber chamber. Liversage has clearly stated that 'it would be hard to find stones that more faithfully reproduced the shape of large crudely split planks' (Liversage 1992, 22, Figures 10–12). Splitting tree trunks with stone wedges and flint axes would not have presented a great challenge to the Neolithic builders, and the massive timber palisades at Sarup provide a clear indication of the carpentry skills available (N. H. Andersen 1997). However, one wonders to what extent the use of split glacial boulders (the so-called 'twin stones'; Chapter 5) in the construction of megalithic chambers is a symbolic continuation of such timber technology; perfect splitting of massive boulders presented a wholly different technological challenge.

The investigations around Flintbek are particularly significant in the context of a juxtaposition of different grave forms, since at least three long barrows here have been shown to have contained several types: timber-built chambers of the Konens Høj type, timber and tree-trunk coffins, and stone-built dolmen chambers. The Flintbek long barrow LA 3 contained at least ten graves: four dolmens, three Konens Høj type timber graves, two tree-coffins and one coffin. Their sequence, based on stratigraphical observations, is as follows: two Konens Høj type graves (A and B) each within its own mound; two tree-trunk coffins to the west (graves C and D), another Konens Høj type grave (E) which is exceptional in having a layer of burnt flint on its floor (one of the earliest examples of this form of flooring, which assumed great importance in the megalithic chambers). The timber-built chambers and the two tree-trunk coffins follow the same longitudinal orientation but, significantly, with the construction of the first dolmen chamber the orientation changes to transverse to the long axis; this is followed by the subsequent dolmens and the later coffin burial.

The LA 37 barrow had at least two extended dolmens and two earth graves, with another possible megalithic chamber slightly to the outside. The LA 4 barrow had three megalithic and three earth graves and was extended on at least five occasions; the polygonal dolmen may have been the earliest grave, followed later by the three timber graves and further dolmen chambers. In each case the internal chronology of the mounds makes it clear that timber- and stone-built chambers alternated.

The data from Flintbek are important in several respects. First of all it is clear that initial covering of early graves could be rather scanty; such small mounds, when not incorporated in a process of aggrandisement as was done here, need not have survived for long and most certainly would have been totally eradicated by modern agricultural activities. Indeed, the many so-called 'earth graves' may well represent such an initial monument building which was not followed up through time. The other significance of alteration and extension is continuity through time – real as well as ritual – where, once chosen, a locality provided a focus for activities over a sufficiently long time to incorporate the changing chamber architecture (from timber to stone) and, in some cases, the creation of an outwardly imposing monument, as clearly also happened at Barkær and Bygholm Nørremark.

While the majority of graves in the north European long barrows contain a

18

single individual, there are examples of multiple burials both here and within the broader context of long barrows in other areas of Europe. There is now good evidence from France to suggest that at least some of the timber chambers were accessible for long enough to permit further bodies to be deposited within them (Midgley 2005, 104–5) and there is no reason why such a practice should not have been present in the north. Such repeated use would also have been possible in the context of the small stone cists, of the kind encountered at Rude, just as it must have been possible with graves nos. 1 and 3 at Troelstrup, since both were provided with a passage (Kjærum 1977).

The preservation of human remains in the north European long barrows is very poor, and generally bodies do not survive. However, often the size of the timber chamber (or coffin) is indicative of a single burial and, where human remains do survive, they usually represent extended single inhumations – individuals placed on their backs with arms stretched out along the sides of the body. There can be little doubt that, at least in northern Europe, this manner of burial is deeply rooted in the preceding Mesolithic tradition (Midgley 2005, 108); indeed, such a custom is continued in many of the so-called 'flat graves' and, as will be seen later, some of the early dolmens also had individuals placed in the extended position.

While the earliest dolmen forms may still have been intended predominantly for individual interments, against the background of practices witnessed in the other stone-built chambers the issue of the possible emergence of multiple burials in the context of the long barrow graves has important implications. While such burials are not common, some long barrow graves did have several individuals buried within one grave, and the question arises as to whether these were simultaneous depositions of several individuals or whether such chambers were kept accessible to accommodate subsequent interments.

At Bygholm Nørremark, four adult males were laid in a large timber coffin, although the arrangement of the bodies – in opposing pairs – suggests a single act of burial (Rønne 1979); similarly, the Skibshøj chamber had remains of five individuals: one adult and four children (Jørgensen 1997b, 8). At least one of the Malice Kościelne graves, southern Poland, had three individuals: a female, a male and a child of about 6–7 years of age (Kozak-Zychman and Gauda-Pilarska 1998, 38).

Due to the vagaries of preservation, estimates of the number of dead interred within the long barrows are fraught with difficulties. As already noted, a majority seem to have had graves designed for a single individual, even if several such graves could be encountered within the confines of a single monument. In Kujavia nine bodies were preserved at Sarnowo and six at Wietrzychowice, while other sites have yielded only one or two remains. From Denmark we have evidence for five individuals at Skibshøj and five individuals from Bygholm Nørremark, but no human remains have survived in north German long barrows. From southern Poland, at Malice Kościelne, remains of about 30 individuals have survived in various stages of preservation within and from the vicinity of the long barrow, although at this stage it is not certain how many date to the TRB culture period, and the six barrows discovered at the cemetery of Słonowice in southern Poland were apparently constructed to contain only one individual each (Tunia 2003).

Irrespective of the number of destroyed long barrows, these figures do suggest that only a minority of individuals were given such an impressive burial. What is equally evident is that both sexes and all ages – from newborn children to mature adults – could be buried within the confines of the barrows. Ample evidence for this derives from the area of the Paris basin (Chambon 1997, 2003a; Midgley 2005, 110) and this is also confirmed in the area of our present study.

What ceremonies were associated with the preparation of the dead for burial is difficult to tell. No evidence for funerary garments survives, although some of the dead from the Kujavian long barrows seem to have been covered with a white calcareous substance which may derive from covering by layers of shells. A beaker from Lindebjerg contained some traces of ochre, and one of the Stengade graves apparently had mineral crust with ochre in it. Strassburg (2000) noted a few other examples of the use of ochre in the Scandinavian barrows, but these are rather sporadic occurrences. The scanty use of ochre thus represents an important change from the previous Mesolithic tradition, in which this raw material played an important role.

We may draw attention to examples of the manipulation of human remains, although this was relatively rare in comparison with the subsequent practices witnessed in the megalithic chambers. Thus two individuals buried at Sarnowo revealed posthumous breakages of the long bones, and partial human remains were also found as debris at the settlement site, just a short distance from the barrow cemetery. These settlement bones were treated differently, as they revealed traces of charring of the bodies at low temperatures (between 100 and 180 °C), although the skulls apparently were subject to exposure to much higher temperatures and suffered breakages that were interpreted as evidence of ritual cannibalism.

A rare example of an isolated human jaw placed on the body of one of the deceased buried in the Skibshøj chamber (Kaul 1994, 44, note 10) foreshadows the presence of unrelated human jaws and other bone fragments in the megaliths. It may be further noted that some of the dead buried in the TRB flat graves in southern Poland reveal evidence of post-mortem manipulations that involved the twisting or crushing of the skulls or cutting-off of limbs (Midgley 1985, 194), and recent study by Kossian of the burials in flat graves in Germany and the Netherlands has also brought to light some burial practices which involved displacement or extraction of human bones (Kossian 2005).

The grave goods are very modest in quantity, and equally scanty in providing any enlightenment on the treatment of the dead. There is no surviving evidence of garments or shrouds; generally a ceramic pot or two, flint tools, some personal jewellery of wild animal teeth or amber beads are the normal grave furnishings. Pottery is more common in southern Scandinavia than elsewhere, but the forms are selective and repetitive: beakers and lugged and collared flasks. The latter – possibly imitations of an inverted poppy head – may well have been receptacles for hallucinatory substances deemed necessary for the journey to the beyond (Chapter 4).

Amber, used in profusion in the Mesolithic, continued to be fashioned into ornaments in Denmark. Many of the long barrow graves have amber beads: tubular, triangular, figure-of-eight or disc shapes which were fashioned into necklaces, sometimes with the use of spacer beads; single amber beads may have been worn as amulets or sewn onto garments as decoration. Amber, in its colour, also provided an attractive locally available medium for imitation of the exotic copper discs perforated along the edges.

Copper, although found only exceptionally in the long barrows and, indeed, in not much greater profusion within the megalithic graves, does nevertheless indicate that these exotic raw materials were making their way northwards from the central European production zone. One of the Leśniczówka barrows apparently had traces of copper, although it was not possible to determine the original form of the item, and one of the dead at the Słonowice cemetery was accompanied by some copper trinkets. Perforated copper discs have been found in several Danish long barrows. At Rude one was apparently attached to the wrist of the deceased, while at Konens Høj and Salten, fragments of copper ornaments were also found (Klassen 2004, List 7). Other ornaments are less common, although wild animal teeth are occasionally present, as evidenced by the wild boar tusks from Sarnowo, Gaj and Malice Kościelne.

The burials in the more northerly latitudes are often accompanied by one or two thin-butted flint axes, which may be a continuation of a custom from the preceding Mesolithic, where exotic Danubian *Schuhleistenkeile* were used in this manner. Sometimes, as in Kujavia, where flint blades and knives are rare, they seem to have been significant more as examples of exotic raw materials – derived from Wolhynia or the Holy Cross Mountains – than as specific tools. Arrowheads, which no doubt represent actual arrows, suggest that not only tools but also hunting equipment were an important accompaniment for the dead; sometimes there are only one or two arrows (for example Sarnowo or Bygholm Nørremark) but up to eight were found in grave D at Flintbek LA 3.

Summary

The evidence discussed in this section demonstrates that the early TRB communities in northern Europe, from the moment of their emergence, imposed their presence on the natural and cultural landscape in a very dramatic way by creating, among other things, monumental structures for some of their dead. The impulse for the creation of monumental cemeteries arose in the southern swathes of the north European plain. Here were the regions where the Danubian tradition – evidenced most clearly in the presence of villages of long houses associated with all the basic agricultural activities typical of early farmers – reached its northernmost limit and where the first farmers lived side by side with the last hunter-gatherers.

It was here also that the Danubian villages offered powerful images of ancestral places. The awareness of these sacred places, imbued with memories of ancestors and times past, provided a symbol which was translated from the domestic to the funerary sphere – from a dilapidated ruined village to the monumental cemetery. In areas outside the immediate impact of the Danubian communities, in Schleswig-Holstein and across the whole of southern Scandinavia, where only echoes of the Danubian presence may have reached via stories and gift exchanges, this idea was also adopted, albeit in a more individualistic fashion, in the form of single or paired monuments rather than large cemetery formations.

The north European long mounds displayed a remarkable variety of forms, as did the grave chambers hidden beneath them. The intimate relationship of these mounds close to or within the disused domestic structures and cultivated fields is such a widespread pattern across northern Europe and beyond that it surely symbolises the newly emerging relationship between mortality, domestic structures and the agricultural cycle – in other words, a new relationship between the living and the dead.

Moreover, throughout the entire TRB culture province, only selected dead were afforded such an extraordinary burial, and these must have distinguished themselves in some way from the rest of the community. Indeed, the contemporary presence of the dead within flat graves, either grouped in cemeteries or placed close by but nevertheless outside the long barrows, as well as of those buried within the settlements, confirms that burial within an imposing long mound was not for everyone.

As I have argued elsewhere, it is the monumentality – either immediate or accrued in sequential construction – that confers a special status on these individuals (Midgley 2005). These dead, by virtue of their placement within monumental barrows which symbolically commemorated past events, were at the same time projecting current religious and social positions for future generations to see. That this message was not ignored is amply demonstrated by the subsequent development of these concepts on a truly grand scale, replacing the relatively short-lived timber with everlasting stone and creating a megalithic tradition which impresses us to this day. It is now time to consider these developments in more detail.

2

MEGALITHS IN
THOUGHT AND SPACE

Preliminary theoretical considerations

It is not necessary to describe here in detail the various typo-chronologies developed for the north European megalithic tombs from the mid-nineteenth century until the present day; the interested reader is referred to my earlier discussion of these schemes (Midgley 1992, Chapter 9). However, research in the past two decades has highlighted the problems that some well-entrenched concepts pose for a meaningful interpretation of the megaliths in their various regional and cultural contexts, and so we will briefly consider some of these issues before engaging in discussion of the archaeological evidence.

We are all familiar with the term 'megalith', which has been in use for more than a century and a half and is deeply rooted in the same mid-nineteenth century tradition that has given us many other terms which continue in use today, such as 'Palaeolithic' and 'Neolithic' (Tilley 1998, 142). The second International Congress of Anthropology and Prehistoric Archaeology, which was held in Paris in 1867, settled upon the term '*monuments mégalithiques*' (Coye 1997, 186) as a generic term for the definition of a specific class of archaeological remains. Initially the term 'megalith' was used in its literal sense to mean great stones, from the Greek *mega* (= great) and *lithos* (= stone); and, unlike other terms of that formative period in the development of archaeology, it did not carry chronological connotations.

Although accepted, the word was used sparingly: it did not feature in the title of James Fergusson's seminal work on megaliths, *Rude Stone Monuments*, published in 1872; it was used rarely and with care by Montelius (1905); and the contemporary German researcher Robert Beltz (1899) hardly ever used it, preferring the traditional local term *Hünengrab* (giant's grave). Indeed Beltz was critical of the trend, expressed among others by Mortillet, of interpreting the megaliths as copies of Oriental burial forms spreading across Europe: '[T]oo often most researchers focus onto common traits which easily lead to wrong generalisations to which belongs the construction of a "dolmen people"' (quoted from translation in Steinmann 2001, 16).

However this trend increased and, in the early twentieth century, the word 'megalith' acquired an extended meaning in terms of singularity of the phenomenon and its chronology. Until the late 1930s it was, for example, perfectly common in Scandinavian and German literature to refer to the TRB culture as the 'megalithic culture'. Thus Nordman's Rhind Lectures, delivered at Edinburgh in 1932, were published under the title 'The Megalithic Culture of Northern Europe', and in the introduction he stated that, although 'there is no uniform European megalithic culture in existence … if the sphere is restricted, as we intend to do, to northern Europe, to Denmark and Slesvig, South and a part of Central Sweden and of the South of Norway, the term covers a cultural unit.' (Nordman 1935, 1–2).

Sprockhoff was equally comfortable with this term, sometimes in the titles and throughout the text of many of his publications (1926, 1938, 1966, 1967, 1975). The term was abandoned in the 1940s, and the subsequent processual approaches developed in Britain during the 1960s–1970s directed scholars' attention to the possibility of several 'independent nuclear areas for the inception of stone monuments' across Europe (Renfrew 1980, 4; see also Renfrew 1976, Chapter 7). When the concept returns today, it is usually in the form of an eye-catching title or as a 'rhetorical question' (Hoika 1999).

Two significant problems emerge here: one concerns the terminology itself, while the other is related to our interpretations of the origins and function of the Neolithic funerary tradition. They are inextricably connected and they stem from the persistent belief that stone-built structures – that is the megaliths – are a singular phenomenon and that their significance, even if it is considered in regional terms, can be somehow understood without any reference to other contemporary sites. However, it has now been demonstrated beyond doubt that in northern Europe timber- and stone-built chambers were contemporary with one another, even if for a short time, and not infrequently constructed within the confines of the same mound. We know that burials within flat graves, while not marked visibly on the surface, were made throughout the entire period of construction of megaliths, and also that related ceremonial activities were conducted at enclosures whose principal architecture involved earthen and timber elements.

When we consider the recent writings of British scholars who deal with 'megaliths', we note that many are quite deliberately using more neutral terms such as 'monument' or 'monumental architecture', or even flexible morphological terms such as 'mound', in order to overcome the nineteenth- and early twentieth-century legacy of research that does not permit us to escape from a terminological *cul-de-sac* (Bradley 1998b, 2002; Tilley 1998, 1999). While not everyone would go along with Chris Tilley's suggestion that we should 'cross out' the word megalith, we may well have misgivings about terminology which has been emerging in the work of some scholars – terminology apparently designed to overcome this 'self-inflicted' problem.

Thus, working within the 'Herzynian' zone, Beier, for example, has for some time now been proposing terms such as 'real megalith', 'sub-megalith', 'pseudo-megalith' in order to overcome the fact that, while some burial chambers were built of large stones, others were constructed using smaller stones or slabs or were constructed in timber (Beier 1995, 90–3). During the international megalithic col-loquium at Bougon in October 2002, Le Roux's proposal that we should develop a 'megalithic terminology' along lines similar to the Linnaean botanical system led to one of the most impassioned polemics of the entire symposium; the typology of megaliths is still a powerful issue in some quarters. However, the solution to this problem does not lie in the ever-evolving verbal permutations on the theme 'mega-lith', but rather in a recognition of the diversity of ways in which one particular phenomenon – in our case the megalith – is interrelated with others.

The study of megaliths has always featured prominently in Scandinavian research, and one of the early classifications was proposed by the nineteenth-century Danish scholar J. J. Worsaae. This classification, which survives in general terminology to this day, distinguished the *Stendysse* (translated into English as dolmen) and the *Jættestue* (passage grave). The visual appearance of the former in the landscape led to a further distinction between the *Runddysse* (dolmen in a round mound) and *Langdysse* (dolmen in a long mound). Oscar Montelius elabo-rated this classification further, distinguishing nine different types of tombs, but only his main types – the dolmen, the passage grave and the stone cist – formed the backbone of typo-chronology of the Scandinavian Stone Age. Nordman, while fol-lowing in principle the scheme of Montelius, was nevertheless conscious of the fact that tomb types were not the best chronological indicators since 'old forms of sepulture … remain in use for a long time, even though new types are introduced side by side with them' (Nordman 1935, 16).

In Germany Sprockhoff, doubtful of the usefulness of the settlement method, concentrated his research on tomb typology. The categories of dolmen, passage grave, *Hünenbett* (his term for an earthen long barrow without a stone chamber) and stone cist, which he first introduced in 1926, were applied by him throughout his working career, albeit with further elaborations. Indeed, Sprockhoff was con-scious of the fact that typology alone was not sufficient, and he emphasised the study of finds and of relative chronology as equally important elements in mega-lithic research. While introducing their own modifications, subsequent German researchers, most notably Schuldt (1972), Laux (1980, 1991, 1996), Hoika (1990, 1999) and Bock *et al.* (2006), followed this general model.

The question of the usefulness of the evolutionary sequence, resulting from the typological paradigm, in the study of megaliths has been raised many times. While tomb typology helps us to navigate around and harness the vast body of archaeo-logical evidence, it is also constraining, with many structures sitting uncomfort-ably outside such a scheme: hence terms such as hybrids, pseudo-megaliths or, as elegantly expressed by Bakker, 'the ingenuity of the builders' (Bakker 1992) to account for monuments which do not fit the typological frame.

Giot pointed out many years ago that 'we are so accustomed to see exposed the inner skeletons of the megalithic monuments that we rather tend to forget when discussing typological or structural niceties that the interiors were no doubt hidden to the profane' (Giot 1981, 22; Figure 2.1). This is precisely the point. In spite of the arguments that some of the megalithic chambers, in northern Europe as

Figure 2.1 The 'inner skeleton' of the Luttra passage grave, Falbygden, Sweden

elsewhere, were left uncovered by mounds (Chapter 5; Bradley 2007, 54), the majority clearly were enveloped in stone or earthen mounds. Thus our typology is based on something which originally was largely invisible – the chambers rarely seen by the community at large. Most people would have experienced the exterior of the monuments – the round or long mounds set within their kerbs – be it through participation in ceremonies outside the megaliths or just passing by them in the course of other daily activities.

Even those privileged to enter the chambers during burial ceremonies would have experienced only some aspects of megalithic architecture. The first use of a chamber may well have involved the actual builders, who would have been familiar with the various architectural and symbolic elements. But subsequent generations would have known only what they could see, although transfer of knowledge about hidden architecture among the privileged members of a community may have been socially and culturally important.

Thus we are faced with the interesting dilemma, not only in respect of northern Europe but in all areas where megalithic structures are found, of reconciling the typological schemes that have become entrenched in our thinking with the need for other forms of discussion to investigate aspects that may have been meaningful to those who built and used them. The simple abandonment of typological terms such as 'dolmen' or 'passage grave' does not provide a solution, and they will not be dispensed with here, since these terms can still be useful shorthand in our narratives. Indeed we need to understand why chamber forms developed and changed over time. But, in addition, we also need other criteria to aid our interpretation of megaliths as places that both reflected and directed everyday social practices, linking the different realms of the living, the dead and the supernatural.

One such attempt may indeed come from phenomenology – from experiencing the monuments the way they may have been seen in the past (Tilley 1994, 2004). The location of a tomb or a group of tombs in the natural landscape, its relationship to other places within the area, the shape and size of the mound, its orientation and the symbolic features of the exterior may well have been more meaningful than hidden morphological characteristics. Such an approach, however, needs to be conducted within the appropriate regional context; transferring phenomenological experiences from, say, Dartmoor or the Atlantic coastline may not be directly relevant to the flat expanses of the north European plain. Similarly, there is a need to continue developing our understanding of the relationships between megaliths and other contemporary places and of how these may have evolved over time. This may include settlements and other sites of everyday economic activities, enclosures, votive localities and other forms of burial site.

On a different level we must think in terms of symbolic meanings locked within the megalithic structures – the internal and external architectural elements and the raw materials used to create these – even if such symbolism is difficult to read against the time gap of several millennia. In contrast to the varying phenomenological conceptualisations of monuments, it is often the more mundane aspects of fieldwork that continue to provide information that helps us to interpret the symbolic and ritual meanings, be it of raw materials or of architectural features of megalithic structures. One may note the remarkable results of research in western France on the quarrying techniques employed in the extraction of large granite blocks for the construction of megaliths as well as stone alignments; these highlight the relationship between the source of stones and the location of monuments and, further, demonstrate that colour, shape and texture played an important role in the choice of raw materials (E. Mens, pers. comm. 2007; Benéteau-Douillard 2006; Sellier 1991, 1995). Similarly, in northern Europe, the restoration projects of the past decade undertaken on the Danish megaliths (Chapter 5) provide a wealth of information on the symbolic use of both raw materials and architectural elements that appear to have no structural logic and yet were clearly very important aspects of megalith construction and use.

Finally, the activities taking place at megaliths involved not merely the placement of the dead but a host of other ceremonial and votive acts that brought them into the overall network of individual and communal Neolithic social practices. Indeed, the monuments themselves provided a medium through which Neolithic cosmology could be given expression both in time and in its spatial, geographical setting. Here, theoretical concepts from sociology and social anthropology may help to explain how past human action was moulded by a dialectic between the structured social context and the way in which the prevailing social norms could be manipulated to individual as well as communal advantage within given situations (Helms 1988, 1993, 1998).

Thus we cannot excuse ourselves from the detailed study of the construction of the megaliths. It is through this work that important new information enlightens us upon their symbolic and cosmological significance, even if such symbolism is difficult to read at a distance of several millennia.

Distribution and location of megaliths in the landscape

Discussion of the north European megaliths in terms of their general landscape setting is problematic; the sheer geographical extent of the area, the variety of natural environments and topography, the number of sites involved, as well as the lack of studies on this subject, impede a proper assessment. Indeed, while such analysis might be appropriate within a regional context, on a larger scale there is a danger that certain local patterns could be imposed on areas where they simply do not apply. The variation between scattered and clustered distributions, for example, must be seen against the background of the historical development of settlement within individual regions and not as some overarching pattern. Similarly, while the placement of tombs in relation to the sea was undoubtedly important to the Danish and Swedish builders and to those along the coasts of the North Sea and the Baltic, it was of no significance further south on the north European plain – with the sea too far away to be regarded as an important landmark. Here other topographical features, such as moraine ridges, river valleys and easily navigable passes from one region to the next, were much more important.

Even a brief glance at the distribution maps suggests that megaliths are by no means evenly distributed (Figures 2.2 and 2.3). There are areas of dense concentrations interspersed with a rather more even spread, as well as zones largely devoid of megaliths. To what extent this is a result of destruction from medieval times onwards we cannot be sure, although figures for the different districts in Schleswig-Holstein reveal how dramatic the destruction rate could be – between 75 and 100 per cent (Hoika 1990, Table 1). Some megaliths may well have been destroyed soon after they were built; Bakker (1999, 148) pointed out that the only dolmen known from the Netherlands was already heavily damaged in the Bell Beaker times, and many megaliths suffered as a result of secondary use.

Nor are the types distributed evenly. Notwithstanding typological issues and possible damage in prehistory, there are very few dolmens to the west of the river Weser. The rather boggy and marshy landscape west of this river may well have been a considerable natural obstacle, creating a natural as well as a cultural boundary; large dolmens also seem to be absent from here, although the German term *Großsteingrab* for any structure built of three or more pairs of orthostats makes identification in literature difficult (Midgley 1992, 420). Dolmen forms are equally rare in the Falbygden area of Sweden, where recent classification of chamber forms by Sjögren has identified only two existing dolmens against the background of 255 certain passage graves. That this is a clear regional trait is shown by the presence of at least 51 dolmens and 32 passage graves in the area of Bohuslän (Sjögren 2003a, Table 6.2). In global terms the distribution of the passage graves tends to gravitate westwards: none were apparently built on Rügen or on the directly adjacent mainland of Mecklenburg, and only sporadically have they been recorded in Poland. On the other hand they are a real *tour de force* along the western stretches of the north European plain and in parts of southern Scandinavia.

Before we concern ourselves with the arrangement of megaliths in different landscapes, let us briefly consider some statistics. Can we estimate the original number of megalithic tombs that might have been built in northern Europe? Denmark presents a truly exceptional case: there are roughly 7000 megaliths known from here, of which about 2000 dolmens and 500 passage graves still survive in one form or another. The estimates for original numbers, albeit conjectural, suggest up to 25,000 tombs (Ebbesen 1985, 40) although even higher numbers, up to 40,000, have sometimes been suggested. The numbers in Sweden

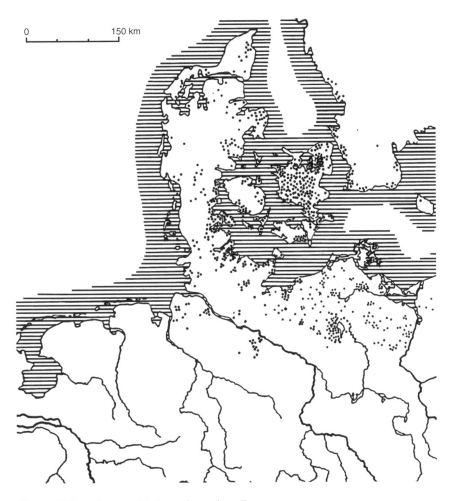

Figure 2.2 Distribution of dolmens in northern Europe

are much smaller: Tilley (1996, 131) quotes 476 surviving certain or probable tombs although, in heavily agricultural areas such as Scania, destructions must have occurred on a significant scale.

Records for over 4500 megaliths exist for north Germany, although the data are very uneven. The early nineteenth-century records for the island of Rügen refer to 254 stone-built chambers (Schuldt 1972, 16). Today only 54 are to be found, which nevertheless is a remarkable survival rate of 21 per cent, but there was neither intensive agriculture nor heavy industrial development on this island. For the area

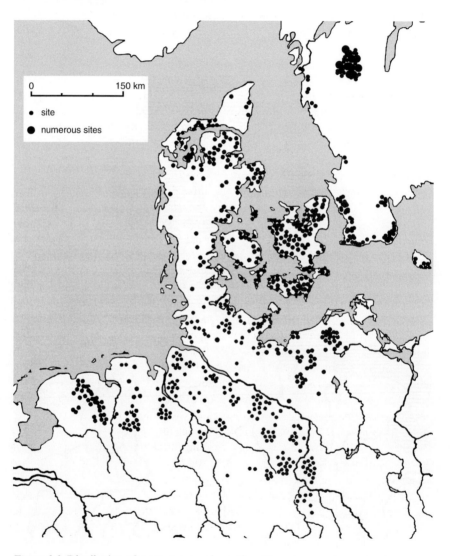

Figure 2.3 Distribution of passage graves in northern Europe

of Mecklenburg altogether, Schuldt recorded 1143 megaliths, of which 443 were preserved (39 per cent). By contrast, Hoika has demonstrated that only 188 of the 3041 known tombs survive in Schleswig-Holstein today (6.2 per cent) and even this varies dramatically between different districts (Hoika 1990, Table 1).

Nelson has quoted 350 sites for Lower Saxony (Nelson 1988, 92) but the numbers must have been much higher, since Schirnig's estimate for the district of Uelzen alone is at least 250 megaliths, although this could represent merely 5 per cent (Schirnig 1979, 223); 69 megaliths survive in the Osnabrück area, and Sprockhoff (1975) recorded about 60 surviving megaliths on the Hümmling in the earlier part of the twentieth century, but the original numbers are difficult to estimate (Schlicht 1979, 44). Bakker (1988 *passim*) has noted 53 existing *hunebeds* in Holland, 22 destroyed and a further 30 problematic or dubious sites; of the 207 megaliths recorded in the mid-nineteenth century by Danneil in Altmark, over 75 per cent are destroyed (Fritsch and Müller 2002, 65). There are no satisfactory data on the number of megalithic tombs east of the river Oder. Megaliths are found sporadically as far east as Kujavia, and archival records in western Pomerania account for about 200 megaliths, of which 150 were noted in an area of roughly 90 km^2 around the modern town of Pyrzyce (Holsten and Zahnow 1920; Jankowska 1999, 220).

Altogether, therefore, there are records for well over 12,000 megalithic tombs in northern Europe and, using the Danish formula loosely, this could easily translate into an estimated minimum of 40,000 megaliths. However, in regions where intensive archaeological fieldwork has been conducted over the past few decades, important lessons have been learned with regard to the number of monuments, lessons which have serious implications for our interpretation of their distribution and density. The most dramatic evidence comes from south-west Fyn in Denmark, in the vicinity of the Sarup enclosure. Before the intensive surveys began in 1975, only three megalithic tombs were recorded in the area between Sarup, Strandby and Damsbo; today 122 new megaliths have been identified there, and the total number of megaliths around the Helnæs Bugt is now about 290 (N. H. Andersen, 1997, 94, Figure 121). Indeed, Andersen has suggested that megalithic tombs may have been built here at a rate of one every two years.

In Schleswig-Holstein near Flintbek field surveys, also begun in 1975, have now provided information on a concentration of about 80 destroyed mounds stretching over a ground moraine ridge 4 km long (Zich 1993, 17). Recent studies by C. Steinmann, using old parish records for five selected regions in Mecklenburg, have increased the number of sites from the 325 originally recorded by Schuldt to 551 (Steinmann 2001, 42). Projecting this for the whole of Mecklenburg would result in just under 2000 megaliths, and future fieldwork and investigation of old records will undoubtedly bring to light many more sites in what has been a rather neglected region in terms of megalithic research. Indeed, there is little doubt that intensive fieldwork would help to identify – even in cases of complete destruction – the hundreds of megaliths that were recorded by von Plön in 1825 in western Pomerania (Holsten and Zahnow 1920).

These few examples of recent increases in the number of megaliths in areas where intensive fieldwork has been undertaken should be sufficient to alert us to the dangers of expressing views on the density of settlement in regions with, and indeed without, megaliths. On the other hand, we should also recognise that field survey and archival research do not always produce the same results: Larsson's work in southern Scania indicated only a handful of probable destroyed megaliths (Larsson 1992, 36).

Location in the landscape

The relationship between the siting of megaliths and the natural landscape formations has always attracted interest; recent phenomenological and other approaches to the study of megaliths in Britain, or along the Atlantic façade, have emphasised the possibly deliberate placement of tombs with a view to choreographing the experience associated with these monuments. Such approaches naturally include the interplay between the architecture and local landscape features such as hills and elevations, the relationship to water (be it along the coast, at lakesides or along rivers) and the vistas available from or leading up to the monuments (Bradley 1998a, 1998b; Cassen et al. 2000; Cummings and Pannett 2005; Cummings and Whittle 2004; Scarre 2002b; Vaquero Lastres 1999). Another theme undergoing a revival is the relationship between the megaliths and the raw materials used in their construction. This variously involves the identification of local or distant sources of stone, the spatial relationship between the location of sites and these sources, and the aesthetics of interior and exterior colour and texture and their symbolism (Cooney 2000; Jones and MacGregor 2002; Scarre 2003, 2006; Tilley 2004; see Chapter 5 for further discussion).

One important feature is the apparent variation between clustered and dispersed distributions in different regions. Thus in Bohuslän the tombs are irregularly dispersed with a few small clusters of up to four graves. Langeland offers a similar picture: using a spatial distance of 0.5 km, Tilley calculated that 60 per cent of tombs are isolated while the rest commonly occur in pairs, although clusters of up to eight monuments are also known (Tilley 1996, 131).

Clustered distributions are typical of Scania, where over a hundred tombs are found in five distinct regional groups, curiously enough all recorded in areas of much agricultural activity, suggesting perhaps that the present distribution approximates to that of the original pattern. Most of the tombs are found within a coastal belt between 10 and 20 km wide, with only occasional examples further inland. In the area between the Saxån and Löde-Kävlinge rivers, for example, the ten passage graves tend to be between 2 and 3 km apart, but some of the dolmens may cluster more closely (Hårdh 1982, Figure 2); they seem to be located at a distance from 0.5 to 1.5 km from contemporary settlements. In the Välabäcken river valley – a tributary of the Saxån – the settlement is in the river valley while the tombs were built higher up, on the southern slopes of the plateau, with votive wetland locations even further on the periphery (Andersson 2004, 172, figure on page 173). A similar pattern is documented in north-eastern Scania, with the passage grave of Fjälkinge about 1 km distant from the Hunneberget settlement (ibid. 175).

32

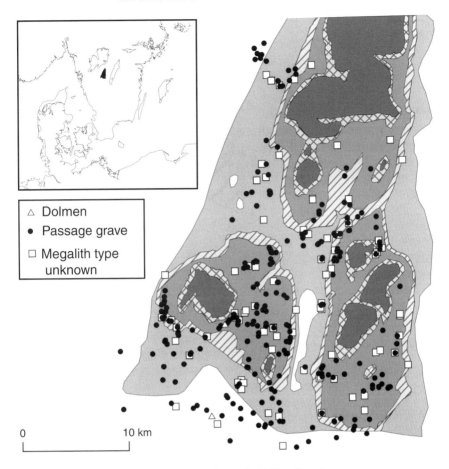

Figure 2.4 Distribution of megalithic tombs on the Falbygden plateau

A powerful concentration of megaliths, almost exclusively passage graves, is found on the Falbygden plateau, in Västergötland, where in an area of about 50 by 30 km over 250 tombs are found (Sjögren 1986, 2003a; Figure 2.4). In the central part of the distribution, for example around Falköping or Karleby, where the largest tombs are to be found, they are no more than 500 m apart (in groups arranged in rows, the distances are often shorter) with tombs becoming smaller and more widely spaced towards the periphery. The Falbygden area is a topographically remarkable landscape, with a flat plateau intersected by ridges of igneous rocks, rising up to 100 m and running roughly north–south (Figure 2.5). Tilley has argued that, because of the lack of earlier cultural landmarks (such as dolmens), the natural landscape created by the mountain ridges served as a reference point for the distribution of tombs, frequently in north–south rows (Tilley 1993, 76). Somewhat contradictorily, he has also argued that the linear arrangements of tombs commemorated the presumed population movements from Scania, where north–south

Figure 2.5 Passage graves at Karleby on the Falbygden plateau, with the Ålleberg mountain in the background

orientations are significant, to Västergötland (ibid. 78), although it now seems that population movement into this region was from western Sweden rather than from Scania (K.-G. Sjögren, pers. comm. 2007).

Indeed, Sjögren suggested that, although the Falbygden topography does explain the linear arrangement of tombs in certain localities (where local groups may range from five to 15 monuments), the relationship to settlement and other cultural activities in the landscape was also important. The tombs were frequently located along the lower edge of a pronounced slope, while the contemporary settlements – as seen in the Karleby area – were well below the tombs, halfway towards the rather marshy valley of the river Åsle. Although the actual distances between the tombs and settlements are not great, at between 300 and 500 m, the tombs are spatially separate, with no inter-visibility between the two types of site. The mediating role, symbolised by the tombs, between the living and the dead reflected their cultural liminality, and the separation of the tombs is further emphasised by their position on the margins of cultivated areas (Sjögren 2003a, Chapter 13). Similar patterns – of tomb and settlement areas separate from one another – have been noted recently in Mecklenburg (Steinmann 2001).

The distribution of tombs in many areas of Denmark is complex, and here it is impossible to consider individual sites as marking a particular territory; rather, it is the clusters which arose over a period of time, sometimes with visible gaps between them, that could be considered as identifying the territories of particular communities. Thus, near the enclosure at Sarup, at least 16 clusters of tombs have

34

been identified around the Helnæs Bugt (Andersen 1997, 100, Figure 130); each cluster, covering on average about 6 km^2, may represent a separate settlement unit as it expanded and contracted over time.

Interesting and contrasting patterns emerge on the southern Danish islands. From Bogø and Møn there are 119 megaliths known, although the original number may have been as many as 300–400 tombs (Dehn *et al.* 2000, 7, Figure 1.1). On Bogø there is a very clear concentration along the coast; on Møn several tombs form long rows leading from the coast inland, and there is a strong concentration in the centre, but towards the coast the tombs are more scattered.

Another very dense concentration of megaliths is in Horns Herred, between Roskilde and Isefjord. Here within an area of about 190 km^2, an area approximately similar in size to Møn, there are about 140 megaliths (57 scheduled) and as many as 500 tombs may originally have existed here. There are five to six groups, each with one or more passage graves (Kaul 1988, Figure 1). The surviving clusters vary in size from seven to 50 tombs, with passage graves present in every one. In the densest scatters the surviving passage graves are found to the north and south fringes of the clusters. However, a double passage grave with a chamber over 22 m in length is located between two distinct concentrations, leading Kaul to consider it as an outlier between two areas, perhaps built jointly by these two communities.

In contrast to the island clusters, megaliths in north Jutland are more dispersed. At Vroue Hede, for example, they display a distinctly linear pattern and, fascinatingly, the arrangement includes not just dolmens and passage graves, but the later so-called stone-packing graves, the entire alignment stretching somewhat less than 2 km (Jørgensen 1977a, Figure 2). Linear arrangements are known elsewhere: the morainic ridge already alluded to at Flintbek, 4 km in length, carries many megaliths in its north-eastern section (Zich 1993, Figure 1). Similar linear patterns are manifest in the Netherlands and certain regions of north-west Germany, for instance on the Hümmling or north-east of Uelzen (see below).

On the subject of water, we should perhaps note that as far as the north European plain is concerned – and this would also apply to large areas of southern Scandinavia – the need for dry rather than wet landscapes may have played a significant role in terms of economy and settlement patterns. With peat extraction and various drainage programmes, some of which date as far back as the Middle Ages, much of the landscape has been altered, with boggy, marshy and waterlogged areas dramatically reduced in size. Thus, although today only 10 per cent of land in Lower Saxony and 12 per cent in Mecklenburg is covered by peatland, in the Atlantic about half of the landscape consisted of raised bogs (Schmatzler and Bauerochse 2003, 217). (Bakker's reconstruction map of the sandy soils, open water and wet deposits in the western part of the north European plain (1976, Figure 6) illustrates this point rather well.) And yet remnants of bogs, such as the former Bourtanger Moor on the present-day boundary of the Netherlands and Germany, the Bissendorfer Moor in the Weser-Aller lowlands, or the Diepholz Moorniederung between the modern towns of Bremen, Osnabrück and Hannover, give some indication of the possible conditions during the Neolithic. Indeed, the famous timber trackways discovered in the 1990s in the Campemoor in the Dümmer area date by and large from the TRB period (Metzler 2003); the majority of the north European votive axe deposits, which today come from the dry land, would originally have been placed in waterlogged landscapes.

This is not to suggest that water was not important – it was indeed essential – nor that it did not play a role in economy or communications, but the recent phenomenological preoccupation with the relationship between megaliths and water has perhaps sometimes overemphasised the deliberate rather than the unavoidable. In large areas of northern Europe, megaliths are found along the coast; this can be seen from the island of Rügen in the east, along the Baltic coastline in Mecklenburg, in Schleswig-Holstein and, of course, in numerous areas of southern Scandinavia such as the southern Danish isles, on Bogø, Møn, along the entire southern and western coast of Zealand, Langeland, south-west Fyn, the Djursland peninsula on Jutland, on the island of Bornholm, in Scania, and Bohuslän, to name but the most obvious areas.

The majority of the megaliths in Bohuslän, west Sweden, are very close to the contemporary coastline (less than 100 m; Sjögren 1986, 253; 2003b, 168, Figure 3) with little arable land around. This has been interpreted in the past as evidence of the importance of marine economy at the time (Clark 1977). Indeed, Bradley and Phillips (2004), in their discussion of the distribution of megaliths on the west Swedish islands of Örust and Tjörn, have emphasised that in the Neolithic, when the sea level was between 25 and 20 m higher than today, many of the tombs were very close to the shore. Tjörn, in particular, would have been a series of small rocky outcrops around the relatively sheltered bay, with tombs dramatically poised on the edge between land and water. They support the idea that boat travel was significant, and relate the location of the megaliths to communication routes and the possible relevance of fishing for the economy of this area.

However, recent analysis of carbon-13 values from several human remains from Bohuslän graves suggests very little marine diet during the time of megalith construction, even though the individuals were all buried in coastal locations. Moreover, Sjögren (2003b) notes that, in contrast to the megaliths, the contemporary settlement sites in Bohuslän are not as close to the shore as the tombs (on average 1–2 km away from the tomb) and that there is generally no inter-visibility between the two types of site. The relationship between the coast and megaliths may have been much more complex than simple marine exploitation; Sjögren has suggested that they may be associated with access routes demonstrating ancestral presences to outsiders.

While in many areas the focus on the sea must have been significant, one notes that in the same regions (for example on Møn) some megaliths are placed manifestly away from the large expanse of water towards the land. An interesting example has been noted by Steinmann (2001, 51–6) in relation to the distribution of megaliths along the Baltic coast and west of Wismar, where both areas are characterised by the presence of moraine ridges. However, in the former group most megaliths are located in the lowlands, focused towards the Baltic Sea, while in the latter the megaliths tend to be built higher up on the moraine ridge. Indeed the builders of the northern group of megaliths at Everstorfer Forst placed the tombs on the moraine ridge, which sloped inland, and thus ignored the breathtaking views across the lowlands towards the Baltic, only a few hundred metres to the north.

Away from the coastline, river valleys were naturally very important, and here another interesting contrast can be shown between two areas in Mecklenburg – the Recknitz and Warnow river valleys – which, once again, demonstrates that local patterns can vary greatly. Along the Recknitz there are large groups of megaliths, for example a group of 20 monuments at Gnewitz/Zarnewanz and 17 monuments at Liepen, both close to the river; smaller groups of up to three monuments and individual sites are noted in the hinterland, a few kilometres from the valley.

The two large groups, on the opposite sides of the Recknitz, show an interesting difference. The Liepen sites are by and large clearly focused on the river valley, overlooking it from prominent slopes or hilltop locations, while of the 20 monuments in the Gnewitz/Zarnewanz group only two have a rather limited view of the valley, with the rest of the sites largely focused away from the river towards the hinterland beyond. Such differential focusing is not apparent from the distribution map and can only be seen by walking among the monuments (Steinmann 2001 and author's personal visit).

The monuments in the Warnow river valley are distributed very differently; large clusters are unknown here, only one small group is close to the river (Klein Görnow), while the rest are scattered between 4 km and 15 km away. The two valleys have very different landscapes: the Warnow valley has some narrow gorges and wet and boggy hinterland, and the low elevation of the river suggests that pastures here would have been liable to prolonged flooding, while the wide valley bottom of the Recknitz and the rolling hinterland would have provided extensive grazing pastures. The zone with the large monument concentrations seems to have offered good soils as well as a safe passage across the river, not hampered by boggy and marshy land. Indeed, as Steinmann suggested, this may have been one of the convenient routes from inland pastures to the Baltic.

However, the Warnow river may also have constituted an important passage from central regions to the Baltic, as a large cluster of megaliths is closely connected with its source higher up the river. Steinmann has suggested that from the river Elbe (where a very good crossing point is known, for example, near the megaliths at Barskamp) one could easily cross along the river Elde towards the head of the Warnow valley. A recent aerial survey has identified here at least four enclosures aligned at 2 km intervals from north-north-east to south-south-west, an alignment that points toward a relatively flat passage which would lead to the Warnow, only 5 km to the north-east. In Steinmann's words, 'No other place in this part of northeast Germany provides a better opportunity to travel north to south and vice versa' (ibid. 57).

That the Elbe was fordable in places has been clearly demonstrated by Bakker's analysis of the distribution of North Jutland axes in the area west of the river Elbe: with a suitable crossing point between Lauenburg and Artlenburg, and another possibly at Hamburg-Altona (Bakker 1976). As already noted, the cluster of megaliths at Barskamp, on the Lüneburger Heide, is found only a few hundred metres west from the only place along this stretch of the Elbe passable with wheeled vehicles (Assendorp 2004a, 340).

The idea that megalithic tombs were important landmarks constructed along frequently traversed routes has a long history, with Müller's initial work in Jutland at the beginning of the twentieth century subsequently followed by others. (Bakker 1976 offers a detailed discussion of the history of research and general issues concerning the identification of prehistoric routes.) Indeed, some of the well-known medieval roads across the north European plain and southern Scandinavia, such as the Haervej-Heerweg in Schleswig-Holstein and Jutland (otherwise known as the Ochsenweg), or the Hondsrug on the Drenthe plateau, clearly follow the courses of much older routes; many have megaliths associated with them and are likely to have been in use at least since the Neolithic.

Safe passage would have been as important in the Neolithic as at any other period, whether it involved travellers, transport of goods or traversing the landscape with animal herds. While in northern Europe there are no obstacles in the form of high mountain ranges, fast-flowing and flood-prone rivers had to be crossed, marshy and boggy terrain avoided and navigated around, and safe routes identified for the transport of goods and animals.

Along the coasts, in the calm seasons, boat travel may have been faster and thus preferred to inland routes; communications between islands of necessity involved crossing stretches of water. The megaliths along the western coast of Bohuslän, or those along the Danish coasts, may well have marked safe harbours and regular landing places from which one could travel inland. Indeed, the Neolithic settlement of the island of Bornholm offers a remarkable testimony to the navigational skills of Scandinavian farmers. The 37-km-wide strait separating this island from the Swedish mainland is known for very strong currents and changing winds, and the crossing must have been one of the most hazardous enterprises of the time. However, at times of inclement weather and in areas where boat travel was not suitable, short- and long-distance overland routes would have been used.

It is difficult to determine how much movement was on foot and how much was by means of ox-pulled carts. That carts were used is evident from the preserved wheel tracks at Flintbek (Chapter 1). The Neolithic trackways at Campemoor do not appear sufficiently wide or sturdy to have accommodated wheeled traffic. However, that carts traversed moorland over wooden trackways is demonstrated at other sites in Lower Saxony, such as the 4-m-wide trackway XV at Meerhusener Moor (Hayen 1987). Here nearly 50 cattle hooves have been found embedded in the timbers; together with fragments of wooden wheels and axles, which must derive from vehicles that broke while driving along the trackway; this demonstrates that ox-drawn carts were in use. Moreover, contemporary iconographic evidence, for example from the well-known pot at Bronocice, Poland (Bakker *et al.* 1999, Figure 7) and from carvings on orthostats at Züschen (Gandert 1964, Plates 1, 3–4), lends further support to the idea of wheeled carts being used in the time of the TRB.

Many linear alignments of megaliths have been interpreted as indicating regularly traversed routes. This theme has been discussed in literature every now and then, albeit in regional contexts, with a broad pan-north-European perspective still awaiting an enthusiastic researcher. Thus the megaliths on the Hondsrug, Drenthe plateau, are clearly the earliest monuments to be aligned along that ancient north–south route from which other routes diverged to east and west (Bakker 1976, 1991; Jager 1985). Schlicht (1961) described several stretches of megaliths on the Hümmling – the longest apparently about 32 km in length – following low watersheds, permitting a reduction in the number of streams and other wet places to be negotiated.

Linear arrangements of megaliths have, in fact, been noted from the nineteenth century onwards: we need only remind ourselves of the two lines of altogether 34 megaliths observed by Von Estorff in the vicinity of Altenmedingen, on the Lüneburger Heide (Von Estorff 1846), or Von Plön's surveys, from 1825 onwards, on chains of monumental cemeteries along the edges of the higher ground around the Pyrzyce basin in western Pomerania (Holsten and Zahnow 1920). In Schleswig-Holstein, apart from the famous Ochsenweg, which in historical periods led from Hamburg on the Elbe to Viborg and Ålborg in north Jutland, other routes have been studied. Hoika's research in East Holstein has indicated that stretches of the seventeenth-century coastal post route were clearly marked with megaliths, and that this may have been a coastal prehistoric route that ultimately led across the Fehmarn Belt to Lolland (Hoika 1986).

Likewise, older researches in Denmark and Sweden have variously attempted to correlate historical and archaeological data to identify prehistoric routes: for example Sahlström's (1935) comparison of megalithic distribution on the Falbygden plateau with the mid-sixteenth-century royally established 'common land routes', or La Cour's (1927) mapping of Bronze Age barrows and megaliths against the background of Zealand's topography.

Naturally, it is not intended here to discuss the overall network of routes across northern Europe during the time when megaliths were constructed. Not only would this be beyond the scope of the present work but, more significantly, research on this topic is largely still to be carried out. However, there are a few general points worth stressing. While alignments of megaliths – with or without later monuments – or groups of megaliths concentrated in the vicinity of important river crossings, are most likely indicative of commonly traversed routes, they can hardly be interpreted in the same way as modern signposts to aid a weary traveller on his way. On the contrary, we need to consider them, alongside enclosures, major settlements, dark and dangerous forests alternating with open fields and pastures, and other locales, as contexts for a network of economic, social and political relationships which operated at the time.

Ethnographic evidence from traditional societies suggests that space and distance, apart from physical dimensions, are also given symbolic significance which, among other things, encompasses both the known and the unknown (Helms 1988). This often highlights the contrast between the familiar life at home and the dangerous world outside; the unknown will naturally be associated with strangers but also with dangerous spirits and activities. Thus, movement beyond the familiar territory may well have been a hazardous activity for those willing or compelled to undertake it.

There is ample evidence, not only in the north but throughout the whole of Neolithic Europe, for circulation of commodities that were either necessary (for example flint and stone tools) or luxurious in nature (amber jewellery, marble rings, copper trinkets), and such goods were clearly distributed through the movement of people. While economic considerations undoubtedly played a role, trade need not have been the sole or, indeed, the most important aspect of long-distance travel. Mary Helms emphasises that within traditional societies travel plays an active element in political, social and religious affairs. Travel can be undertaken for knowledge (ritual, esoteric, in order to develop ideological powers, to observe performances of other groups or to acquire specific skills), to exchange information and news, or to acquire self-realisation and individuality that were not possible at home (the Kula exchanges offer the most dramatic ethnographic example of such institutionalised long-distance travel), and to acquire personal prestige by sharing one's experiences with those who cannot travel. An ancestral role in providing protection and facilitating travel is an important consideration and will be explored further in Chapter 6.

Megaliths and agriculture

There is very little doubt that megalithic tombs were built in an agricultural landscape. This is demonstrated by the various pollen analyses and, more particularly, through the preservation of ard marks under the protective mantle of the mounds. Indeed, as was noted in Chapter 1, the custom of placing burials in association with cultivated fields commenced with the construction of the long barrows, and the subsequent location of dolmens and passage graves continued this tradition. The presence of ard marks is really only well documented in Denmark, where they have been known since 1963. They are found in all parts of the country, from north Jutland to the southern Danish isles, and the recent programme of restoration of passage graves has brought to light many more examples (Figure 2.6). Elsewhere, ard marks are encountered only sporadically; we have already noted their presence at Flintbek, Schleswig-Holstein, and they are also known from beneath the secondary Bronze Age mound at the Skogdala dolmen in Scania (Jacobsson 1986, 108, Figure 14).

The reason for such an uneven distribution lies, naturally, in limited excavation and poor investigation of surviving old land surfaces rather than in different agricultural practices in the TRB culture. However, sometimes the original Neolithic land surface was removed prior to the construction of the chamber, as was the case at Jordehøj on Møn, where the chamber floor was dug below the old land surface and the ard marks survived only between the kerb and the external walls of the chamber (Dehn *et al.* 2000, 81–6, Figures 3.31–3.33). Indeed, at the double passage grave of Klekkendehøj the entire area underneath the mound had been

Figure 2.6 Plough marks under the chamber discovered in the process of restoration at
Maanehøj passage grave on south Zealand

stripped of the original surface prior to construction. On the other hand at Kong
Svends Høj, which was constructed directly upon the original Neolithic surface,
ard marks survived beneath the chamber as well as outside it (Dehn *et al.* 1995, 37–
9, Figures 36 and 37).

Analyses of soils preserved underneath some of the Dutch megaliths, conducted
over a quarter of a century ago by Casparie and Groenman van Waateringe (1980),
indicated that all were built in an environment altered by agricultural practices. Of
the 14 megaliths analysed, a majority were built either on abandoned arable land or
on arable land that subsequently had been used for grazing; in a couple of cases the
area had been abandoned long enough for heathland to be developing.

Recent investigations in Denmark have amplified this picture quite dramatically. There was clearly a huge labour investment in land management to create
fields and pastures; of necessity this involved the removal of erratic boulders (to be
used as construction materials) and the burning, sometimes repeatedly, of secondary forests was an important aspect of agriculture at the time megaliths were
constructed.

Naturally, the precise conditions varied from area to area. Study of ancient surfaces from the Vroue Hede region in north Jutland, where long barrow, dolmen and
passage grave soils have been analysed, concluded that here the early land use
(EN) involved the burning of the original lime and birch forest to establish grazing
land and birch coppice woods. These were utilised in rotation, with pastures being
regenerated through periodic burning of coppice woodlands. Even more intensive

41

grazing was postulated for the period during which passage graves were built, with heath areas now also taken into grazing (S. Th. Andersen 1995).

Analysis of samples from Klekkendehøj has revealed that hazel-dominated secondary woodland was burnt in order to create fields. Barley and possibly einkorn and emmer were grown, and the quantity of surviving pollen suggests that the fields must have been quite extensive. However, grazing here was slight, which contrasts with apparently heavy grazing around Jordehøj. The clearing of land through burning is indicated at many other megaliths, for example at Ormshøj on Møn, where lime, hazel and birch woodland was burnt, and at Kjephøj or at Skelde in south Jutland, where hazel groves were burnt (S. Th. Andersen 1988; Dehn *et al.* 1995, 166; Dehn *et al.* 2000, 154).

In the vicinity of Sarup there are now several dolmens and passage graves where clear traces of ard marks have been encountered and pollen analyses carried out. During the time of Sarup I, when the dolmens were built, fields and pastures were created in clearings where birch woods had been burnt, with hazel, lime and alder stands all around. During the time the passage graves began to be constructed, contemporary with Sarup II, the hazel and lime coppice woods had been burnt for further cultivation and grazing. Ard marks clearly indicate the presence of arable land and, in many instances, there is evidence that fields were ploughed two or even three times before the megalith was built. The passage grave Sarup Gamle Skole II was erected in a locality which had been ploughed at least twice, where barley was grown and where weeds of cultivation included cornflower, and such is the case with several other dolmens and passage graves around Sarup (N. H. Andersen 1997, 94, endnote 56). Several ploughing episodes have been recognised elsewhere: at least two episodes were noted at Jordehøj and possibly three at Kong Svends Høj; ard marks have also recently been noted beneath the passage grave at Tustrup (T. Dehn, pers. comm. 2007).

While the placement of a monument upon a ploughed field can be demonstrated practically, the interpretation of this phenomenon has been polarised in archaeological literature between ritual ploughing and accidental survival of a fragment of a field. On the one hand, this is seen as an example of ritual ploughing, a symbolic initial stage in the preparation of the ground for the construction of a funerary monument (Rowley-Conwy 1987). The opponents of this theory argue that the presence of ard marks is nothing more than a fortuitous circumstance of survival, the preservation of a fragment of a field under an earthen mound that was built soon after the ploughing took place (Thrane 1982, 1989; Kristiansen 1990).

This relationship first began with the long barrows, and the subsequent dolmens and passage graves continued to mark the ancestral land by being constructed upon ploughed fields; in this sense, as Kristiansen once suggested (1984, 80), the megaliths became a ritualised extension of the organisation of agricultural production. However, there is another way of looking at this phenomenon that may help to explain the close relationship between cultivation and the dead, and there need not be a contradiction between the symbolic and practical, between the sacred and secular. We shall return to this theme later, in Chapter 6.

3

TO BUILD A MEGALITH

General considerations

Building a megalith required many activities, of both a practical and a ritual nature. While a detailed discussion of the construction of different chambers – dolmens and passage graves – will follow later, many aspects of construction are common to all megaliths and may conveniently be introduced here. Initially, it undoubtedly involved prolonged consultations among the community members on appropriate location and auspicious time, negotiations with master builders and workforce, choosing the design of the tomb, remuneration, etc. These processes, for which there is hardly any archaeological evidence, were at the core of any megalithic building activity and could have been just as long and complicated as the actual construction of the tomb.

In practical terms, megalith building involved the identification and selection of appropriate building materials in the vicinity of the site. Large boulders, each weighing several tonnes, were needed for the construction of the chambers and the kerbs of the surrounding mounds. Sandstone and other rocks had to be quarried to provide slabs to fill in the gaps between these big stones. Smaller stones, flint, earth, sand and clay had to be collected in order to stabilise the chambers and build the mounds. While timber is rarely discussed in relation to megalith building, it was an equally important raw material for carrying out the work: trees had to be cut to provide rollers for transport of large stones, to build pulleys for raising them, and for scaffolding within and around the chambers; strong ropes had to be manufactured to aid the process; tree bark had to be stripped and prepared.

Once the appropriate raw materials had been selected, they had to be transported to the building site. In most cases this would not have involved great distances, but some rarer materials, such as the unusual quartz blocks used in the Danish megaliths, may well have come from further afield. The boulders had to be dragged on rollers or sledges; earth, clay, sand and smaller stones were most probably transported on carts pulled by oxen. Once amassed, the raw materials had to be prepared. While many boulders were used in their raw state, some were split to the required shapes, while stone and flint had to be broken and crushed into smaller pieces. The construction work on site would involve levelling the ground,

43

sometimes raising a platform; pits were dug to embed the uprights before erecting them, slabs for dry-stone walling had to be cut to appropriate shapes and sizes, capstones were raised, and subsequently the mound was piled up within the surrounding kerb. These were some of the most obvious building tasks that took place at simple as well as elaborate megaliths.

Estimates for the amount of work required for the construction of a megalith and discussion of methods employed in construction are a common pastime among archaeologists. There are ample, if not always consistent, data derived from ethnographic sources, as well as from modern experiments in handling raw materials employing methods that would have been available to Neolithic builders, to give us some idea of the work efforts involved (see insert below).

Work estimates for the north European megaliths

Within the context of north European megalith building, Johannes Müller has suggested possible workloads for the construction of two German megaliths: a passage grave at Kleinenkneten 1, near Oldenburg in Lower Saxony, and a passage grave at Drebenstedt in Altmark (Müller 1990a, 1990b; Fritsch and Müller 2002). His work has been followed in Sweden by Karl-Göran Sjögren's estimates for the construction efforts in Bohuslän and Falbygden (Sjögren 2003a). Müller's criteria for a 'mega-work' programme (1990a) are averages extrapolated from a variety of data derived from nineteenth-century ethnographic records and archaeological experiments. The basic principles are as follows.

RAW MATERIAL PROCUREMENT

Stone extraction*	330 kg per man-hour
Earth extraction	676 kg per man-hour

* Granite and gneiss require 40% more effort than limestone and sandstone

---

TRANSPORT OF RAW MATERIALS

Stone and rubble	50 kg over 1 km per man-hour
Earth	455 kg over 100 m per man-hour
Boulder transport	1000 kg over 1 km per 132 man-hours

WORK ON SITE

Pit digging	675 kg per man-hour
Erection of uprights	1000 kg per 65 man-hours
Placement of capstones	1000 kg per 35 man-hours
Creation of stone/earth mound	400 kg per man-hour

Kleinenkneten 1 chamber is built of nine uprights, weighing on average about 2 tonnes each (one orthostat weighs 5 tonnes), and three capstones of about 15 tonnes each; the boulders used in the passage weigh altogether about 4 tonnes. The long barrow surrounding the chamber has 69 kerbstones (average 2 tonnes each) and originally contained 700 cubic metres of earth. Using the criteria outlined above, the overall estimate for the construction of this monument (procurement, transportation and building) is 109,500 man-hours. This means that, accepting a ten-hour working day, a hundred persons would have needed about three and a half months to build this tomb.

The Drebenstedt megalith was smaller: 61 kerbstones, 12 orthostats, five capstones but only about 138 cubic metres of mound earth. Müller's estimate is between 35,000 and 40,000 man-hours, and thus about 40 days for the construction of this site.

Karl-Göran Sjögren has used some of Müller's criteria for estimates of labour in the construction of megaliths in Bohuslän and Falbygden, Västergötland, adding data from other experimental work (for example Mohen and Scarre 2002) as well as estimating labour needed for transporting earth and stone using ox-driven carts (Sjögren 2003a, Tables 10.6–10.12). His estimate of the work for Karleby 57 passage grave relates principally to the transport of raw materials, thus not being directly comparable to estimates for total construction of Müller's model. Nevertheless overall results are similar, with between 50 and 100 individuals required for cooperation in tomb building.

However, Palle Eriksen has recently provided an interesting critique of the known ethnographic examples and modern experiments in manoeuvring large heavy stones, concluding that the lifting of heavy stones could have been performed with a relatively small workforce provided there was appropriate leadership: 'a foreman with ingenuity, coordination and determination' (Eriksen 2002, 98, Figure 24).

Building materials

One of the features of the natural landscape across the whole of the north European plain and southern Scandinavia during the Neolithic period was the abundance of glacial boulders. These huge gneiss and granite rocks – originally suspended in ice sheets that formed in the far north, subsequently crushed and dragged along southwards, and finally left behind as the glaciers melted and retreated northwards – provided the most obvious building materials for the megalithic chambers: the

Figure 3.1 Großer Karlstein megalithic chamber, Osnabrück, Lower Saxony

walls, the roofs and the kerbs of covering mounds. While occasionally sedimentary rocks such as sandstone or limestone were also used for the 'megalithic' components of tombs, as seen at the magnificent passage grave from Lower Saxony known as Großer Karlstein, which was built of massive sandstone slabs (Figure 3.1), there is only one area in which sedimentary rocks were used in preference to others for megalith building. The geology of the Falbygden plateau, in Västergötland, makes slate, sandstone and limestone plentiful there and it was these rocks that were predominantly chosen to provide the raw materials (Sjögren 2003a, Table 10.5).

While most erratics were probably relatively small (Figure 3.2), there are still some extraordinary boulders left, giving an impression of their possible original size. One of the largest surviving may well be the so-called *Giebichenstein* at Stöckse, near Nienburg/Weser, estimated to weigh 330 tonnes (Caspers *et al.* 2005, 46; there is an interesting '*Findlingsgarten*' at Hagenburg where such glacial boulders are displayed in a garden setting; ibid. Figure 3). At Halskov Vænge, on the island of Falster, many megalithic tombs were constructed using local stones, but one glacial boulder still survives intact to this day (Figure 3.3). It is called *Spejder Stenen*, standing in an artificial hollow dug by locals curious to see its size (an informal estimate by a Danish colleague put the weight at about 80 tonnes); it has two cup-marks which most probably were carved during the Bronze Age.

Discussion of raw materials used in the construction of megaliths is important for several reasons. The size of the boulders, which has fascinated antiquarians and archaeologists alike, had a bearing on the size of the chambers, particularly in

Figure 3.2 J. J. Assendorp by the glacial boulder at Karlstein, near Neu-Wulmstorf,
Lower Saxony

Figure 3.3 Spejder Stenen glacial boulder at Halskov Vænge on the island of Falster

Figure 3.4 Capstone employed to its limits at the passage grave of Soderstorf, Lower
Saxony

terms of their width, which depended directly on the size of stones available for
capstones. Clearly some huge stones were available, since the capstone covering
the passage grave at Vedsted, south Jutland, is close to 30 tonnes in weight. That
many may have been of medium rather than large size is indicated by the 'minimal-
ist' approach evidenced at some sites, where the capstone length is employed to the
limits (Figure 3.4), a factor which may have been responsible for the collapse of
some chambers, once the protective stone and earth mantle had eroded or been
removed.

Although analysis of the different raw materials features in some excavation
reports, the significance of various raw materials generally has not been an integral
part of the study of megaliths in northern Europe. 'The Megalith Campaign'– a
project, begun in 1991, whose purpose is to restore some of the Danish protected
megalithic sites – has given rise to new archaeological investigations of principles
of construction (Dehn *et al.* 1995, 7). While these investigations are in practice
limited to relatively small excavations at megalithic monuments, they have brought
to light a wealth of data on construction principles, which in turn may stimulate
new discussions regarding the symbolic and aesthetic aspects of megalith buildings, as well as practical solutions to architectural problems.

Thus, while the large boulders were clearly significant, other raw materials were
also used in the construction, and the architectural, i.e. aesthetic, qualities such as
the juxtaposition of colours and textures are an equally important feature. Moreover it seems that many building materials – and not just the visible components

highlighted in some post-modern approaches – carried important symbolism in terms of their exotic nature, provenance and relation to other ritual activities, and thus were incorporated in the construction precisely for these reasons (Chapter 5).

Packing materials outside chambers and mounds

Mound surfaces, as we observe them today, hardly reflect their original appearance. Many have been altered in subsequent periods either by extensions or by superimposition, most commonly in the Bronze Age, while others have completely disappeared over the course of several millennia. While it is difficult to determine precisely when the mound destruction process began, some of the north European megaliths were certainly devoid of their mounds by the early eighteenth century. (On early damage, see p. 28.) This is well illustrated by an engraving from J. H. Nunningh's *Sepulchretum gentile* of 1714 (Schnapp 1996, figure on page 206). It depicts diggers busily exploring a round mound but, in the background, there is a perfect Lower Saxon passage grave with capstones freely balanced on the uprights, completely devoid of its mound. This engraving suggests that destruction of megaliths did not always begin with the extraction of the large stones for other building purposes. It is possible that some of the chambers were never covered or that the mounds simply decayed naturally; it is not inconceivable that the earth was also sought after as a suitable practical or symbolic raw material.

The absence, or at least partial disappearance, of mounds at some megaliths has naturally given rise to the suggestion that not all megaliths were completely covered. This argument appears every now and then and has surfaced once again in recent Danish literature, with suggestions that some chambers may have been free-standing and others were covered only up to their capstones (Eriksen 1999, 76; N. Nielsen 2003, 139–49). We shall return to this issue later but, for the moment, we should note that the mounds in the Falbygden area are commonly assumed not to have covered the chambers entirely; the outer stone mantles were quite low and the massive capstones are believed to have protruded above. However, irrespective of the above controversy, there are still many megaliths, dolmens as well as passage graves, which remain fully covered by their mounds, making it quite clear that the majority of chambers must have been fully hidden from view.

The mound surfaces are equally difficult to reconstruct. In some cases they were made of an additional dense capping of stones: good examples survive at Klekkendehøj, Bigum, and the extended dolmen at Wilsen (Dehn *et al.* 2000, 74–6; Schuldt 1972, Plate 39b); such stone mantles may in due course have been covered up naturally by drifting sand and earth. On the other hand, Michaelsen's excavations at Kleinenkneten 1 (Michaelsen 1978, 234) have demonstrated that, once the chamber was stabilised by layers of granite cobbles, the entire mound was composed of an estimated 700 cubic metres of earth, creating a flat upper surface. Thus, many megaliths may have been covered with mounds composed largely of earth.

Natural decay of the mounds, as well as the effects of ploughing and other disturbances, further obscure the fact that some chamber mounds were constructed

Figure 3.5 Dolmen at Poskær Stenhus on the Djursland peninsula, Jutland

on raised platforms. Such platforms or multi-tiered constructions are rarely seen, but a high chamber entrance, raised well above the surrounding ground, is a good indication. Raised mounds are common throughout the Falbygden area in Sweden. Many passage graves here have a two-tiered construction, with a wide raised platform serving as a base for the erection of the mound proper (Tilley 1996, 144, Figure 3.22). At Hjelmar's Cairn, for example, the platform is about 25 m in diameter with a central 12 m large mound on top (Persson and Sjögren 2001, 43), and such platforms can still be perceived today, for example in the Karleby area (Figure 2.5). Since in many cases the megaliths are constructed in an already elevated position, this feature accentuated the location even further.

Recent restoration work at Danish passage graves has also recorded artificial platforms at a number of sites (Dehn *et al*. 2000; Hansen 1993). Thus at Klekkendehøj the outer part of the mound was made up of stone packing arranged in three steps; the outermost formed a wide berm which protruded all the way round the foot of the mound and served as a platform for votive offerings (Dehn *et al*. 2000, 45, Figures 2.4, 2.38 and 2.39). Similar raised terraces below mounds are suggested by the passage graves of Gundsølille on Zealand, Moreshøj on Fyn, at long dolmens at Ormstrup on Langeland, Sarup Gamle Skole X on Fyn, and several other dolmens throughout Denmark. The outer kerb at the well-known polygonal dolmen at Poskær Stenhus, for example, is so highly elevated above the surrounding ground that an original platform to the outside seems a strong possibility (Figure 3.5).

50

Evidence from other areas is difficult to interpret. Bakker does not discuss this feature at all with reference to the Dutch and west German megaliths, but Schuldt comments on a number of mounds in Mecklenburg (round as well as rectangular) where the chamber is placed high in the mound, for example at Nadelitz 2 (Schuldt 1972, Plate 21), or at Wilsen (ibid., Plate 39b) where the chamber effectively sits atop the round cairn. At Serrahn (ibid., Plates 9 and 38) the chamber is surrounded by three circles of large stones – an arrangement reminiscent of that at Klekkende-høj – but the plan and cross-section are too schematic to indicate whether or not the outer layer was visible outside the stone cairn.

Stone kerb settings

Most mounds were surrounded by boulders set up on the outside, with gaps between them also filled with dry-stone walling to create a continuous stone kerb. Where kerbstones have not survived, they can usually be identified by the presence of stone holes and small wedging stones. The kerb boulders vary in shape: flat sides may face the outside, or else the stones are placed deliberately to display their naturally rounded surfaces. Generally they are medium-sized, not matching the height of the chamber; for example at Everstorfer Forst (Naschendorf 2) where the kerbstones are only half as tall as the chamber uprights (Figure 3.6a); at Grønnehøj on Zealand, where the kerbstones are even smaller than those in the passage (Figure 3.6b); at Jordehøj on Møn (Dehn *et al.* 2000, Figures 3.25 and 3.37); or the half-metre-tall stones around the great dolmen at Vedsted, south Jutland (Ebbesen 1979, 20).

Oval enclosures, so typical of the western region – Lower Saxony and the Netherlands – sometimes have a double kerb that displays an interesting pattern. At the double oval enclosure at Thuine in Emsland, the stones of the inner kerb appear to be even lower than their outer counterparts (Figures 3.7 and 3.8). The same has been noted at the long dolmen of Stokkeby on Langeland, which was also surrounded by a double kerb: the inner row was composed of stones smaller than those of the outer kerb (Skaarup 1985a, 296). Eighteenth-century descriptions also suggest a smaller inner kerb for the Poskær Stenhus polygonal dolmen in Jutland (Eriksen 1999, figure on page 23).

The very long enclosures at Visbeker Braut and Visbeker Bräutigam, near Wildeshausen, Lower Saxony, provide examples of interesting contrast between the low and high kerbstones. Visbeker Braut is a slightly trapezoidal enclosure 80 m long, whose kerbstones increase in size from north-east to south-west, culminating in a massive façade of four uprights at least 2 m in height. Although the Visbeker Bräutigam rectangular enclosure of 108 m in length does not display such a progressive change in the size of the stones on its long sides, the western façade has stones 1.4 m tall and the eastern façade once again towers over the entire setting, with massive boulders up to 2.4 m in height (Sprockhoff 1975, 137; Figure 3.9a and b).

The nearly 100 m long dolmen of Grønjægers Høj, on Møn, has a massive kerb of closely set boulders 1.5 m tall and even taller stones at its western façade, which

Figure 3.6 (a) Dolmen (Naschendorf 2) at Everstorfer Forst, Mecklenburg;
(b) Passage grave at Grønnehøj on western Zealand

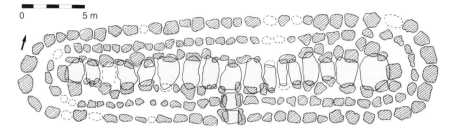

0   5 m

Figure 3.7 Plan of the passage grave in a double stone setting at Thuine in Emsland

Figure 3.8 Passage grave at Thuine in Emsland

create a gable end (Figure 3.10), and the same feature can be observed from
A. P. Madsen's 1887 drawing of the Kong Humbles long dolmen on Langeland
(Skaarup 1985a, 151, Figure 134). Similar arrangements have been noted during
the restoration of Kong Svends Høj passage grave. The rectangular mound is set
within a kerb whose long sides are built of stones between 1.6 and 1.7 m in height.
The two façades are slightly concave, and here the stones increase dramatically in
size, with the tallest in the middle, rising 2 m above the basic kerb. This arrangement also suggests that the mound was roof-shaped, tallest in the middle. The
stones in the south-eastern gable, although they differ petrographically (two
of granite, two of porphyry and one pegmatite), were chosen specifically for
their very strong reddish colour; the north-western gable unfortunately was not
complete but the restorers thought that, in contrast, it was distinctly grey in character (Dehn *et al.* 1995, 142; Figure 3.11).

53

a

b

Figure 3.9 Massive façades at (a) Visbeker Braut and (b) Visbeker Bräutigam, near
Wildeshausen, Lower Saxony (Ute Bartelt kindly provides the scale in both
pictures)

Figure 3.10 Grønjægers Høj long dolmen on the island of Møn

Apart from the impressive kerb, many rectangular and trapezoidal mounds have so-called guard stones (from the German word *Wächtersteine*) – conspicuously large monoliths associated with the corners. In most cases the chamber contained within the mound is a dolmen, but some passage graves with this feature are also known. Sometimes only the actual cornerstones appear larger, for example at the reconstructed long mound at Munkwolstrup, Schleswig (Figure 3.12a), or at Mankmoos 1, Mecklenburg (Figure 3.12b), but true guard stones protrude beyond the kerb at one, or occasionally both, ends of the mound. The north-western façade of Kong Svends Høj originally had two outliers – the so-called 'horns' or guard stones. On present knowledge this is a rare phenomenon in Denmark, and Kong Svends Høj is the first passage grave at which this feature has been observed (Dehn *et al.* 1995, 78–9, Figures 89, 91 and 92; Figure 3.13).

The trapezoidal long mounds on Rügen provide truly dramatic examples of such an arrangement, for instance at Nobbin, Dwasieden or Nadelitz (Schuldt 1972, Plates 10, 20, 21). The guard stones at Nobbin are very large: over 3 m in height and weighing about 25 tonnes each, they contrast dramatically with the kerbstones, which do not exceed 1.5 m in height and six tonnes in weight; the guard stones, in addition, display a distinctly red tint (Figure 3.13).

The facades may be straight, as at Nobbin, or curved as at Naschendorf 4, where the western façade is concave (Figure 3.14a and b). Schuldt's investigations at some of the sites suggest that the guard stones may have been integrated with the corners of the façade by the presence of dry-stone walling (traces of thin slabs were observed at Lancken Granitz 1, Nobbin and Dwasieden; ibid. 69). Such façades

55

Figure 3.11 Reconstruction of Kong Svends Høj passage grave on the island of Lolland

would have been particularly impressive: the juxtaposition of massive vertical boulders alternating with the horizontally arranged red sandstone slabs was a dramatic aesthetic device creating a theatrical setting for rituals and ceremonies.

The dolmens

The simple rectangular dolmen is the commonest form of megalithic chamber and, with the possible exception of the area west of the river Weser, found in large numbers across the whole of northern Europe (Figure 2.6). Such chambers have walls built of between four and six boulders of roughly equal height, and one massive stone, reposed longitudinally upon them, usually serves as a capstone. The chambers may be slightly subterranean, that is to say partly dug into the old land surface; good examples of this are provided by several of the dolmens in the Everstorfer Forst (Figure 3.15a), and Mankmoos 1 in Mecklenburg, at Kläden (Figure 3.15b) and Haaßel in Lower Saxony, and at the Ølstykke dolmen in northeast Zealand (Figure 4.2a). The majority, however, seem to rest on the old land surface, for example the Kellerød chamber in the long dolmen in west-central Zealand (P. O. Nielsen 1984, 378; Figure 4.2b), but without proper investigation it is often impossible to determine which is the case. While the size of individual structures varies, we should note that normally they are only large enough to accommodate one extended human body. Such chambers were not intended to be reused, and further access could only be gained by removing the capstone.

It is generally assumed that closed dolmens are the earliest megalithic structures

a

b

Figure 3.12 (a) Reconstructed long dolmen mound at Munkwolstrup, Schleswig;
(b) Long dolmen no. 1 at Mankmoos, Mecklenburg

(N. H. Andersen 1997, 97; 2000, 17); the accessible stone chambers came to be built later, became larger and displayed a wider range of forms. Whereas larger rect-angular and trapezoidal dolmens were built everywhere, in Schleswig-Holstein, Denmark and Sweden oval, polygonal and the so-called pear-shaped chambers

57

Figure 3.13 Christoph Steinmann at one of the guard stones at the great dolmen of Nobbin on the island of Rügen

were also built. Some chambers became quite large and, independently of the typo-chronological connotations, they may indeed be termed great dolmens.

The form of the larger dolmen chambers, be they rectangular, trapezoidal, polygonal or pear-shaped (Figure 3.16), may well have been guided by a range of considerations: local community tradition, desire to innovate or to create a contrast, availability of building materials within a specific locality, etc. However, there are two aspects that should be considered as particularly important: the accessibility of the chamber and the possible symbolic meaning of the increased size.

The development from a closed to an accessible chamber is not simply an architectural, but rather a functional change, which permitted easy access to the chamber's interior, facilitating subsequent interments (should such be required) and creating a focus for ceremonies designed to honour the dead. Indeed, N. H. Andersen has observed that the chambers which were accessible, especially those with passages, have the most profuse votive deposits placed in front of them (1997, 314). While such votive depositions took place in other contexts throughout the landscape, the megalithic tombs were incorporated into this process, culminating ultimately in the massive votive deposits in front of and around the passage graves (Chapter 4).

As for the size of the chambers, we need to consider its possible symbolism; size need not be expressed in a metric sense (that is length and width) but rather in terms of an increase of the basic architectural units that went into the construction. Thus the number of pairs of orthostats, the number and positioning of capstones, or the different impression of volume created by a polygonal or trapezoidal shape,

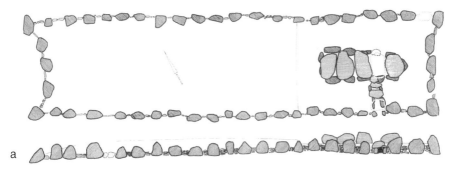

a

b

Figure 3.14 (a) Plan of the passage grave (Naschendorf 4), Everstorfer Forst,
Mecklenburg; (b) Western façade at Everstorfer Forst, Mecklenburg

could have been as important as the actual physical size. In practical terms – say
the available floor space – a simple rectangular chamber could be larger than an
extended dolmen, but in symbolic terms the latter would be larger because of the
greater number of architectural components and the different mode of construction.

In order to enable access to the interior, a variety of entrance arrangements were
employed: either via a short passage with or without a threshold stone or, more
commonly, through an opening at one of the chamber ends. This could involve an
end stone that was smaller than the rest, creating a narrow gap either above or
alongside it. Such chambers also tend to have the wall stones placed upright, thus
increasing the height of the interior. We find them throughout the entire dolmen
distribution area – the numerous *erweiterte* dolmens in north Germany, such as
Mürow (Figure 3.17a), Naschendorf 2 (Figure 3.17b) and Bavendorf 3. Further

a

b

Figure 3.15 Simple dolmen chambers: (a) Everstorfer Forst (Naschendorf no. 1), Mecklenburg; (b) Kläden, Lüneburger Heide; (c) and (d) Two dolmen chambers from the Stokkebjerg Skov long dolmen, north-west Zealand

c

d

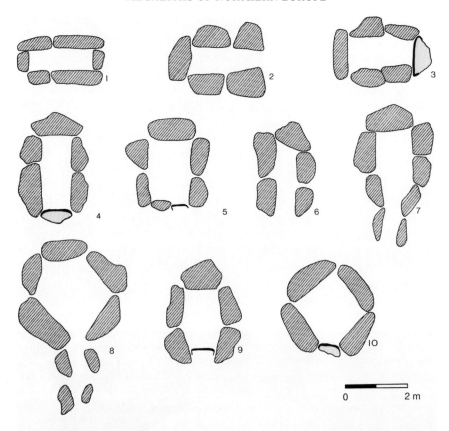

Figure 3.16 Plans of dolmen chambers

west are the chambers on the Lüneburger Heide at Barskamp and Haaßel; that at Seedorf is one of the more westerly examples, although Bakker has described the chamber from G5-Heveskesklooster also as a dolmen built of seven orthostats and three capstones (Bakker 1992, 108–9, Figure 5; 1999, 147–8, Figure 1). In Schleswig-Holstein, the recently reconstructed chamber at Munkwolstrup, near Flensburg, is an excellent example of a chamber that was entered over a half-height end stone (Figure 3.17c) and the dolmen of Poppostein has a short passage (Figure 3.17d). These openings, when not in use, were usually closed with a door slab, a small orthostat or a packing of smaller stones.

It would be impossible, and indeed unnecessary, to describe all large dolmens but, throughout the distribution area, there are some interesting regional styles of chamber that merit our consideration from the architectural point of view. We may thus profitably consider the polygonal dolmens of southern Scandinavia, the great dolmens of that region as well as their counterparts further south and across the Baltic Sea; a few unconventional examples provide insights into the constructional ability and ingenuity of the builders.

Some of the larger south Scandinavian dolmens appear truly dramatic as they stand in the landscape today, devoid of the covering mounds (Figure 3.18). While the rectangular and trapezoidal forms are found everywhere, the main distribution of the polygonal dolmens is in north-west Zealand and, across the Kattegat, on the Djursland peninsula, with an additional scatter along the south-western Swedish coast in Bohuslän. Elsewhere polygonal dolmens are found sporadically, with none, apparently, south of the river Eider in Schleswig-Holstein.

The orthostats are usually placed with the flat sides towards the interior, slightly inclined towards the top to counterbalance the weight of the capstones placed upon them. Although many dolmens have lost their capstones (for example the two polygonal dolmens at Tustrup, one of which has a capstone replaced as part of recent reconstruction; Figure 3.19a, b and c), the sheer size of some that survive, far beyond what was needed to provide a roof, suggests that massiveness was the order of the day. Figure 3.18 shows some examples of such large capstones, and the question of whether these dolmens were entirely covered by earthen mounds is indeed worth considering. The polygonal dolmens were easy to cap with just one massive stone, as seen at Poskær Stenhus (Figure 3.18b) or at Grovlegård. The Poskær Stenhus capstone weighs just over 11 tonnes, the Grovlegård cover is close to 19 tonnes; they were split from the same boulder and used on chambers that are just under 2 km apart. (While the use of split boulders in megaliths has been known for quite some time, the symbolic significance of their use in construction in northern Europe is only now beginning to receive attention; more discussion in Chapter 5.)

Among the Swedish dolmens, the chamber at Haga on the island of Orust, Bohuslän (Figure 3.20), must rank among the most evocative megaliths in northern Europe and is one of the largest and best-preserved round dolmens in the region. Strictly speaking, the plan of the chamber floor is nearly square (2.1 m across at maximum) and the four thin slabs lean inwards towards the top to support, at a height of 1.8 m, a relatively thin capstone over 3 m in length; entry was made through a short passage with a threshold just within the chamber. Once again, the covering of a chamber of this size and height with a mound apparently only 8 m in diameter is questionable.

Some of the great Danish dolmens set within round mounds have long passages of the sort normally associated with passage graves: that at Brejninggård in north Jutland was 4.5 m long, and the one at the Vedsted great dolmen, south Jutland, was 3 m in length and had a threshold just before the chamber (Ebbesen 1978, 50; 1979, 19). The latter was a substantial chamber of 3.75 × 1.75 m, built of eight orthostats with flat faces turned inwards and covered with one massive and two smaller capstones.

Schuldt wrote extensively on the subject of the great dolmens that he excavated in Mecklenburg, and he attempted to distinguish separate settlement groups based on local architectural styles (Schuldt 1972, Map 9). Unfortunately, such spatial groupings were contradicted by his strict typo-chronology of chamber development, with the spatial and temporal dimensions never reconciled. Nevertheless the great dolmens in Mecklenburg exhibit some interesting regional traits. In principle the chambers are rectangular or slightly trapezoidal (some could easily be

a

b

Figure 3.17 Accessible dolmens: (a) Mürow, near Prenzlau, Brandenburg; (b) Everstorfer
    Forst (Naschendorf no. 2), Mecklenburg; (c) Munkwolstrup, Schleswig;
    (d) Poppostein, Schleswig

c

d

Figure 3.18 South Scandinavian dolmens: (a) Toftebjerg, north-west Zealand; (b) Torben Dehn at Poskær Stenhus on the Djursland peninsula; (c) Svend Hansen at Bakkebølle, south Zealand; (d) Hofterup, south-west Scania

c

d

Figure 3.19 Megalithic centre at Tustrup, Jutland: (a) SE dolmen prior to placement of the capstone; (b) SE dolmen after recent reconstruction with a capstone placed on top; (c) NW dolmen without capstone; (d) cult house

c

d

Figure 3.20 Dolmen at Haga, Island of Orust, Bohuslän

described as pear-shaped forms), usually consisting of more than three pairs of uprights. The local features showed themselves, among other things, in different ways of constructing an entrance: for example an antechamber was typical of great dolmens built around the river Schwinge, while a porch arrangement using red sandstone slabs was developed to perfection on the island of Rügen.

The island of Rügen, in fact, displays a great variety of chambers, from relatively simple dolmens covered by a single capstone, for example at Nobbin, to very elaborate extended dolmens such as at Lancken Granitz 4. The great dolmens here, as elsewhere, are built of erratics. The passages, however, have their walls and covers made of thin red sandstone slabs (on average 0.8 × 0.6 m wide and 0.2 m thick) creating a rather delicate and elegant entrance, which contrasts with the massive boulders. The individual pairs of passage walls may be of the same height (Lancken Granitz 1), or the outermost set of passage stones may be taller with the arrangement decreasing in height towards the chamber (for example at Lancken Granitz 4, Figure 3.21). This sort of passage arrangement does seem to be very much a local characteristic.

Within the general dolmen category there are also some sites where the ingenuity and skill of the builders, in combination with boulders of particular shapes, has occasionally led to construction of chambers that stand out from the general pattern. They cannot be 'fitted' into any of our typological standards but, at the same time, they offer exciting insight into the ingenuity and skill of the builders. A unique example comes from Utersum, on the north Friesian island of Föhr (Figure 3.22). The chamber, 1.8 m high and constructed of eight orthostats and three

Figure 3.21 The entrance arrangements at the great dolmen of Lancken Granitz 4, seen from inside the chamber, island of Rügen

capstones, was entirely subterranean and had two passages (3.5 m and 7 m long) running in roughly opposite directions to one another, rising to the surface. The passages' capstones were later used in the construction of a Bronze Age stone cist that overlay the earlier structure (Kersten and La Baume 1958, 320; Hoika 1990, 60).

Another curious subterranean dolmen has recently come to light at the enclosure of Sarup Gamle Skole, in south-west Fyn, only about half a kilometre away from the Sarup enclosure itself. Here a miniature dolmen (112 × 73 cm internally) was built at the bottom of one of the enclosure ditches. Although the capstone had been removed in the course of ploughing, the small chamber was built (and used?) in exactly the same manner as its larger counterparts on the surface (N. H. Andersen 2000, 29–30, Figure 7).

Although architecturally simple, the south Scandinavian dolmens were nevertheless very sophisticated constructions, employing elements that would continue to be used throughout the time of megalithic building, culminating in the elaborate passage graves. Dry-stone walling filled the gaps between the orthostats of all forms of dolmen chambers; sometimes the chambers were additionally protected. A good example is offered by the two stone chambers at the long dolmen at Grøfte; these demonstrate most eloquently that the builders were concerned to keep the chambers dry, since both were surrounded by flat split slabs angled around each chamber to divert the rainwater to the outside, away from the chambers and into the mound (Ebbesen 1990, Figures 5 and 10–12).

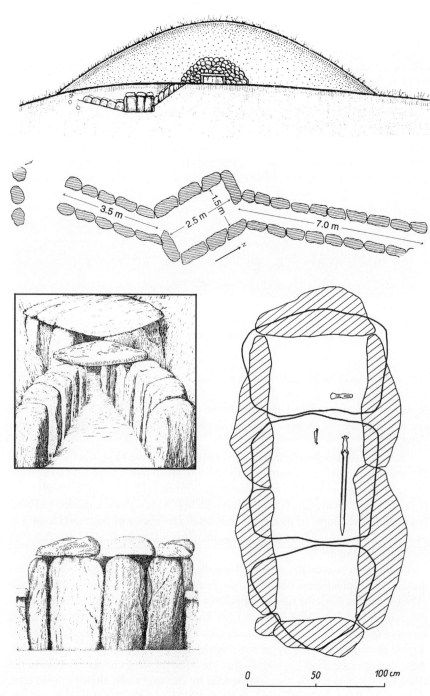

Figure 3.22 Dolmen from Utersum, island of Föhr

Passage graves

The passage grave, as previously indicated, is the other major type of chamber occurring throughout the whole of northern Europe (Figure 2.3). By the time these structures were built, from about 3300/3200 BC, there was already a great store of skill and knowledge regarding the handling of raw materials, solutions to architectural problems and understanding of the symbolic meaning of both. This experience was translated into architecture which, even today, cannot fail to impress. A well-built passage grave is an almost hermetically closed chamber, sure to stand for at least 5000 years; in some areas passage graves represent the ultimate achievement in megalithic architecture. (During my megalithic tour of Denmark in the autumn of 2004, I was frequently tested by Danish colleagues in the art of distinguishing a well-built passage grave from one where 'corners had been cut'. Initially it was hard but, in due course, I learned to appreciate the intricacies of passage grave construction and to distinguish a gem from a mediocrity.)

Regional variants

In the north European typological nomenclature, a passage grave is recognised as a chamber entered by means of a passage which is at an angle to the long axis of the chamber and thus leads from one of its long sides (Figure 3.23). This is in direct contrast to an open dolmen, where the entrance, with or without a passage, is the continuation of the long axis, so that the chamber is entered from its end (Hansen 1993, Sprockhoff 1938). This change in the position of the entrance is a significant feature – not only did it create new architectural and constructional challenges but it clearly also must have been related to changes in the way people used burial chambers and conducted ceremonies within and around them.

Most passage graves are rectangular and trapezoidal in shape. These are encountered everywhere: from the Drenthe plateau in the west to Mecklenburg in the east, from the Falbygden area in Sweden, to Altmark and the middle Elbe–Saale region. Sporadically passage graves are found further east, with isolated examples known as far east as central Poland (Bakker 1992, 73–6; Midgley 1985, Figures 52 and 53). In addition to these common forms, oval chambers are known in parts of Schleswig-Holstein and throughout Denmark and Scania, but they are not encountered elsewhere.

However, within the vast area of the north European passage grave province, there are many regional variants that can be recognised on the basis of ground plan, three-dimensional appearance, and size. Irrespective of the arguments about the visibility or invisibility of dolmens, or the Swedish passage graves, the number of passage graves totally concealed beneath their mounds makes it quite clear that the majority were not meant to be seen. Thus the regional variants assume a double significance; on the one hand they give us an indication of the different architectural schools and building approaches to the same problem across northern Europe, and on the other hand they offer a paradox of the passage graves being sacred

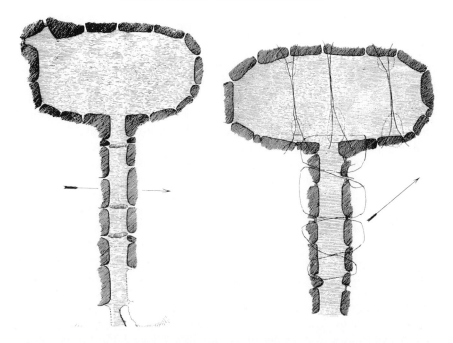

Figure 3.23 Two passage graves from the island of Zealand, showing the position of the passage in relation to the chamber

architecture, hidden from public view and penetrable only by those few who had access to the interior and to the spiritual world of the ancestors buried within the chambers.

The majority of chambers, irrespective of their ground plan, are of medium size, between 8 and 10 m in length and 2 to 2.5 m in width (Hansen 1993, 21; Schuldt 1972, 29). The construction of oval chambers may well have depended on the relationship of length to width for overall harmony and stability. In rectangular and trapezoidal chambers, however, the length was by and large a question of multiplying the architectural units (orthostats, or their pairs, supporting the capstones) and, in theory at least, there was no limit. Although we have already noted that metric dimensions need not necessarily reflect the concept of size as it was understood by the megalith builders, some chamber lengths and widths are very impressive indeed.

Although various sizes of chambers are encountered on the boundary of Lower Saxony and the Netherlands, this is also an area where the longest north European passage graves are found. Thus we may note chambers 20 m long at D27-Borger, 27.5 m at Werlte and 32 m at Damme (Bakker 1992, 12; Knöll 1983, 5). For large chambers, many orthostats were needed: ten pairs at D53-Havelte, 15 pairs and the same number of capstones at Werlte and Lähden, and at Thuine this is increased to 18 pairs (Figures 3.7 and 3.8).

The width of the chamber was also an important element, as this was crucial to

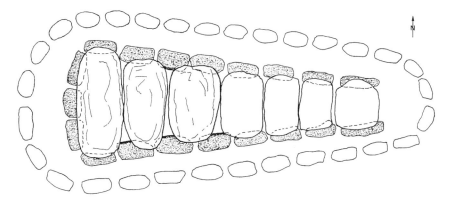

Figure 3.24 Reconstructed plan of the chamber at König Surbold, on the Hümmling, Lower Saxony

its stability, but it also depended on the size of the boulders available for capstones. Hansen notes that there are optimal forms of construction and that average Danish passage graves are generally between 2 and 2.5 m in width (Hansen 1993, 21). Thus it is further significant that the most dramatic examples of chambers of great width come from the same region where we witness the greatest lengths: from the area of the Hümmling and around Osnabrück, in Lower Saxony. Here many very wide chambers are known. The chamber at Großer Karlstein is 3 m wide (Figure 3.1), as is the south chamber at Hekese, while the north chamber is 3.5 m wide at its south-east end, and the chamber at Haltern is 3.8 m wide at its eastern end (Laux 1991, 56, 58). One of the widest may well have been the chamber at König Surbold, destroyed towards the end of the eighteenth or beginning of the nine-teenth century; if the existing early documentation is to be believed, the chamber was 17 m long, expanding from 1.6 m in the east to the mighty 6-m-wide interior at its western end (Laux 1989, 119; Figure 3.24).

Interestingly, Bakker has argued that it was not so much the desire to create exceptionally wide chambers, but rather the opportune presence of large, unusu-ally shaped boulders that led to this curious development. Sometimes the largest capstones are in the middle, causing the chamber walls to 'bulge' outwards at this point. In an unusual move, the builders of the passage grave known as Heiden-opfertisch at Visbek (Figure 3.25a) laid the capstone lengthwise over the chamber – in a manner normally typical of dolmens – since it was clearly too large to be placed across; a similar solution was used at Molbergen-Teufelssteine (Bakker 1992, 27) and also at Stöckheim, in Altmark (Figure 3.25b). Opportunistic form is well demonstrated in one of the chambers from a rather isolated small group known as Sieben Steinhäuser, near Fallingbostel. Of the five chambers known here, four are typical small to medium passage grave chambers, but the fifth one (known as chamber D) is a nearly square structure covered by an unusual slab 4.6 × 4.2 m wide and 0.5 m thick, with the squareness of the chamber further accentuated by the square stone setting around it (Figure 3.26). The builders in Lower Saxony

Figure 3.25 Passage graves with longitudinally arranged capstones: (a) Heidenopfertisch, near Wildeshausen, Lower Saxony; (b) Stöckheim, Altmark

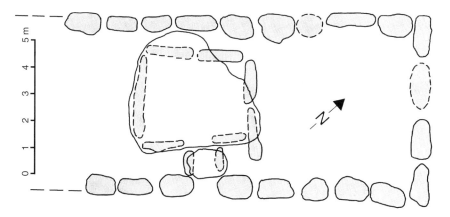

Figure 3.26 Passage grave D at Sieben Steinhäuser, near Fallingbostel, Lower Saxony

clearly exercised their skill and ingenuity using what was close at hand, rather than deriving inspiration from the distant '*dolmen angevin*' (Laux 1984a; Bakker 1992). Whichever came first – the desire or the opportunity – they were responsible for some exceptionally large chambers.

Oval chambers have a wide distribution in southern Scandinavia: they are found in Jutland (especially Himmerland and on Djursland), in northern and western Zealand, in Scania and, to a lesser extent, in Schleswig-Holstein. Some small chambers are nearly circular, but usually they are up to 3 m long, 1.5 m wide and not tall enough for one to stand up in the interior. Rectangular chambers (Figure 3.27a) tend to be larger, easily up to 10 m long and 2.5 m wide, with some sufficiently high to accommodate a standing individual.

While there is only a scatter of rectangular chambers in north Jutland with isolated examples along the east coast, they are very common on the Danish islands; many are known from north Fyn, from north, west and south Zealand and all the smaller islands. Some of the chambers from this part of Denmark are quite large: the Danish passage grave at Lustrup, on Falster, is about 16 m long, as is the passage grave at Låddenhøj, in mid-Zealand, which was built as one chamber and subsequently divided in the middle (Hansen 1993, 27–8, Figure 36). A passage grave at Græse, north Zealand, was 12 m long; 27 orthostats were used for its chamber and 14 for the passage. Similar lengths – up to 16 m – apparently can be reached in Västergotländ (Tilley 1999, 14).

Not all such chambers are strictly rectangular. Lolland is home to the slightly trapezoidal chambers with sometimes rather asymmetrically placed passages – in plan resembling a hafted axe – for example Kong Svends Høj (Figure 3.28) and Frejlev Skov. Similarly shaped chambers are known on south Zealand (Knudshoved Odde). Indeed, some of the Mecklenburg chambers also display a ground plan very similar to a hafted axe (for example the passage graves at Naschendorf or Jamel; Schuldt 1972, Plates 24 and 26b); far from being a barrier, the Baltic Sea

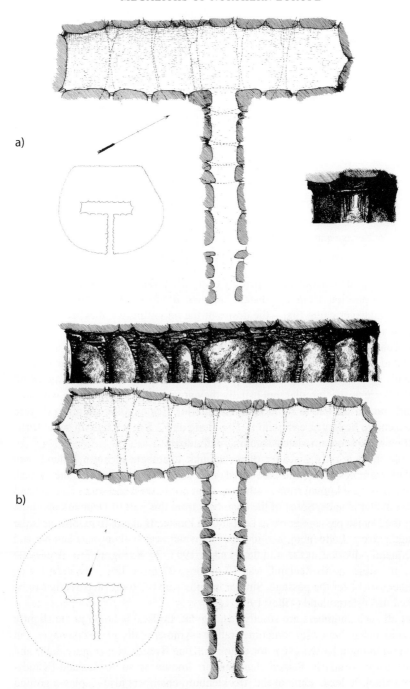

Figure 3.27 (a) Rectangular passage grave at Hjelm, island of Møn; (b) The so-called 'foot-shaped' passage grave at Sparresminde, island of Møn

Figure 3.28 Plan of the axe-shaped chamber at Kong Svends Høj, island of Lolland

seems to have facilitated communication between southern Denmark and Meck-lenburg. While there are some very large rectangular chambers to be found on the island of Møn, such as the 13-m-long chamber at Kong Askers Høj, other cham-bers here are unusual – referred to as 'foot-shaped' – with rounded ends and a clear narrowing in the middle; such ground plans are also encountered in south Jutland (Figure 3.27b; Hansen 1993, 27–28).

Apart from the regional peculiarities of chamber form, Denmark is also home to two other types: the twin and the bi-chambered forms. The twin passage grave, of which about thirty examples are preserved, seems to be a unique Danish develop-ment. (This form of double passage grave is now frequently called 'twin chambers' in Danish literature, and I shall use this term here to distinguish it from the so-called double passage grave.) Two passage graves, each with its own passage, are built sharing a common wall of one or two orthostats (Figure 3.29), and this type represents one of the most sophisticated forms of passage grave construction. Each chamber is an independent space, but the whole structure was conceived and built as one; the intermediary layers are well integrated and sometimes a capstone lies directly on the 'common' orthostat, serving both chambers. Indeed, in a few of the most remarkable cases the ground plans of the two chambers are mirror images of one another. Such passage graves are common in north and west Zealand, and most

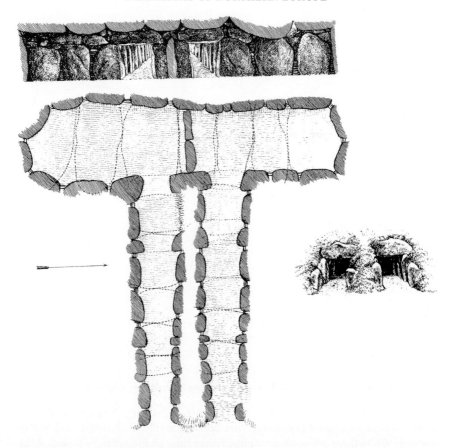

Figure 3.29 Twin passage grave of Klekkendehøj as drawn *c*. 1880, island of Møn

probably arose there; a few isolated examples are also found on the south Danish islands, and possibly in north Jutland (Figure 3.30).

Twin passage graves should not be confused with monuments where two chambers, covered by a single mound, are essentially two separate structures, for instance at Snæbum, north Jutland (Figure 3.31). Ebbesen has listed about thirty such monuments of a generally northern distribution, with concentrations along the Roskilde and Hjarbæk fjords (Ebbesen 1978, 60–1). The bi-chambered version has a very clear, albeit equally restricted distribution: Ebbesen has identified 25 such chambers in north Jutland (particularly around the Limfjord area), with two examples each on Zealand and Lolland (Ebbesen 1978, Figure 45). Two, occasionally even three, connecting chambers are constructed one behind the other, and access was by means of a single passage leading to the chamber in front (Figure 3.32).

As already noted, the Swedish area of Falbygden represents a very special region where the construction of passage graves was strongly influenced by the nature of local raw materials, making these chambers unique within the north

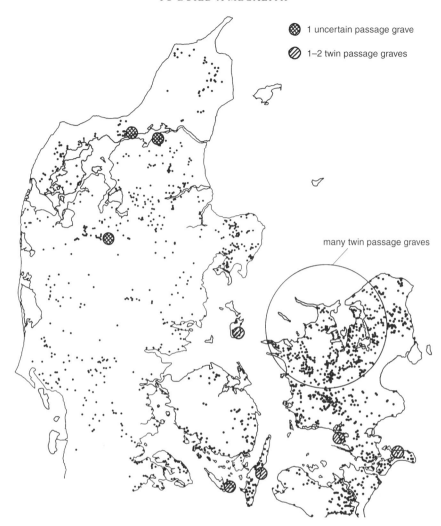

Figure 3.30 Distribution of twin passage graves in Denmark

European megalithic tradition. There are about 250 monuments known in the area, with particular concentrations around Karleby, Falköping and Gökhem (Figure 2.5). The rectangular chambers (Figure 3.33) are between 4 and 17 m long, and between 1.5 and 2 m wide. The passages, between 4 and 8 m in length, tend to be built of smaller stones. Christopher Tilley has commented on the fact that the different properties of sedimentary and igneous rocks, used in the construction of chambers, created an interesting contrast between the capstones, which seem 'natural', and the chamber walls, which give a somewhat standardised and artificial – almost prefabricated – appearance to these chambers (Tilley 1996, 124; Sjögren 2003a, 238, Table 10.5).

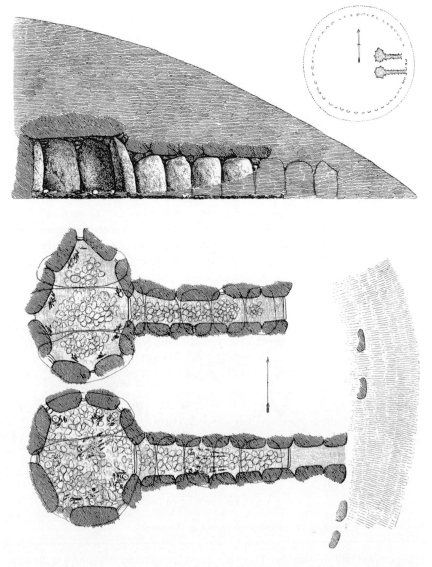

Figure 3.31 Two separate chambers covered by a single mound at Snæbum, north Jutland

Principles of chamber construction

As already indicated, construction of megalithic chambers was a complicated engineering feat. Irrespective of the form of the chamber, there are certain general principles of construction, which required similar technology and had similar objectives. First of all, accessible chambers had of necessity to be stable and, if they were to serve the community for several generations, they needed to be well sealed and

Figure 3.32 Bi-chambered type of passage grave from Suldrup, north Jutland

kept dry. Figure 3.34 illustrates the principal architectural elements of a megalithic chamber – in this case a complex passage grave. While not all chambers display such complexity or contain all the features, they were built according to the principles illustrated here. Some elements were clearly technological and absolutely necessary, others may have been irrational in terms of technology but nevertheless, although hidden from view, seem to have been equally significant in their presence.

Figure 3.33 Tony Axelsson at Karleby 4 passage grave, Falbygden

Orthostats

Orthostats made up the fundamental framework of a chamber, and their arrangement was essential to the chamber's stability. They were placed in shallow pits,
their bases wedged with slabs or small stones, flat sides turned to the interior and
slightly inclined inwards towards the top. Boulders were inclined even in the simplest of dolmens, such as at Ølstykke (Figure 4.2a), and at the polygonal dolmens –
for example at Poppostein and Poskær Stenhus (Figures 3.17d and 3.18b) – and
this was essential in the complex passage graves, where they supported the
massive capstones; the majority of chambers in northern Europe have the wall
orthostats inclined to the inside (Figure 3.35).

While it is now evident that some of the boulders were split and may even have
been worked to a desirable shape (Chapter 5), many were used in their natural
state, although the flat faces show that efforts were made to locate such shapes.
Often the orthostats were placed alternately: some rested on their broader ends
while others were placed on their narrower ends. This can be seen, for example, at
the great dolmens of Poggendorf 3 (Schuldt 1972, Plate 53) and Burtevitz 1 (ibid.,
Plate 64). It is a common feature of many passage graves.

At Ostenwalde, only the passage cornerstones and those at chamber ends were
placed on their broader ends, while the rest had their narrower ends towards the
floor (Tempel 1978, 9). Many Danish passage graves display this alternation:
Klekkendehøj, Jordehøj, Korshøj, Hjortegårdene, Regnershøj, Ubby Dysselod and

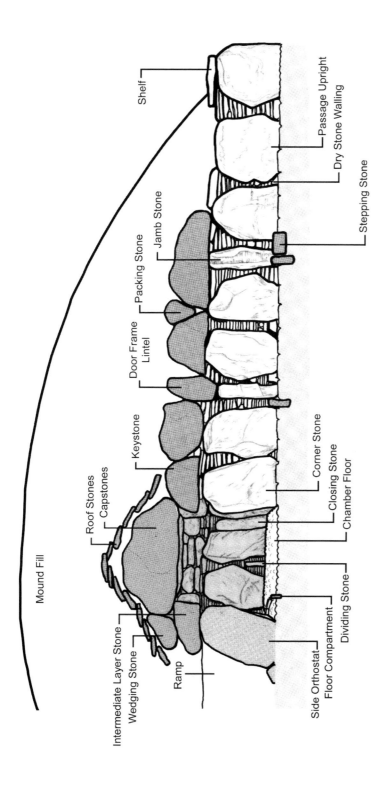

Figure 3.34 Principles of chamber construction

Figure 3.35 Chambers displaying the arrangement of orthostats inclined inwards at the top: (a) Sprove dolmen, island of Møn; (b) Röra dolmen, island of Orust; (c) Troldstuerne passage grave, south chamber looking towards the right from the entrance, north-west Zealand; (d) Knudshoved passage grave looking towards the left from the entrance, south Zealand

c

d

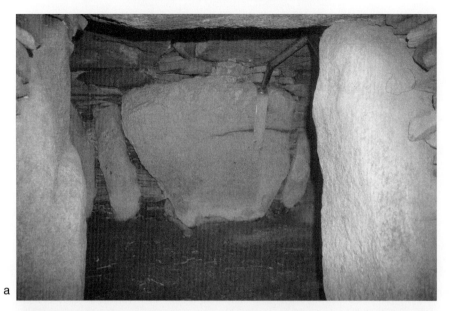

a

b

Figure 3.36 Passage graves displaying examples of boulders placed on narrower ends:
(a) Sparresminde, island of Møn; (b) Ubby Dysselod, north-west Zealand

Sparresminde (Figure 3.36a and b) are some of the best Danish examples of such
positioning. Such arrangements were structurally difficult, with the vertical faces
of the orthostats often staggered rather than placed in line with their neighbours
(Kjærum 1969, 14) to add further stability, but the arrangement also creates an

aesthetically pleasing effect: standing massive boulders on their ends may well have been socially significant in terms of prestige in the community.

From his long and intimate experience of studying and restoring passage graves, Svend Hansen has suggested that the orthostats were placed in the chamber in a specific sequence (Hansen 1993, 22). Accordingly, the two cornerstones at the entrance to the chamber were placed first and those at the back of the chamber, directly opposite the entrance, were next. Thus the chamber's principal width was established and the remaining boulders could be placed to achieve the desired shape and size. In some chambers the cornerstones and their opposites also supported the heaviest and largest capstones, and their positioning was critical to the overall stability.

Throughout the construction process it would have been imperative to access the interior, manoeuvre the orthostats, check that the slabs of dry-stone walling fitted properly and, especially, to guide the massive capstones into place. Thus many chambers (this includes some of the larger dolmens) have the so-called closing stone. This is usually a relatively small and narrow orthostat, often found at the end of the chamber. The gap filled by this stone was sufficient for a person to pass in and out of the chamber and supervise the necessary work (Figure 3.36a). This very last stone, effectively sealing the chamber, not only was important from the construction point of view but, being the final sealant of the chamber, may also have had a symbolic significance.

Dry-stone walling

Dry-stone walling was used to fill the gaps between the boulders making up the walls of the chambers, adding further stability and also as the first stage towards making them earth-free and impervious to water. The commonest material was red sandstone, and it was used everywhere, although other materials were also occasionally employed; gneiss, slate, arkose, shale, porphyry and granite have all been recorded, albeit in small quantities (Strömberg 1971, 210; Hårdh and Bergström 1988, 47; Bakker 1992, 28; Paulsen 1990, 26). Generally the dry-stone walling was of true form; thin slabs, on average between 5 and 3 cm thick, were appropriately shaped and wedged horizontally from behind the orthostats, contrasting dramatically with the vertical boulders (Figure 3.37); at floor level the dry-stone walling often commences with a rather thick slab – the so-called sole stone. Well-preserved dry-stone walling shows clearly that the slabs were cut and shaped on the spot as the building work progressed. The slabs fit perfectly, and even the smallest spaces were filled in; where spaces between the orthostats were particularly wide, additional vertical sandstone slabs were inserted to reduce the gaps. Occasionally clay, loam, chalk and even birch bark have been found in between the horizontal slabs; this would add strength to the slab arrangement, absorbing some of the shock from the placement of heavy capstones, but also could have had a symbolic and aesthetic function.

Figure 3.37 Dry-stone walling in Danish passage graves: (a) Knudshoved, south
Zealand; (b) Sparresminde, island of Møn

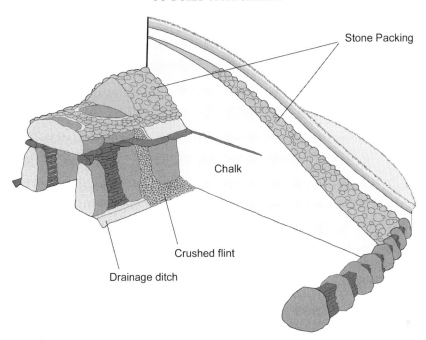

Figure 3.38 Schematic mound stratigraphy at the passage grave of Jordehøj, island of Møn

Packing materials outside the chambers

Hand in hand with the construction of the chamber went the process of stabilising and protecting the structure on the outside. While each site where the mound has been explored offers a slight variation, the general principles (Figure 3.38) – irrespective of whether this was a round or a long mound – involved creating an envelope around the chamber, beginning with a layer of cobble or stone packing at the base; such material would usually surround the entire chamber in a variable band of up to 12 m in thickness. While stones and cobbles were commonly used in the area from the Netherlands to Mecklenburg (Michaelsen 1978; Bakker 1992; Schuldt 1972), flint was an important substitute in Schleswig-Holstein, Denmark and Scania.

The use of flint in megalithic mound constructions was noted as early as the mid-nineteenth century. Danish archaeologist L. Zinck carried out in 1865 an excavation, extraordinarily advanced for that time, of a small dolmen at Kalundborg. In his report he commented on the presence of crushed flint outside the chamber. Zinck further observed that such a mass of flint was an integral feature of dolmen construction, and thought its role was to protect the chamber from rodents (Dehn *et al.* 1995, 39).

Crushed flint as packing material is common in most dolmens and passage graves in regions where flint was available: Scania, Denmark and Schleswig-Holstein (Strömberg 1971; Dehn *et al.* 1995, 2000; Hoika 1990). Recent repairs to the Kong Svends Høj passage grave on Lolland give a good idea of this type of construction. Large flint blocks were crushed on the spot, packed tightly around the chamber and between the capstones, sometimes additionally supported in place with round stones. Apart from the stabilising effect, such flint packing also served to keep the chamber and the area around it dry, allowing drainage and perhaps even absorbing some of the moisture (Dehn *et al.* 1995, 40–1). It has been estimated that between 20 and 30 tonnes of crushed flint were used to construct this mound. The outer layers of such packings, especially at the height of the capstones, often had flat slabs placed overlapping one another, in the manner of tiles upon a roof (Figure 3.34), providing additional drainage at the most vulnerable point.

The stone or flint packing was usually surrounded by softer materials. Where clay was locally available, it was used to provide a virtually impervious cover over the flint packing; it could be pure or mixed with stones. When clay was not available, loam or earth extracted in the neighbourhood of the site would be used. On the North Friesian Islands – where the core packing could consist of a mixture of granite, gneiss and quartzite – a local marsh soil called *Marschenklei*, the best and most fertile soil of the region, was used (for example at Nebel, Kampen or Denghoog; Kersten and La Baume 1958, 21); it turns very hard when it dries, but the possible symbolic significance of incorporating such agriculturally important soil should not be forgotten. (I thank Christoph Steinmann for detailed information on this type of soil.)

Not all chamber surrounds, however, were built to such high standards. Birkehøj, on account of its sophisticated chamber construction and dimensions – nearly 12 m in length and with a remarkable height of up to 2 m – is an exceptional chamber. However, recent restoration has shown that corners may have been cut when it came to building the mound. Here, instead of using flint, the builders went for a much cheaper solution: they built a stone wall at a distance of 0.5 to 1 m from the chamber and filled the cavity with pebbles which, judging by the quantity of crushed cockle shells, must have been brought from the nearby beach. The restorers wondered if this could perhaps be one of the oldest examples of jerry-building! (Dehn *et al.* 2004, 163; Figure 3.39.)

To further ensure that chambers were kept dry, drainage trenches were sometimes dug just outside the chamber, and overlapping flat slabs were additionally placed above and around the chamber creating a sort of tiled roof. Drainage ditches immediately behind the orthostats are known from Jordehøj and Lundehøj on Møn, 20–30 cm deep and filled with crushed flint, and on other sites basal layers of flint may well have had the same function (Dehn *et al.* 2000, 87–8, Figures 3.35 and 3.36). A good example of additional waterproofing is offered by the two stone chambers at the long dolmen at Grøfte, which demonstrate most eloquently that the builders were concerned to keep the chambers dry, since both were surrounded by flat split slabs, angled around each chamber to divert the rainwater to the outside, away from the chambers and into the mound (Ebbesen 1990, Figures 5 and 10–12).

A section through the mound during Kjærum's excavation at Jordhøj (Mariager Fjord, Jutland) showed that the capstones were totally covered by multiple layers of

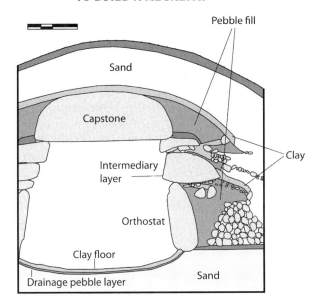

Figure 3.39 Unconventional construction of a mound at Birkehøj, north-west Zealand

overlapping flat slabs, and this arrangement continued in a sloping fashion for at least 2 m outside the chamber (Kjærum 1969, 17, Figure 8). The great dolmen at Vedsted had its capstones covered in identical fashion (Ebbesen 1979, 18, Figure 11).

Similar arrangements have been noted elsewhere during the recent restoration of Danish passage graves, for example at Horslunde (Dehn *et al.* 1995, 160) and Jordehøj (Dehn *et al.* 2000, 73–4, Figure 3.19). At Denghoog, on the island of Sylt, the chamber was coated with about seven layers of smooth stones that were laid out 'like a shingle roof' (Hoika 1990, 70). Other drainage arrangements may involve a flint-filled channel sloping away in the mound, between layers of packed clay, as observed at Klekkendehøj (Dehn *et al.* 2000, 47, Figure 2.60). At Kong Svends Høj there is no overlapping layer of slabs over the chamber, at least not in the excavated sections, but the clay mound was covered with a layer of stones that slope outwards, away from the chamber to a stone foundation at the bottom (Dehn *et al.* 1995, Figures 31 and 32). Such waterproofing solutions are, of course, only encountered at sites where mounds have been well preserved and where the excavators were consciously seeking all the details of mound construction; one wonders what other solutions were employed at megaliths where only remnants of the chamber survive.

Placement of the capstones

We have already noted the extraordinary size and weight of the boulders covering the chambers. The placing of the capstones, normally between 7 and 12 tonnes but in some cases reaching up to 30 tonnes in weight, was one of the most critical moments in the construction, and the techniques of manoeuvring such stones onto the chamber walls have long been a matter of speculation.

No less illustrious an investigator of megaliths than Frederik VII, King of Denmark, had concerned himself with this matter in the middle of the nineteenth century and presented papers on the subject to the Royal Society of Northern Antiquaries. Frederik VII suggested two different hypotheses on how the capstones may have been placed: initially he argued that the capstone could have been placed on a natural elevation and that the chamber was excavated below; later he suggested that a ramp led from the ground to the top of the orthostats and the capstones were pulled up the ramp on wooden beams. In his own words:

> By means of wedges and levers, mallets, beams, and the efforts of men and beasts of burden, they could succeed in rolling up the covering stone along the inclined plane as far as the stones of the wall. The latter being, so to speak, stayed up by the earth rammed down inside the chamber and outside, could not tumble over, nor move to one side or the other ....
>
> Frederik VII 1862, 11

It is reasonable to assume that the capstones were placed only after the chamber had been fully stabilised on the outside. Indeed, while there is little direct evidence, we can assume that both internal and external timber scaffolding and supports were used. The former would have kept the orthostats in place, while the latter would serve to raise the capstones to the required height and then move them into position.

The builders tried to create a relatively level surface, with the tops of the boulders roughly at the same height, and this was most commonly achieved by varying the depth of the stone holes into which they were placed. Although many chambers, as we have already noted, survive only in fragmentary condition, the position of the capstones does suggest that frequently they were simply placed on the tops of orthostats. This applies to dolmens as well as passage graves; Figures 3.15b and d, 3.17, 3.18 and 3.37a illustrate some of these examples.

In many cases the capstone's length was exploited to the utmost – with minimal overlap – and the fact that so many are still in their precarious original position demonstrates that the balance of weight distribution was thoroughly worked out, as seen at Listrup on Falster or Luttra in Falbygden (Figure 2.1). At Olshøj, where two separate chambers are found 1.25 m apart, the western chamber is the larger of the two (6.5 × 2.5 m in size) and the capstones' length is also exploited to the maximum over the orthostats (Dehn *et al.* 2000, 161, Figure 8.4).

Sometimes the shape of the chamber was such that supporting stones were needed to keep the capstones level and occasionally, when these were not long enough, to extend the underlying support. Schuldt (1972, 57) noted numerous instances in Mecklenburg where stones were placed under capstones to provide a more level surface. At some of the Danish passage graves this art, of supporting capstones at the desired height, had been developed to perfection by means of the so-called intermediary layer; some of the passage graves in Scania, such as Gillhög, also display this constructional feature (Figure 3.40a). In order to raise the height of the chamber, the builders resorted to placing between one and four horizontal layers of large stones, perfectly balanced, over the tops of orthostats and over one another (Figures 3.40 and 3.41a–b). If we are appreciative of the difficulties in placing heavy capstones on top of firmly wedged orthostats – as was the case in the majority of the north European megaliths – we can barely envisage the problems of manoeuvring capstones, of a dozen or more tonnes in weight, upon what in effect was a loose pile of stones.

As far as I am aware, this method of construction was not used anywhere else in north-western megalithic construction. This is not just a simple matter of corbelling, where regular slabs overlap one another in an orderly fashion to create a relatively small gap to be covered by one large stone, as is commonly found in the British Isles and western France. In the Danish passage graves the intention seems to have been to increase the height without decreasing the volume of the chamber; thus the inward slant is almost imperceptible and the large stones are placed more or less vertically one above the other.

At the twin passage grave of Klekkendehøj, the orthostats in both chambers alternate between tall and low, and very good use is made of the intermediary layer to even out the differences; even the two partition orthostats have intermediary boulders placed beneath the capstones (Dehn *et al.* 2000, Figures 2.13 and 2.17).

While most of the large stones within the intermediary layer are just ordinary stones, collected in the fields for their size and shape, the intermediary layers sometimes also include a selection of stones which had previously been used in other contexts – namely corn-grinding and axe-polishing stones. Thus, at Birkehøj two grinding stones supported one end of the biggest capstone and, directly opposite this, two other grinding stones were placed below, each within its own dry-stone walling. As the restorers noted, the remarkable symmetry of this arrangement was unlikely to be accidental (Dehn *et al.* 2004, 168).

Hansen notes the presence of axe-polishing stones wedged below a capstone at Lundehøj and at Milhøj (Hansen 1993, 52). Sometimes axe-polishing stones were also used in the exterior construction. At Kong Svends Høj the original top of the dry-stone walling between the orthostats of the façade seems to have been covered with a layer of large, thick sandstone slabs, creating a sort of horizontal shelf – a feature known at a number of other mounds. One of these shelf-stones was a large piece of an axe-grinding stone (Dehn *et al.* 1995, 77). During the reconstruction of the long mound at Karlsminde, Rendsburg-Eckernförde, Paulsen noted that complete as well as fragmentary axe-polishing stones had been incorporated in the dry-stone walling between the kerbstones (Paulsen 1990, 26).

In these exceptional chambers the point at which the passage joined the chamber was crucial and must have been completed early on in the building process. Often the cornerstones support a massive lintel (sometimes referred to as a keystone; Figures 3.35d and 3.40a) which subsequently provides support for the central capstones. This sequence has been confirmed at Kong Svends Høj, since there is a

a

b

Figure 3.40 Examples of intermediary layer construction in south Scandinavian
passage graves: (a) Torbjörn Ahlström at Gillhög, Scania;
(b) Nissehøj; (c) Maglehøj; (d) Rævehøj (all on Zealand)

c

d

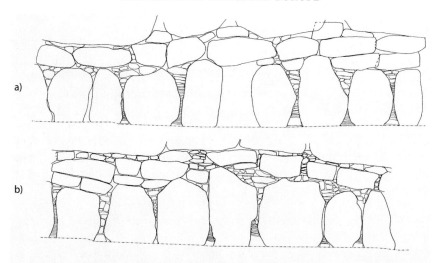

Figure 3.41 Elevations of the northern chamber at Troldstuerne passage grave on
north-west Zealand, showing construction of intermediary layer:
(a) entrance wall; (b) back wall

sightline behind the orthostats at the back of the chamber to guide the position of
the passage (Dehn *et al.* 1995; Figure 3.31). Sometimes, for example at the axe-
shaped chamber at Glentehøj, instead of the keystone, a capstone large enough to
span both cornerstones was used (Dehn *et al.* 2000, Figure 9.11); the Lolland
chambers do not, in fact, have intermediary layers.

Perhaps the most complicated construction was that of the bi-chambered monuments. Here, not only was the transition between the passage and the chamber an
important point, but the transition from the outer to the inner chamber(s) was
equally significant and had to be established before the rest of the chambers could
be built. The best example of the architectural solution is offered by a passage
grave at Vilshøj, which in fact has three interlocking chambers (Hansen 1993,
Figure 70). The capstones were interlocked with one another in such a sequence
that the capstone of the middle chamber was laid first and subsequently locked
by that of the outer chamber. Although according to Svend Hansen (ibid. 48) the
small back chamber was built last, its capstones were still interlocked with those of
the middle chamber – in his words 'this structure was built by experts of great
skill'.

In chambers with an intermediate layer, the keystone not only provided a reference point for the alignment of the intermediary layer but was very often an
unusual type of stone, different from the remaining orthostats. We have already
alluded to the presence of unusually coloured stones, either used as capstones on
dolmens or employed in the external kerbs. Equally, inside some of the passage
graves it is possible to indicate examples of rather unusual stones – lintels, cornerstones or casing stones in the passages – which were exceptional types of rock,
specifically chosen. Thus, for example, white limestone boulders, most probably

dragged up from a nearby beach, were used as casing stones at Ormshøj, Grønne-høj and Ubby Dysselod, while one of the cornerstones at Klekkendehøj contained a large amount of quartz (Dehn *et al.* 2000, 30–1). We shall return to this theme in Chapter 5.

Throughout northern Europe, there are only very meagre indications of possible timber arrangements for construction. Traces of post holes are known from several Dutch and Lower Saxon megaliths, and similar evidence has recently come to light in Denmark. The position of post holes immediately to the outside of the chambers' orthostats, observed by Gabriel during his excavation of Tannenhausen (Figure 3.42a), suggests that they were part of a contemporary structure related to the building of the chambers, and may well have formed an external scaffolding for the placement of the capstones. The post holes along the entrance to the eastern chamber, however, are generally thought to represent a timber passage leading from the edge of the mound (Gabriel 1966, 91; Bakker 1992, 32). They correspond to Schuldt's discovery of a similar arrangement at the entrance to the passage grave of Neu Gaarz, where four pairs of posts indicate a passage 2 m long and 0.8 m wide (Schuldt 1972, Figure 23). The post holes discovered at D43-Emmen were found underneath two fallen boulders of the kerb (R17 and R18; Bakker 1992, 18, Figure 12). While some distance away, their position in relation to the central orthostats of the chamber, and in line with the central capstones, may represent remnants of a capstone-raising contraption.

Recent restorations in Denmark have confirmed the presence of timber struc-tures for the raising of capstones. At Røverkulen, in south Jutland, an impression of a post was found in a small trench when a fallen orthostat was being re-erected (Hansen 1993, 23), and traces of posts were also noted in connection with one of the passages at Uglhøj (T. Dehn, pers. comm. 2007). Recent work at Birkehøj revealed that the clay and pebbles of the packing around the chamber's north side were cut to near the intermediary layer by a post hole, 40 cm wide and surviving for 60 cm depth. The post hole had a curious hourglass cross section, suggesting that the post moved back and forth in its position. Its location, above the intermediate stone layer, suggests once again that this is a rare example of a structure for raising and pulling the capstones (Dehn *et al.* 2004, 167).

Passages

Passage grave chambers, obviously, were accessed by means of a passage and there are many variations in how this was achieved, although the passages are gen-erally low. Chambers covered by rectangular or oval mounds tend to have short passages: between two and three pairs of orthostats were usually sufficient to achieve this, for example at most of the Dutch or the Lower Saxony chambers. Even the very long chambers are usually set within a kerb that is only a short dis-tance from the chamber itself; for example only one pair of orthostats was needed at Groß Berßen and Kleinenkneten 1, two pairs at Thuine and for the eastern chamber of Kleinenkneten 2 (Schlicht 1979, Figure 4; Michaelsen 1978, 224,

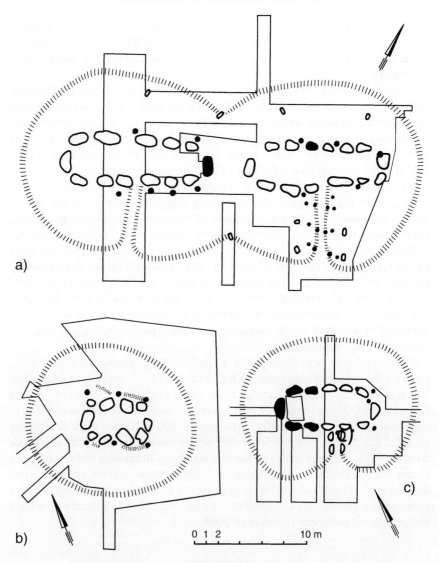

Figure 3.42 Post holes in association with megalithic chambers: (a) Tannenhausen;
(b) Tinaarloo; (c) Noordlaren

239). In Mecklenburg, the longest passage identifiable from Schuldt's excavations
seems to be four pairs of orthostats, but even then the actual length is not great.

Only the chambers covered by large round mounds required long passages, and
these are, by and large, seen in southern Scandinavia (Figures 3.6b and 3.43). In
Denmark there are examples of passages built of up to eight pairs of orthostats; one
of the longest passages, leading to the western chamber of the twin passage grave
at Korshøj, was at least 8 m long (Dehn *et al.* 2000, 110, Figure 4.4); in Falbygden,

on account of mounds with large diameters, the passages can reach up to 16 m in length (Tilley 1996, 152).

Like chambers, the passages were built of orthostats whose flat sides were visible, with dry-stone walling between them, and generally they were covered with capstones, albeit not as massive in size as those covering the actual chambers; sometimes the passage orthostats close to the exterior were left uncovered. Internal structures within the passages include threshold stones in the floor, jamb stones fitting between the orthostats, and casing stones up above in the ceiling; up to three such sets can be found within a single passage (for example at Gundsølille and Mutter Gribs Hule (Dehn *et al*. 2000, Figures 11.7, 11.8 and 16.3).

We assume that passages were closed after depositions took place in the chamber – many were filled with earth and stones, although this may have been the result of secondary use of megaliths – and that all the closing arrangements were put back in place each time after the chamber was reopened. Indeed, the presence of more than one set of closing elements suggests that it was not merely a matter of physical access and security of the chamber, but rather an important *rite de passage*. Negotiating these closures in succession – quite apart from the practical problems of manoeuvring the closing stones in a very tight space – must thus have been a powerful emotional experience, each action bringing those entering the chamber closer to their ancestors.

Floor constructions: materials and arrangements

It was on the floor of the chamber that burials were placed and grave goods deposited, and for that reason the construction of the floor was very important. In practical terms it needed to be relatively flat and dry, but it also seems to have been imbued with symbolic meaning, expressed in the structure of the floors, the presence of niches and compartments as well as the raw materials employed in such arrangements.

Generally, the clay or sandy ground inside the chamber – depending on the natural local conditions – was trampled down and sometimes additionally affected by fire. In some chambers nothing else appears to have been placed, for example at Hjelmar's Cairn in Falbygden (Persson and Sjögren 2001, 238). Normally, however, some sort of artificial floor was constructed. Such floors variously include a layer of cobbles or flat slabs of red sandstone, limestone or granite, and generally are carefully laid out; they can be single or multiple. In many chambers there are double floors which were clearly a primary feature and should not be confused with later floor layers resulting from the secondary use of chambers in the later Neolithic. Such multiple floor structures may well emphasise further the invisibility and complexity of certain constructional elements.

In Lower Saxony and further west, head- to fist-sized field stones were commonly used to make a pavement: fine examples come from Oldendorf I, II and especially IV (Laux 1980, Figures 12 and 13). At Radenbeck the chamber floor was made of a layer of slabs, covered with a double layer of field stones and granite

Figure 3.43 Passages at Danish passage graves: (a) Knudshoved, south Zealand;
(b) Kong Askers Høj, island of Møn

Figure 3.44 Reconstructed dolmen chamber at Munkwolstrup with burnt flint covering the chamber floor, Schleswig

grit above, and at Holzen two layers of stones were separated by granite grit (Laux 1980, 203, 206). The use of granite grit is typical of the area west of the Elbe, and it must be seen as a complementary material to burnt flint, which was commonly applied in Mecklenburg, Schleswig-Holstein and throughout southern Scandinavia.

The already-mentioned mid-nineteenth-century excavation of the dolmen at Kalundborg documents a section of the chamber which is one of the early examples of the now frequently encountered sequence of a chamber floor with a stone layer followed by a layer of burnt, shattered flint (Dehn *et al.* 1995, Figure 38). Burnt white flint, in contrast to the crushed flint used in the stabilising of mounds, seems to have been used where it would be seen – even if only by a handful of individuals – on the floor of the chambers as well as outside the chambers; we shall see later that it was also used outside the chambers as part of ceremonies conducted around the burial mounds.

That burnt flint had been used in chambers from a very early time is demonstrated by the presence of flint layers in very simple early dolmens in Denmark, Schleswig-Holstein and Mecklenburg (Figure 3.44). Thus the Ølstykke dolmen, investigated by Sophus Müller in 1890, had a floor laid with crushed flint which, judging by the quantities of charcoal found upon it, may well suggest that there was strong fire burning in the chamber prior to any burial activities (P. O. Nielsen 1984, 377). Similarly, the polygonal dolmen of Klokkehøj had a sophisticated floor which, in places, was covered with white burnt flint, and these concentrations were associated with charcoal. Since the clay below the flint was burnt red and black, it is again reasonable to assume that strong burning took place *in situ* (Thorsen 1981, 112).

Schuldt's excavations in the two groups of megaliths in Everstorfer Forst confirm this early use of shattered and burnt flint which, as a raw material not available locally in this region, was clearly brought from elsewhere (Schuldt 1972; Gehl 1972). In the northern group the small dolmen (no. 5) had, in the middle of its floor, a pile of crushed burnt flint in an area of about 30 × 40 cm (Schuldt 1968, entries 11 and 12), and in the extended dolmen close by (no. 1) a thin clay floor layer was covered with a layer of flint 3 cm thick (Schuldt 1972, Figure 25b). Numerous examples of such dolmens are known from Mecklenburg: for example a 10-cm-thick layer covered a sandy floor at Friedrichsruhe (ibid., Figure 25), or at Mankmoos, where a floor made partly of cobbles and small red sandstone slabs had burnt flint on top (Schuldt 1967, entries 14 and 15).

The great dolmens also demonstrate the use of burnt flint in the chambers. At Vedsted, an area 1.75 × 1 m was defined by vertically placed slabs and covered by burnt flint (Ebbesen 1979, 19). The great dolmen at Liepen (no. 3) had three compartments in its western end that were cobbled and covered with burnt crushed flint; while in the passage grave no. 3 from the south group in Everstorfer Forst, not only the five partitions but the rest of the chamber were covered with burnt crushed flint.

In the passage graves at Liepen (no. 1) and at Katelbogen the crushed burnt flint is mixed with charcoal. At Liepen over three cubic metres of flint covered the floor in a layer 20 cm thick; it seems to have been crushed and burnt on a cobbled platform near the entrance. It is curious, however, that on the island of Rügen, where flint was amply available and indeed mined in vast quantities during that time, it was not thought necessary to provide the floors of the megalithic chambers with this material at all.

Many Danish passage graves, where the original floor of the chamber and passage was laid of flat sandstone slabs or larger rounded stones, generally had a layer of crushed burnt flint 10 to 25 cm thick. Such deposits are known in north Jutland, for example from the passage graves at Sødalshøj, Snæbum, Bigum and Maglehøj as well as from Tustrup on Djursland, where a small internal 'cist' was floored with flat slabs and filled with burnt flint. Examples from Zealand include among others: the passage graves at Mutter Gribs Hule, Ormshøj, Gundsølille and Knudsskov, Kinderballe on Langeland and Kong Svends Høj on Lolland. Sometimes the chamber floors have a multiple layer of white slabs (chalk or limestone) with burnt flint placed on top: such was the case at the Zealand passage graves of Troldstuerne and Regnershøj, at Hulbjerg on Langeland and at Klekkendehøj on the island of Møn (Dehn *et al.* 1995; Dehn *et al.* 2000; Hansen 1993).

Thus it seems that the provision of a chamber floor with a layer of burnt material – be it flint or granite – was a significant requirement of the ritual associated with burial. Such burnt rock material, in practical terms, may well have contributed to the maintenance of dry conditions in the interior. However, the use of burnt flint or granite in accessible (as well as occasionally hidden) parts of the monument must have had a strong symbolic significance.

Many chambers, in addition to carefully laid out floors, display additional arrangements of the interior such as niches, shelves and, above all, vertical slabs built into the floor, which create internal compartments. Niches, found in north Jutland and Zealand, most commonly are created by recessing an orthostat; for example at Mutter Gribs Hule, the south-western orthostat is set 70 cm further back from the rest, creating a little niche (Dehn *et al.* 2000, Figures 16.3–4, 16.6). At Jordhøj, just to the left of the passage, the two orthostats are set further apart from each other and the dry-stone walling between them is recessed by 40 cm to form a small niche which, moreover, had a shelf of red sandstone slab wedged into the dry-stone walling, about 60 cm above the floor (Kjærum 1969, Figure 4).

The early-nineteenth-century excavation, by the captain of Swedish artillery Anders Lindgren, at the passage grave of Onskulle is well known in literature on account of a drawing published in 1806 which showed seated skeletons enclosed in eighteen roofed compartments all along the chamber walls (Figure 4.1). However, as Ahlström pointed out, Lindgren's original drawing did not in fact show any roofing slabs (Ahlström 2003, 254); it seems to be one of the earliest recognitions of compartments in megalithic tombs in northern Europe.

Compartments within chambers are known throughout most of northern Europe, although they seem common only in Mecklenburg, Scania, and Västergötland, while elsewhere such divisions are encountered more sporadically. It is, of course, possible that such divisions may have gone unrecognised in the early investigations, or were sometimes executed in organic materials such as timber and have not survived.

Compartments vary in size, shape and number. Only a few Danish passage graves seem to have this feature, and usually it is just one or two compartments. The double passage grave at Ormshøj has a small niche in the eastern chamber and a compartment, 1.6 × 0.9 m in size, defined by vertically placed sandstone slabs against the back wall of the western chamber (Dehn *et al.* 2000, Figure 7.11). The rectangular chamber at Hulbjerg on Langeland has its southern corner divided from the rest by vertical white limestone slabs (Skaarup 1985a, Figure 188); both Hansen (1993) and Ebbesen (1978) note several other examples of such divisions in Jutland and on Zealand. Similarly, for the area from the Netherlands to Altmark, Bakker (1992) quotes only seven examples of chamber division, usually separating the western part of the chamber by means of a low wall or a few slabs; none of these spaces are larger than that which could accommodate an individual.

In Västergötland the passage graves are divided into segments by upright slabs, which protrude from the floor and stand at right angles to the walls of the chamber; these are just vertical slabs, and the segments are better described as niches rather than fully closed compartments. At Hjelmar's Cairn (Figure 4.12) some of these niches are in fact so small that they could never have contained a whole body (Persson and Sjögren 2001, 238). At Rössberga the twenty niches still surviving

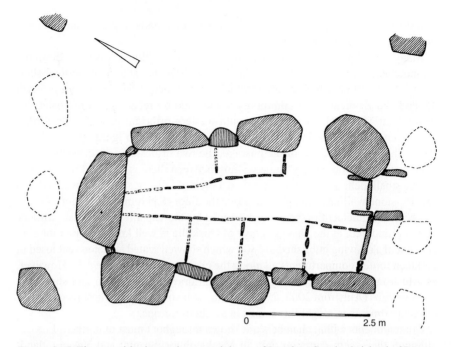

Figure 3.45 Floor partitioning at the great dolmen of Lancken Granitz 2, island of Rügen

are located along the walls as well as protruding into the centre of the chamber. Similar niches are known from a number of passage graves in Halland, for example at Snöstorp (Tilley 1999, 127, Figure 4.8).

In contrast, the compartments in Scania and Mecklenburg divide the whole or part of the chamber into clear separate units. In Scania, only passage grave chambers seem to be divided, while in Mecklenburg both dolmen and passage grave chambers are known to be partitioned (Figures 3.45 and 3.46). The number of compartments varies: in Mecklenburg three is a common number in extended dolmens, up to nine in passage graves (Neu Gaarz); in Scania up to thirteen have been noted (at Tågarp; Tilley 1999, 99).

An important feature is the different flooring associated with such compartments. Thus at Carlshögen these were variously covered with diabase and quartzite stones, clay, limestone and tufa (Tilley 1996, 127). In Mecklenburg the compartments were carefully built of red sandstone slabs, and often these were the only parts of the chamber floor to be paved: at the great dolmen at Liepen the three compartments had cobbles covered with burnt flint. At Zernin 2 the compartments were built of vertical, alternating with horizontal, stacks of red sandstone slabs; the floors were also paved with them and flint was scattered on top; the remaining parts of the chamber floor were not covered. Similar arrangements are also known from passage graves, for example the floor constructions at Gnewitz and Liepen (Schuldt 1972, 48–9).

106

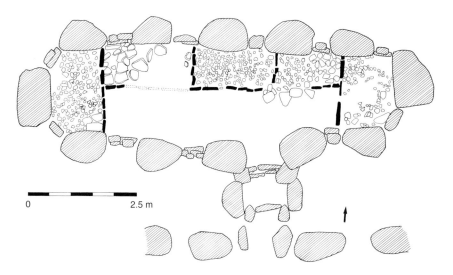

Figure 3.46 Partitioning and floor slabs arrangement at the passage grave of Gnewitz 2, Mecklenburg

These compartments structured the interior of the chambers, in many cases providing defined areas for deposition of human remains and, in regions where this practice was employed, this must have been one of many ways in which the relationship between the dead and the living could be expressed.

Conclusions

In summary, the evidence discussed in this chapter demonstrates that north European megaliths rank among the most extraordinary structures surviving from the Neolithic. The skill and ingenuity of the builders are seen not simply in their ever-increasing ability to manipulate massive boulders in an enterprising fashion, but also in the successful solutions to architectural problems presented by these structures, which define the existence of various 'architectural schools' as seen through regional variants of chambers and enclosing mounds. That practical considerations were not the only dilemmas facing the builders is seen in the tension between the constructional and the symbolic requirements of these structures, which demanded ritually appropriate raw materials to be incorporated in different parts of chambers and mounds in order to create conditions appropriate to the deposition and veneration of their dead. Before this symbolism is considered further, it is first necessary to consider the evidence for burial, the ritual practices that accompanied the placement of the dead inside the chambers, and those that were carried out in the immediate vicinity of the monuments.

4

BODY AND SOUL

Megalithic chambers in northern Europe contain human remains, even if the frequency of preservation is low, and uneven from one area to the next. Moreover the ambiguity of some burial deposits tends to raise questions rather than provide answers. But megaliths are also burial monuments that featured in the wider social realm of the Neolithic communities. Indeed, as we have already noted in Chapter 1, apart from burials the earliest monumental structures of the TRB – the earthen long barrows – had already provided a focus for many other activities, perhaps only obliquely associated with burial ritual *per se*.

Thus, whatever went on within the megalithic chambers themselves, we need to consider activities on the outside of the megaliths – particularly the deposition of pottery, flint and stone tools by the entrance to the chambers – that in many cases appear to have continued after the chambers themselves became obsolete. These deposits were part of a wider network of ritual acts performed in the vicinity or the more distant surroundings of the monuments. The latter include various activities taking place at settlements, within ceremonial enclosures, by rivers and lakes and in marshy locations, along routes of daily passage from one task to the next. Indeed, ritual acts could take place anywhere and at any time, involving single individuals or groups acting together.

In order to appreciate the significance of megaliths within the TRB culture, it is necessary to review briefly the evidence for the whole range of activities that can be deduced from the investigation of megalithic tombs – both within and outside. Therefore this chapter will first of all explore the evidence from the interior – burials and the goods that the living bestowed upon the dead – and then consider the range of activities which took place outside and in the immediate vicinity of the chambers.

Burial within megaliths – general considerations

One of the most frequent comments made by early excavators of the megalithic chambers referred to the 'chaotic' nature of the human remains encountered therein. It was this 'chaos' which, in the nineteenth century, gave rise to the idea of megalithic chambers as ossuaries. The Swedish archaeologist Bror Emil

Hildebrand, following his excavations at two passage graves in Västergötland where he encountered chaotic spatial arrangements of human bones, suggested that bodies were defleshed elsewhere and that dry, disarticulated bones were introduced into the chamber until it became full; and that it was at that point that capstones permanently sealed the chamber (Ahlström 2003, 255). This idea, which continues to have many supporters to this day, is opposed by those who argue that complete bodies were being placed inside the chambers and that what some scholars consider as 'chaos' is in fact the result of processes of dynamic decomposition and bone fragmentation.

However, to polarise the discussion between these two extremes would be to ignore the available evidence as well as to oversimplify the funerary practices. There is no a priori reason why different practices could not have operated in different areas of northern Europe and, indeed, why they should not be subject to changing tradition in the course of nearly a millennium. There is ample evidence that different rituals were practised side by side throughout the TRB, that the funerary traditions changed, and that regional and chronological parameters must be taken into account in the overall interpretation. The issue, therefore, is not so much complete burial versus fragmentary skeletal deposition, but rather the variation and dynamism of funerary practices as they are evidenced in a spatial and temporal framework. The evidence is mixed, with interment of complete human bodies in simple closed dolmens and in some passage graves, as well as piles of bones clearly selected from the already skeletonised bodies. Indeed, this variation is emphasised by the similar, albeit less frequently discussed, treatment of the dead who were buried outside the megaliths – in flat graves, in enclosures, on settlement sites and in bogs, to mention but the most obvious locations.

The general pattern of funerary practices within northern Europe during the late fifth and early fourth millennia BC does represent a shift from the initial single complete inhumation to a later communal deposition of fragmentary skeletal remains within the burial chambers. This pattern is sometimes interpreted as signifying a transition from predominantly funerary rituals to those that concern themselves substantially with ancestors (Barrett 1988). However, this general trend is supplemented throughout by other ways of dealing with the dead, some of which may signify an expression of formal burial or of ancestral cults, or other activities in which human remains played a role, such as sacrificial offerings to spirits and gods.

Preservation of human remains

Taking into consideration the number of extant megalithic tombs in northern Europe, the chambers with preserved human remains are but a small proportion. On the one hand the natural conditions, in particular acidic soils, have clearly been responsible for the poor preservation of human remains. The repeated use of many chambers by subsequent cultural groups, especially the Globular Amphora and the Corded Ware cultures, may have resulted in the removal of earlier burial deposits, in the trampling and damaging of delicate parts of skeletons, and in the dilapidation of some chambers, contributing to the further destruction of skeletal material. In many instances, the attribution of human remains to a particular cultural horizon is difficult, to say the least.

Regional considerations reveal a very irregular pattern of bone preservation. As early as 1893, Krause and Schoetensack were remarking on the apparent absence of human skeletal remains in the region of Altmark, although Fischer did find small amounts of human remains in two of the Leetze passage graves (Fischer 1956, 79–80). Hoika mentions 48 chambers in Schleswig-Holstein, where some human remains have survived, but too often in such a poor state that no analyses of any kind are possible (Hoika 1990, 88). Very small bone fragments are known from a few of the Dutch and the adjacent west German passage graves, but not enough to give an inkling of the actual manner of burial, although the large quantities of ceramics of different chronological phases suggest that chambers were entered repeatedly and depositions made; presumably these accompanied burials, but the manner of these is not known (Bakker 1992, 47).

Thus the best evidence derives from Mecklenburg and southern Scandinavia. Schuldt found human remains in about one-third of the hundred or so chambers he investigated in Mecklenburg (Schuldt 1972), to which some older and some more recent evidence can be added (Steinmann 2001). Human remains in the Swedish passage graves have been recorded from the eighteenth century onwards (for example the 1788 report on a seated burial in the passage grave at Dala, Västergötland (Ahlström 2003, 254)). However, as elsewhere, early reports are often insufficient, confusing and, as the already-mentioned example of the Onskulle passage grave from the Axvalla district in Sweden demonstrates, present images that became entrenched in the archaeological literature and persist to this day (ibid., 254; Masset 1997; Figure 4.1). Nevertheless the nineteenth-century investigations, coupled with more recent research in Denmark and Sweden, provide the best evidence of the burial practices within the megalithic chambers in northern Europe.

Human remains in the north European dolmens

It has been demonstrated in Chapter 1 that during the early TRB the majority of graves within the long barrows, or indeed the so-called earth graves, contained single inhumations, although some multiple burials were also present. The dead were buried fully articulated, laid out in an extended position on their backs – a practice which, as I have previously argued, was deeply rooted in the preceding Mesolithic burial tradition (Midgley 2005, 108). Even in instances where timber chambers were accessible, the additional burials appear to have followed the same mode.

It has generally been assumed that the small closed dolmen chambers were equally intended for single interments, and that the change from single to collective burial practices took place at the time of the construction of extended and great dolmens with permanent access to the interior. There are only a very few chambers

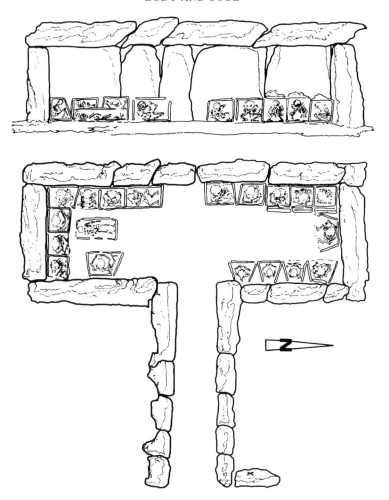

Figure 4.1 Idealised version of Lindgren's drawing of the passage grave at Onskulle,
Sweden, as popularised in megalithic literature

known today where primary deposits may be regarded as representing individual
interments, although some of these were excavated a long time ago. Thus, Sophus
Müller's excavations at Ølstykke in 1890 and Thorvildsen's report on the 1933
excavation at Kellerød, both involving simple dolmens on Zealand, concern single
individuals. At Ølstykke a partly preserved extended skeleton was found on the
floor of the chamber, with its head to the south and with one collared and one
lugged flask standing at the opposite end of the chamber; fragments of human bone
within the slightly sloping lugged flask were assumed by Müller to have been a
result of animal activity (P. O. Nielsen 1984, 376–7; Figure 4.2a and b). At
Kellerød, where the dolmen chamber was partly filled with earth, a disturbed
extended skeleton of an adult male lay in the same position, with a flint knife by the

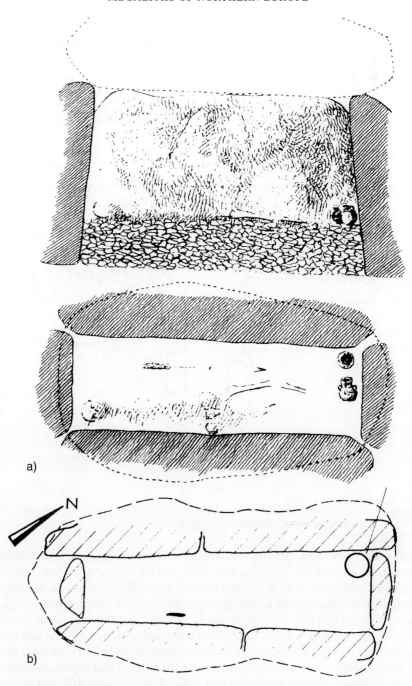

Figure 4.2 Early Danish dolmens: (a) section and plan of the Ølstykke dolmen, north-east Zealand; (b) plan of the Kellerød dolmen, west Zealand

right arm and a broken lugged flask by the feet (ibid., 378), and from Bogø, A. P. Madsen described a long dolmen which revealed a similar arrangement: the dead individual lay extended on the back and surrounded by grave goods on both sides (A. P. Madsen 1896; Figure 4.15).

The small size of many closed dolmens supports the idea that they were indeed intended for individual interments and, once the body was deposited and all the rituals conducted, the great capstone sealed the chamber. The bodies were not meant to be disturbed, but this does not necessarily mean that the living were unaware of the dead. In some cases the massive capstone, for example the huge quartz cover at Grønjægers Høj (Figure 3.10), may have remained visible, providing a powerful reminder of the dead beneath and permitting the living to associate with the 'house of the dead'. Indeed, there is evidence that even the small closed chambers provided a focus for other ceremonies, and that in some cases at least, in continuation of the tradition which commenced at the façades of the long barrows, votive deposits were placed outside.

Evidence from other dolmens is much more ambiguous. The two Grøfte chambers were both small, each measuring 1.7×0.8 m in floor space. They contained primary burials in the sense that they had not been disturbed by any later cultural activity (Ebbesen 1990, 66; Figure 4.3). Chamber A contained 23 identifiable bones belonging to two adult males. There were also three teeth, of which at least one was identified by Bennike as belonging to a young person between 15 and 25 years of age and another to an adult (Bennike 1990, 70). The bones were lying haphazardly on the chamber floor; there were two lugged flasks at the southern end of the chamber. Chamber B contained remains, similarly scattered over the floor, of one adult woman between 35 and 55 years of age. There was some doubt, on account of the differential tooth wear, whether the upper and lower jaws both belonged to this individual. Not a single rib, foot- or hand-bone survived in either of the chambers, and from the plan it appeared that the larger bones in chamber A were 'collected' in the middle.

Some of the bones revealed gnawing marks of small rodents (Bennike 1990, Figure 2) and the lack of small bones was also attributed to animal activity. Although the anthropological report concluded that originally complete bodies were placed in the Grøfte chambers and that the partial condition of the skeletons and the position of the bones were a direct result of animal activity, nevertheless a number of doubts remain. While animals may have been responsible for devouring the smaller bones, it is curious that the two male skulls were all but consumed, while the female skull was largely preserved; the tooth of a young individual may have belonged to a third person, the two jaw halves did not really match, and Bennike reported that other specialists did not necessarily agree on their attribution to one individual (ibid., 70). It is therefore possible either that the Grøfte dolmen chambers contained remains of more individuals, or that the burials involved parts of bodies already in skeletal form.

The change in the funerary ritual, which indicates a gradual transition in the status of the dead with increasing emphasis on their ancestral qualities, takes place

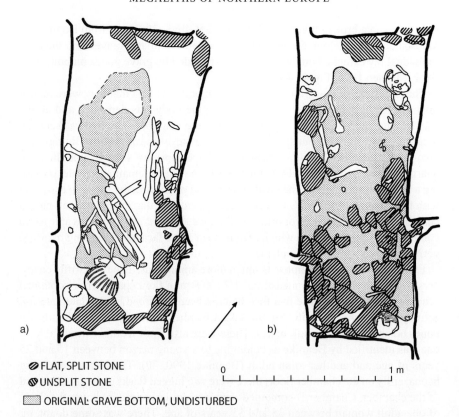

FLAT, SPLIT STONE

UNSPLIT STONE

ORIGINAL GRAVE BOTTOM, UNDISTURBED

0   1 m

Figure 4.3 Human remains in the Grøfte dolmen, south-west Zealand: (a) Chamber A;
(b) Chamber B

at a time when chambers acquire means of access in the form of openings and passages. It is a matter of interpretation whether the desire to access the chamber interior is a direct result of society's changing attitude to the dead, whether it reflects
changing religious ideas which influenced that attitude, or whether some other
ideological factors were responsible. That this process was most probably a prolonged one is seen from the fact that some of the timber chambers were also
equipped with passages, for example at Troelstrup (Kjærum 1977). Indeed, fragmentary human remains were also being placed in association with otherwise complete bodies (for example the inclusion of a child's lower jaw at Skibshøj; Kaul
1994, footnote 10), and elsewhere we have evidence that rituals involving human
remains were also carried out at settlements. Thus skull fragments, as well as burnt
upper limb bones, are known from Bistoft (Johansson 1982) and this tradition may
go even further back, as the skulls from the Sarnowo settlement, in close proximity
to the long barrow cemetery, reveal not only breakages but also exposure to relatively high temperatures (Midgley 2005, 111)

Before we consider further evidence from the open dolmens, it is perhaps worthwhile to note that, from this transitional period, there is also evidence that some individuals buried outside the megaliths were subject to bodily manipulation, be it skeletonisation prior to formal burial, partial deposition, or deliberate rearrangement of the normal anatomical order. A particularly significant example comes from the Fakkemose dolmen on Langeland (Skaarup 1985a, 207–8, Figure 222). The round mound here protected an earlier grave pit containing two strongly crouched individuals placed there in skeletal form, albeit assembled in the grave in more or less anatomical order; of the lower extremities, one leg bone was missing and another placed the wrong way round. Two metres to the west of this double grave there was another pit with an isolated skull of a 16-year-old individual.

Similar finds, of fragmentary human remains sometimes accompanied by a small quantity of objects, are also known from beneath several of the Scanian passage graves. These are normally interpreted as foundation deposits prior to the chamber construction, although partial burials whose location remained known within a community for quite some time, and which subsequently provided an appropriate spot for the erection of a chamber, should not be excluded. Moreover, fragmentary deposits that lack certain bones need not be too surprising; apart from a possible symbolic significance of certain body parts, ethnographic evidence suggests that sometimes there is no great effort made to collect all the bones for a secondary burial ceremony, and that a handful is sufficient (Metcalf and Huntington 1995, 101). Partial burials also need to be seen against the background of circulation of bones as relics among the living, or of their use in other ceremonial contexts.

Kossian's recent survey of burials in flat graves from Germany and the Netherlands has added a number of examples where either the anatomical order of the bones was deliberately altered or, indeed, the burials involved disarticulated bodies (Kossian 2005, 144). At Wartin D1 at least one of the crouched burials, resting on a pavement of pottery sherds, was put there in a disarticulated state; a slab cist at Malchin 46 contained remains of three children, none in anatomical order; likewise, the bones from two skeletons buried in a pit at Düsedau 1 were laid out without anatomical order, with skulls to the south, the arm bones lying north–south, leg bones lying east–west, and other bone fragments in between the extremities. Some complete bodies were also, it seems, subject to rearrangements of body anatomy. The clearest evidence comes from the flat grave cemetery at Ostorf, near Schwerin. Here some of the dead had their right forearms turned through 180 degrees, suggesting either deliberate cutting of the tendon or possibly a partially skeletal state prior to burial.

Although the five chambers at Strandby Skovgrave excavated by N. Andersen were badly damaged through ploughing (Andersen 1997, 94–6), the better-preserved Klokkehøj dolmen in the same area, dating to the time of the Sarup I enclosure, may be illustrative of precisely this transitional process. The principal burial was that of a man between 20 and 35 years of age, laid out extended with feet towards the entrance. However, the skeleton lacked its head and four uppermost vertebrae, suggesting that the individual was decapitated before he was put into the

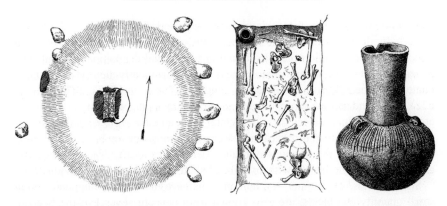

Figure 4.4 The disarticulated burial in the closed dolmen at Hjortegårdene, north Zealand

chamber and before the body was defleshed; two halves of a jaw were lying either side of the remaining neck vertebrae (Thorsen 1981, 118). In addition there were a few bones of another adult, and the skull of a five-year-old child was found nearby. These are therefore partial burials of several individuals that herald the new custom. The reasons for the removal of the head are not clear, although ethnographic evidence suggests that one way in which the dead are transformed into ancestors is through the removal of their skulls. Indeed, skulls and jaws appear to have had special significance; we shall return to this theme in due course. The secondary layer within Klokkehøj had three piles of bones, of which two were presumed to have been deposited towards the end of the TRB; in both of these, large fragments of skulls and all the limb bones were broken into pieces, while the smaller bones were not. Although 13 adults and nine children were represented, not a single individual was identified as complete.

Other dolmens also reveal evidence that strongly argues for partial burial and also for a deliberate manipulation of bodies (Figure 4.4), although the sequences are not always clear. The two pear-shaped dolmen chambers at Oldenbjerggård, on Langeland, were excavated by Jens Winther during 1883–4. The western chamber apparently had remains of two skeletons, one of which lay extended in the northern part of the chamber and was covered by a pile of stones. The eastern chamber, however, had five deposits of discrete piles of bones, each representing one individual, placed carefully on a large flat stone with a skull lying on top – a pattern to be encountered in very many of the Danish chambers (Skaarup 1985a, 132–3, Figure 104).

The Trekroner dolmen, east Zealand, excavated by Fleming Kaul and regarded as late in the dolmen tradition, contained remains of at least ten individuals – five adults and five children – almost none in anatomical order. Although the chamber had been robbed of stones, the burial deposit seemed relatively untouched. No individual was complete, each being represented by a few bones only; this was particularly clear in the case of the children (aged between 3 and 13 years) who were first and foremost represented by their jaws. The long bones and skull fragments were sparsely present, and there were not enough arms and legs to account for ten individuals. Kaul further noted that preservation conditions at Trekroner were good, since even some of the small hand and foot bones had survived well. The presence of some fatty, slightly sticky soil implied that the bodies may have been buried with their flesh, and Kaul suggested that, after a time, parts of the bodies were extracted from the chamber and moved elsewhere (Kaul 1994, 9–11).

None of the dolmens excavated by Schuldt in Mecklenburg have provided evidence of complete bodies, although the small Basedow chamber is said to have contained a large and a small skeleton (an adult and a child). The typologically early sites – the two *Urdolmen* at Everstorfer Forst, Barendorf 2 and Naschendorf 1 – both contained fragmentary human remains. Naschendorf 1 is an early simple dolmen, and on the floor there were disordered remains of two individuals (Figure 4.5a): the skull in the north-west corner lacked its jaw; another skull was slightly east of the middle of the chamber; the two jaws were found slightly to the west of the centre; and other broken bones – vertebrae, ribs, finger bones – were scattered in between; very many bones were missing. Barendorf 2 is an *Urdolmen* with an entrance where, in a corner, there was a small bone deposit containing part of a skull, some upper and lower long bones, a few vertebrae and ribs; a collared flask stood at the entrance to the chamber (Schuldt 1972, 71–2).

A similar deposit derived from an extended dolmen at Friedrichsruhe, where two piles of bones representing two separate adult individuals were found; skulls were fragmentary and the extremities were broken up. The position of these bones on a chamber floor cannot under any circumstances be considered as badly-disturbed extended inhumations – the bones were placed in their small piles (Figure 4.5b) and the chamber seems to have been intact, being filled to the roof with gritty sandy soil.

The great dolmens from Mecklenburg continue the story of fragmentary deposits. At Liepen, the end compartment had remains of three individuals: no skull was complete, they all showed old fractures, and only two lower jaws were present. The compartments along the sides had similar deposits: one damaged skull and some bones in the south, two skulls and some other bones in the north. The passage between the compartments also had a bone pile with fragments of a skull (Figure 4.6; Schuldt 1972, 72–3). Disarticulated bundles of bones have further been found at Ziesendorf and Lancken-Granitz 2 on Rügen (Steinmann 2001, 96; Schuldt 1972, 73).

Human remains in the north European passage graves

With the possible exception of chambers in Sweden, the pattern of partial human remains observed in the dolmens continues within the passage graves. Where they do survive, their disarticulation is so consistent that most scholars accept that they represent secondary burials after the flesh had disintegrated through some form of primary storage. Complete skeletons, sometimes encountered in the upper levels of chambers or in the passages, commonly indicate secondary use by the

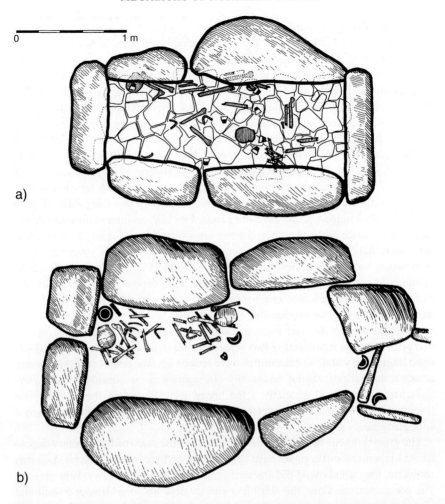

Figure 4.5 Burials in *Urdolmen* in Mecklenburg: (a) Everstorfer Forst (Naschendorf 1);
(b) Friedrichsruhe

subsequent Globular Amphora and Corded Ware populations. Nevertheless, the presence of complete squatting bodies described by Anders Lindgren from his 1805 excavation at the Onskulle passage grave, Västergötland – so dramatically if somewhat exaggeratedly represented in a published drawing of Lindgren's orig-inal plan – appears to have some support. Anthropological analyses of skeletons from some recent excavations in this region suggest the placement of whole bodies in squatting or flexed positions (Ahlström 2003).

The number of individuals represented in the chambers varies considerably. Some Swedish passage graves are known to have contained remains of in excess of one hundred individuals: at least 128 were found at Rössberga, about a hundred at Hjelmar's Cairn, 60 at Carlshögen, 40 at Ramshög, and from the recently excavated

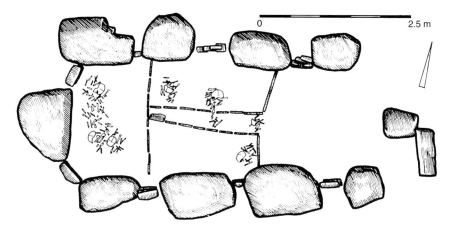

Figure 4.6 Burials in the great dolmen at Liepen, Mecklenburg

chamber at Frälsegården, Gökhem, a presence of at least 80 individuals is estimated (Ahlström 2001; Persson and Sjögren 2001). Danish passage graves may
also originally have contained remains from a large number of individuals, for
example 92 at Rævehøj, at least 90 at Uggerslev, between 50 and 60 at Troldstuerne, a minimum of 25 individuals at Kinderballe, 22 at Gundsølille (Bennike
1985, 473; Dehn *et al.* 2000), although it is difficult to be certain precisely how
many of these date from the TRB culture.

No such large numbers survive outside southern Scandinavia. The maximum of
individuals in Mecklenburg passage graves does not exceed 20 (at Liepen 1;
Schuldt 1972, 73); the 40 or so individuals from the great dolmen at Mönchgut on
Rügen cannot all be attributed to the TRB, and the find from chamber B at Sieben
Steinhäuser, in Lower Saxony, is exceptional for this area in preserving the
remains of more than 15 individuals (Jacob-Friesen 1925, 15).

In the majority of passage graves, however, human bones either do not survive at
all or are found in scanty quantities that cannot approximate to the original number
of interments; for example a skull and a few bones at Wechte 1 appearing unrea-
sonably low in number against the background of the 536 vessels found within the
interior (Knöll 1983, Plate 2b; Bakker 1992, 47); a couple of skulls and a few other
bones at Oldendorf II and IV (Laux 1980, Figures 36 and 43); fragments of human
tibia in the passage at Kleinenkneten 2 (Bakker 1992, 52); a fragment of a lower
jaw, a thigh bone, a few ribs and a tooth found by Raklev at Kong Svends Høj
(Dehn *et al.* 1995, 20); a few bones from two individuals at Øm (B.-J. Johansen
2003, 57). In Mecklenburg, remains from single disarticulated individuals have
been noted at Qualitz 1, Klein Görnow 1 and Ziessendorf 1, 2 and 4 (Steinmann
2001). The massive Katelbogen chamber contained only two skulls (an adult and
juvenile) in the western compartment, and a few bones scattered some distance
apart opposite the entrance (Schuldt 1967, 7).

It is hardly conceivable that such paltry survivals, as well as many empty chambers, represent the original state of affairs with respect to funerary rituals. It has often been claimed that TRB burials were habitually cleared out from the passage graves by subsequent users. While it is not impossible that some of the chambers may have been emptied of their deposits, with the old bones being moved and employed in ceremonies at other locations, human bones found in the forecourts and in front of the passages are more plausibly interpreted as a part of ritual activities taking place outside the chambers, rather than as material removed from within them (see **Votive deposits**, p. 148).

In chambers where human remains do survive, the most frequently encountered arrangements can be aptly described as piles of bones (frequently displaying old breakages), which either were arranged in discrete concentrations or lay scattered over the chamber floor. Skulls are frequently present, sometimes amassed in a pile or grouped in a corner. Such skull arrangements are best documented in the Danish passage graves, but they are also found elsewhere. In the Nebel 2 chamber, on Amrum, there were five skulls – two lying side by side against the north end wall, while the remaining three were near the middle of the long south wall (Figure 4.7; Kersten and La Baume 1958, 140). At Oldendorf II and IV the skulls appear to have been placed side by side with the cranium uppermost (Laux 1980, 156 and 164; Figure 4.16).

From Denmark, assemblages of skulls are known from several passage graves. The already-mentioned Uggerslev chamber displayed a remarkable arrangement: three discrete bone piles were resting against the western end of the chamber, each with a skull on top, while the huge pile of bones in the eastern part comprised remains of at least 80 individuals (Figure 4.8). The skulls here were frequently close to or above one another, surrounded in all directions by leg, arm and other bones. That they were arranged rather than just thrown haphazardly is clear from Madsen's statement that, as a rule, the skulls were face down and with crown to the top (A. P. Madsen 1900, 8).

Piles of skulls are known from other chambers: nine skulls, but only four mandibles, were piled up with other bones in a corner at Rævehøj; twenty skulls piled into a corner at Kyndeløse; and two piles of bones with 14 and seven skulls respectively at Frejlev Skov (Kaul 1994, 22). Raklev's investigations in 1933 of the Kinderballe passage grave on Langeland brought to light many human remains, which apparently lay in two separate layers (although these may be a result of his excavation technique; Dehn *et al.* 2000, 149). Raklev's plan (Figure 4.9) shows that disarticulated remains were concentrated mostly in the northern half of the chamber and comprised mainly long bones and skulls; the upper part of the deposit had 12–13 badly disintegrating skulls, and 12 more skulls were found in the lower part. One skull with a few bones was also found in the south-western part of the chamber; none displayed any anatomical order.

The importance of different parts of the human body in the funerary or other ritual contexts is clearly seen, even if their interpretation is difficult. In their discussion of human remains from Ramshög and Carlshögen passage graves in Scania, Shanks and Tilley have emphasised the deliberate selection of left or right,

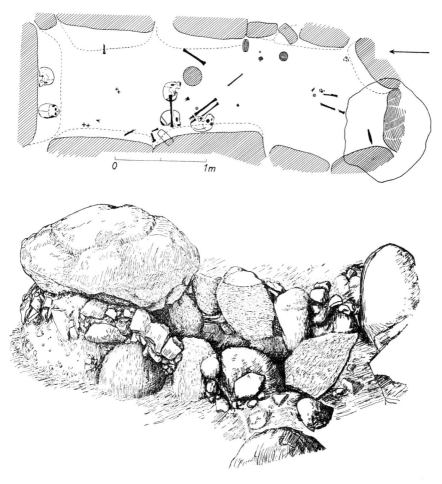

Figure 4.7 Disarticulated remains in the chamber of the passage grave no. 2 at Nebel, island of Amrum

upper or lower body parts, but have not offered any particular interpretation of this pattern (Shanks and Tilley 1982; Tilley 1996, 228–30). However, one could suggest that, while emphasis on right or left parts of the body may be of signifi-cance (Hertz 1960), human skulls most certainly would have featured prominently in the rituals. The removal of the head from the body buried at the Klokkehøj dolmen is a rare example of decapitation, but such practices may have been common. There is clear emphasis on skulls within the chambers, either by crown-ing the piles of bones or by amassing in the corners, in the occasional presence of skulls as the only surviving human remains, and in their frequent presence in other contexts such as depositions during rituals taking place in front of megaliths, in causewayed enclosures, or on settlement sites.

We have already noted that the shift from complete inhumation to communal

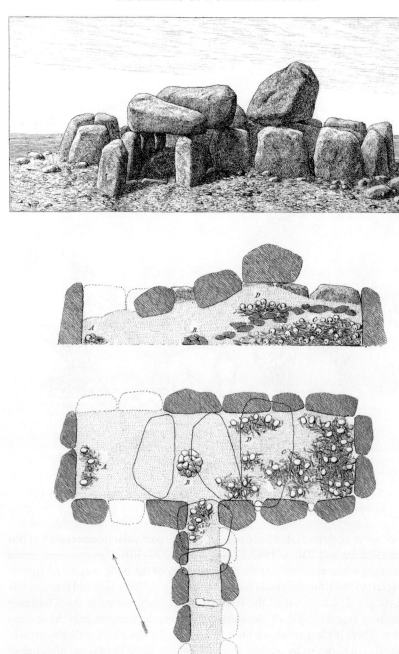

Figure 4.8 Human remains piled inside the passage grave at Uggerslev, island of Fyn

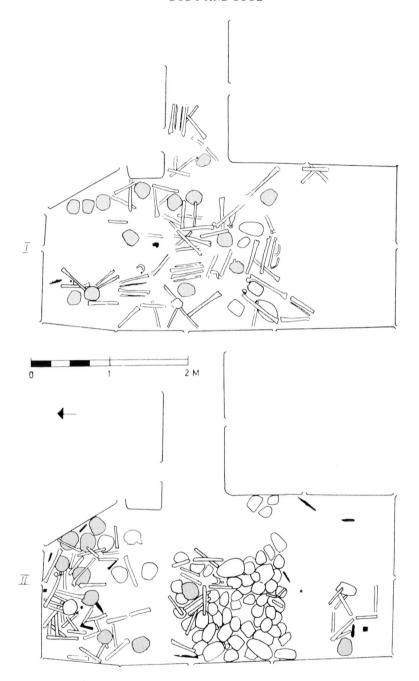

Figure 4.9 Raklev's plan of his excavation at the passage grave of Kinderballe (the two
levels apparently represent excavation layers rather than two separate
horizons), island of Langeland

deposition of fragmentary skeletal remains may herald the increasing importance of ancestral rites expressed, among other things, through burial. Thus skulls could have been periodically displayed in front of tombs or at enclosures during ancestral rites, or they may have been brought out, perhaps decorated to create a truly awesome sight, during initiation ceremonies. While rare, skulls with traces of skin cut away in strips are known from TRB contexts, for example from the settlement at Basedow and from the enclosure at Bundsø (Asmus 1987; Kossian 2005, 145; P. O. Nielsen 1982, 43). Such evidence may reflect the preparation of a skull for display rather than the commonly suggested cannibalistic practices. Indeed, the rather bizarre shaping of human skulls into utensils, for example a skull made into a bowl at Bundsø or a similarly fashioned bowl and spoon from Ringsjörn-Sjöholmen, all of which showed traces of use (Brøndsted 1957, 268; P. O. Nielsen 1982, 43, figure on p. 41), and the presence in the megaliths on the Danish islands of the so-called 'face pots' – vessels clearly decorated with facial motifs which plausibly could imitate such special organic containers – may be regional expressions related to feasts in honour of ancestors.

Jaw bones may also represent another part of the body with significance for rituals. Sometimes they are missing completely, or else their number is insufficient to account for the number of the dead in the chamber. When present, they often seem to derive from children or young persons, and are commonly encountered in votive placements in front of tombs. Being one of the more robust parts of the skeleton, and belonging to young individuals whose loss to a community may have been particularly painful, they may have circulated as relics among the living.

Skulls and jaws, in combination with other select bones, also have been encountered beneath some of the Swedish passage graves. The tripartite pit at Carlshögen contained an adult skull, a collection of vertebrae, and another group of mixed bones; the vertebrae and the skull being central to the body, these deposits have a particular significance (Strömberg 1971, 58–60, Figure 36). Several similar deposits have been noted at Ramshög and Tågarp (Strömberg 1971, 94–5, Figure 55; Tilley 1996, 232). It is possible that these were bones removed from other chambers to consecrate a location for a future one but, as noted above, it is equally plausible that they may represent earlier burials of fragmentary remains in locations that were known and revered in the community.

A subsequent decision to build a megalithic chamber in such a place need not be surprising. Indeed, recent investigations at Nissehøj revealed that the stone paving for votive offerings in front of the entrance to the chamber covered an earlier Neolithic earth-grave, and this could hardly have been unknown to the builders (Hansen 1993, Figure 17). Such juxtapositions are, in fact, much more common than is generally recognised in archaeological literature. A number of German and Dutch megalithic chambers were built upon, or in the immediate vicinity of, earlier burials. Such are known from Mecklenburg (for example at Serrahn), from Schleswig-Holstein (at Rastorf, Schwesing and Buensen), from Lower Saxony (at Gudendorf, Nenndorf, Rohstorf and Deinste) and from the Netherlands (at Odoorn D32, Glimmen G2 and Emmen D43; Kossian 2005, 123–6).

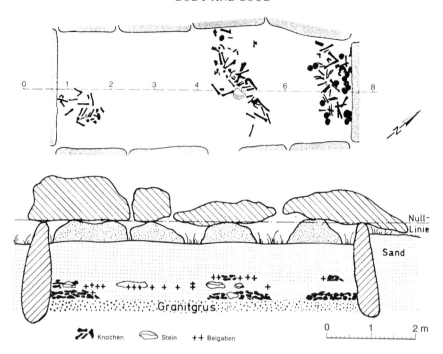

Figure 4.10 Disposition of human remains in Chamber B at Sieben Steinhäuser, near
Fallingbostel, Lower Saxony

Evidence from further south on the north European plain, from Lower Saxony
and Mecklenburg, by and large confirms the pattern of partial interments discussed
so far. Thus at Sieben Steinhäuser (chamber B), in a rare example of surviving
burials in Lower Saxony, Jacob-Friesen encountered on the original floor three
piles of bones: one in the middle, not far from the entrance, and the other two both
at one end of the chamber (Jacob-Friesen 1925, 15; Figure 4.10). The piles comprised mostly long bones and skulls; at least 15 skulls were found in the pile to the
right of the entrance. What is curious here is the fact that, although this primary
deposit of bones was covered with a layer of sand about 20–25 cm thick, subsequent bone deposits overlay precisely the earlier bone piles; either there were some
markers set into the sandy layer, or the position of the earlier deposits was known
to those who placed further bones in the chamber at a later stage. Indeed, as
Schirnig remarked (1982, 46), perhaps new anthropological analysis would help to
establish the relationship between these deposits.

An interesting deviation from this pattern is offered by the megalithic chamber
at Rheine, Westfalen. This chamber was only partly investigated by Eckert in 1983
and, in the excavated section, he encountered skeletal remains belonging to 12
individuals. The short report does not provide sufficient information on the condition of the preserved bones, but their analysis points to the presence of a six-
month-old foetus (*in utero*) which suggests that at least one of the six females

125

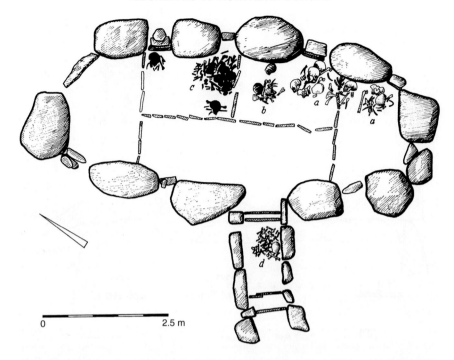

Figure 4.11 Disposition of human remains in the passage grave at Liepen 1, Mecklenburg

identified there must have been buried as a complete individual – a fact which Eckert used to argue strongly against the ossuary theory. A further peculiarity of the bone deposit was the additional presence of about 250 fragments of lightly burnt human bones which, according to Eckert, also belonged to the TRB group using this chamber (Eckert 1999, 101–2). (I am indebted to Ute Bartelt for drawing my attention to this megalithic chamber.)

Human remains in passage graves in Mecklenburg vary between one and twenty individuals (Schuldt 1972, 73–5). Arrangements at Liepen 1, where only TRB materials have been discovered (Figure 4.11), display a sequence of depositions that involved several separate events: remains of two disarticulated individuals were placed on the original floor (a skull and bones of a young individual and, at a distance but in the same compartment, a skull and some bones of a child seven or eight years of age). Then, upon the secondary floor, mixed remains of three individuals were placed, and at some stage a pit was dug from this floor to the lower level, in which broken bones belonging to five persons were placed. A mixed bundle of bones and skulls belonging to six individuals – but only three jaws – was found 40 cm above the secondary floor; and, in the passage, mixed remains of between three and five individuals were found covered with sand.

Mecklenburg also offers evidence of contemporary disarticulated burials outside the megalithic chambers. Protected by one of the barrows at the Bronze Age barrow cemetery at Groß Upahl 1, in the Warnow river valley, a smaller round barrow covered eight graves (Schuldt 1972, 75; Steinmann 2001, 97–9). One of the graves – a stone-framed pit – contained disarticulated remains of about 21 individuals, possibly placed there in two stages. At the top there were six skulls and bundles of long bones, lower down there were two piles of bones from seven individuals each, and in between these two piles was one fully articulated body.

Another of the graves had remains of five persons in the upper part, with long bones clearly sorted into bundles; below, there were three layers of stones covering disarticulated fragments of eight persons in one half, and three partly articulated remains in the other half of the grave pit. A decorated TRB beaker gives a clear cultural indication, suggesting the later MN period. Three further graves had disarticulated remains of one person each, while one stone setting had a complete, crouched inhumation. These grave pits could represent 'emergency' storage: while some bodies were ready in their 'bone bundles' to be moved to the appropriate chamber, their association with an articulated body suggests that for some reason this was not possible and that the bodies, in their various stages of decomposition, were temporarily covered. Steinmann's remark (2001, 97) that some of the graves were most probably visible on the surface supports this idea.

We should also consider that burial of complete bodies within the megalithic chambers would not in any sense preclude the performance of secondary burial rites at an appropriate stage: subsequent rearrangement of bones, removal of certain skeletal parts to other locations or addition of new bones at other times. Indeed, while decomposition of many bodies undoubtedly took place outside the megaliths, the 'within the chamber' scenario receives some support from the Swedish passage graves and has also been argued for some of the Danish chambers.

However, recent investigations of Danish passage graves have led to conflicting interpretations. On the one hand, in the intact TRB burial layers from Aldersro, on Zealand, no complete skeletons have been found in spite of good preservation. The full osteological report on the human remains is still pending, but the TRB deposits here – sealed off from the subsequent interments – are claimed to have been incomplete: hands and feet were largely missing, although other fragile bones such as ribs, vertebrae and scapulae appear to have been present. Poor preservation was excluded as a cause of such bone distribution, and Holten has argued that the incompleteness of the individuals was a result of deliberate human action (Holten 2000, 289).

In contrast, at the passage grave at Sarup Gamle Skole II the original floor had only a few human bones, but upon the second floor, 10 cm above, several bodies were discovered. Although the bones were disordered, Andersen stated that all skeletal parts were represented and thus that complete bodies must have been deposited there (Andersen 1997, 117). Indeed an analysis of even later TRB burials (from the time of Sarup IV) in one of the dolmens at Damsbo Mark, with bones also ordered in piles, suggests that these individuals were related to one another (ibid., 125, note 87).

The evidence from the passage grave at Hulbjerg has also been claimed to indicate burials of full bodies. Here the two TRB layers were sealed with stones and thus at least partly separated from the subsequent interments of the Corded Ware culture. Fatty organic materials in the lower part of the chamber have been interpreted as deriving from slowly decomposing bodies; many of the bones – segments of vertebrae columns, hands and feet – showed at least partial articulation, and Bennike (1985) has argued that burial involved complete bodies. (See Midgley 1992, 454 for comments on the disparity between the apparent archaeological stratigraphy and the lack of osteological analysis in accordance with cultural contexts.) On the other hand, although some skeletal fragments retained their anatomical attachment, Skaarup also emphasised the sorting of limb bones and skulls into piles and noted the stacking of shoulder blades in the passage (Skaarup 1985a, 195). Thus the two processes – deposition of full, or possibly partial, bodies and subsequent reorganisation of the bones in the chamber – could plausibly reflect two separate aspects of funerary ritual.

Indeed, the chambers may have provided the most secure and controlled environment in which decomposition could take place. We have already noted that many chambers were built to create impervious structures, with no effort spared to protect the interior from seeping or rising water, to minimise animal intrusion and to protect against other disturbances (Chapter 3). The presence of closing devices, occasionally multiplied several times across the passage, is generally seen as representing symbolically important markers in different stages of access by the living; it could equally well have indicated stages in the 'departure' of the soul of the dead for the world beyond. But such devices also served the practical purpose of keeping the tombs closed. When closed, megalithic chambers offered stable atmospheric conditions – constant temperature and low humidity all year round – in which the decomposition process would have been slow and the time needed for a total decomposition could be predicted (Gräslund 1994, 24). Moreover, Ahlström has argued that in these conditions the process of decomposition did not so much involve putrefaction but rather mummification and formation of adipocere (Ahlström 2003, 261).

The idea that complete bodies were buried in the Swedish passage graves is commonly accepted by Swedish archaeologists, with the dead envisaged as seated resting against the upright slabs of the niches (Strömberg 1971, Chapter VIII; Malmer 2002, 54). We have also noted already the Onskulle passage grave, famous for its images of seated bodies. The earliest reference to such a practice dates from 1788, when the passage grave of Dala in Västergötland was excavated by Gottfried Hilfeling. Ahlström has compiled a list of about a dozen sites with references to 'seated' burials in Sweden (Ahlström 2003, Figure 2).

Indeed, it is worth noting that old reports referring to 'seated bodies' do exist in other areas. Thus the Andemosehøj chamber on Langeland, opened around the middle of the nineteenth century, was reported to have had ten individuals 'seated' with their backs against the chamber wall and legs across the floor (Skaarup 1985a, 144), and the Brandsbjerg chamber on Zealand, opened in 1890, was described as having about 30 skeletons also perceived as 'sitting' in a row along the long chamber walls, although these are regarded as dating to the Late Neolithic. The Mecklenburg antiquarian Friedrich Lisch also described the burials found at Blengow as 'sitting bodies' on account of the fact that the skulls and the vertebrae were found lying in between the legs, and similar sentiments were expressed by Beltz with reference to bone piles in the centre of the chamber at Lenzen (Steinmann 2001, 88, 96). While these descriptions lack supporting illustrative documentation and are difficult to verify today, the possibility of such burial practices outside Sweden, even if rare, should not be discounted altogether.

Malmer has argued that the niches within the Swedish chambers indicate kin groups or families (Malmer 2002, 57), but this really would have to be tested through anthropological analysis. Future DNA studies of human remains from individual chambers may further enlighten us on this aspect. However, from a purely functional point of view, the presence of niches is suggestive of somewhat different arrangements for placing the skeletons inside chambers. Marta Strömberg has argued that the compartments at Carlshögen – some of which were delineated by vertical slabs – were certainly large enough to accommodate a seated, squatting body, and that there were remains of between three and ten individuals in such sections. At Ramshög most of the human remains were found in the centre, directly opposite the entrance, and in the northern end of the chamber (Strömberg 1971, 44–58, 93); whether the chamber had niches was not entirely clear.

The bones from the Rössberga passage grave, excavated in 1962 by Cullberg, have recently been reanalysed by Ahlström (2001). The minimum number of individuals who had been interred here is estimated at 128; the fragmentary condition of the material is assumed to have resulted from taphonomic processes, with wrist and finger bones under-represented. Cullberg identified at least 17 niches inside the chamber (Figure 4.12b; although more may originally have existed) but, interestingly, the quantity of bones within each bears no relationship to its size: thus the relatively small niche no. 17 had the most human remains, while the large niche no. 6 had few bones. Ahlström has suggested that bodies were decaying in defined parts of the chamber: the southern part of the southern half, where the passage entered the chamber, and the northern part of the northern half. Skeletal parts were mostly deposited to the north and south of the entrance.

This interpretation is interesting for two reasons. First, we may envisage functional differentiation within the Rössberga chamber: decay of bodies and deposition of skeletal fragments resulting from this process seem to have taken place in separate, clearly defined areas. This suggests that, even if entire bodies were placed inside the chamber, the bones were sorted at some stage and moved from the decay to the deposition zones. Thus, in contrast to Ahlström's statement, human factors may well have contributed to the ultimate fragmentation and distribution, resulting in over- or under-representation of certain bones in parts of the chamber (ibid., Figure 4.12).

Moreover, such a practice could help explain the anomalies that have been noted in the distribution of the upper and lower, left and right body parts, discussed by Shanks and Tilley with reference to the Ramshög and Carlshögen passage graves

129

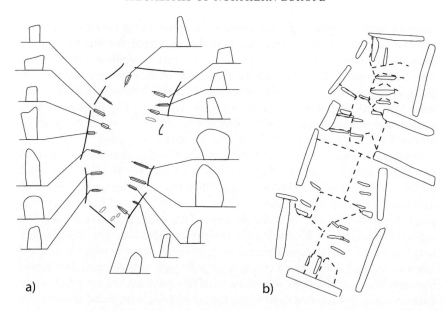

a)   b)

Figure 4.12 Arrangement of niches within the Falbygden passage graves: (a) Hjelmar's Cairn; (b) Rössberga

in Scania (Shanks and Tilley 1982). Such arrangements need not be a result of deliberate selection of upper/lower and right/left body parts, but may reflect the movement of skeletal parts from the 'decay' to the 'deposition' sections of the chamber – depending on where the bodies were placed originally, the various skeletal fragments being moved to the nearest deposition area, for example some upper skeletal parts being moved in one direction, and lower parts in the other.

Recent excavation of a passage grave at Frälsegården, Gökhem, in Västergötland, in which there were between eight and nine niches and where the burial deposit appears to have survived intact in the middle of the chamber, was undertaken precisely with a view to analysing the spatial distribution of human remains (Axelsson and Sjögren 2001). All bones were measured three-dimensionally and marked in a field in such a manner as to permit a close relationship between spatial arrangements and the subsequent osteological analysis (Ahlström 2003, 256). Of the 9502 bones recovered, 7004 were human and anatomically determined. Ahlström's analysis demonstrated that two of the bodies were complete, four were partially complete, and that there was a substantial amount of other articulated skeletal material.

His analysis centred on the hypothetical pattern of decomposition of bodies which would have been placed in a seated position, bound or wrapped in hides and supported by the vertical stone slabs placed in the chamber floor. Some of the bodies appear to have collapsed during the decomposition process: at least two of the skeletons fell backwards (Figure 4.13) and one disintegrated vertically, creating a pile of bones which, according to Ahlström, is the phenomenon described

Figure 4.13 Collapsed skeleton of a female aged 40–50 years, discovered just inside the entrance to the chamber at Frälsegården, Falbygden

previously in literature. The latter does indeed look very convincingly like a vertically collapsed skeleton (ibid., Figure 12) but it does not bear any resemblance to the piles of bones, with their skulls neatly placed on top, seen in some of the Danish chambers. The study of the six skeletons from Frälsegården does nevertheless make a reasonably convincing case for these individuals having been placed in a seated position. What is now needed is a study of the disposition of the other, partially articulated fragments, to permit an understanding of arrangements made with completely decomposed corpses.

One more site from the Falbygden area, Landbogården, should be mentioned in connection with seated bodies. Landbogården is one of the smallest passage graves in the area and, within one of its niches, four bodies appear to have been placed one on top of the other, apparently seated (Figure 4.14). The lowermost individual (E), reasonably well-preserved and displaying lower and upper body articulation, is thus the oldest known seated (?) body found in a Swedish megalithic chamber (dated to 4755 ± 100 BP; Persson and Sjögren 2001, 82–3, Figure 70). There are several possibilities here: the chamber may have started as a dolmen and been rebuilt later, or the body was preserved – possibly mummified elsewhere as an important ancestor – to be finally buried in the family or group chamber (Persson and Sjögren 1996, 75). While the small size of the chamber may have influenced the location of each new interment, one on top of the other, two other individuals

131

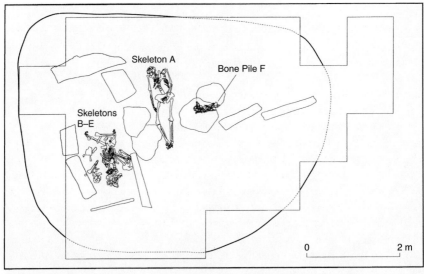

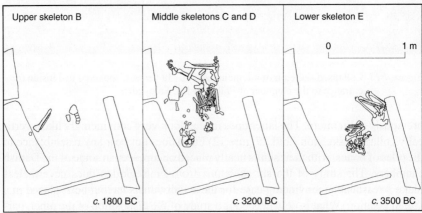

Figure 4.14 Plan and sequence of burials in the passage grave at Landbogården, Falbygden

found within it suggest that the positioning within one particular niche may have been dictated by considerations other than space; family connections, even if they spanned a generation or two, should not be left out of consideration.

Against the background of the above discussion it has to be conceded that information on the age and sex of individuals interred within the megaliths is entirely inadequate for any discussion of demographic issues, be it in terms of local group size, mortality rates or related questions. Only human remains from the closed chambers, which are undisturbed and contain grave goods, can definitely be assigned to the TRB, and these rarely amount to more than a couple of individuals.

Theoretically all open chambers could have chronologically mixed human deposits although, as we have seen, primary and secondary interments can sometimes be distinguished. The disintegration of the osteological material poses major problems in the identification of age and sex, as also does the manner in which analyses take place, often treating the chamber bone material en masse; this applies not only to the older analyses but, as we noted earlier, even to relatively recently excavated chambers, as seen at Hulbjerg. Moreover, as the continuous use of flat graves demonstrates, very many individuals were buried outside the megalithic chambers; and this is an important issue, rarely raised in the literature.

However, it can be said that neither age nor sex appears to have been a discriminatory factor, as adults of both sexes and children were all buried in the megaliths. The relationship between the sexes is difficult to ascertain because of extremely limited data; in a recent table compiled for southern Scandinavia and Mecklenburg by Sjögren (2003a, Table 10.4) only 68 males and 51 females are identified. The inclusion of children is important in individual monuments: earlier, children had been buried in the long barrows (Chapter 1), and they are found in dolmens, for example at Klokkehøj, Trekrone and Basedow. Scanian passage graves demonstrate well the presence of children: two of the three foundation deposits beneath the floor of Carlshögen contained bones of young individuals, and every chamber compartment but one contained bones belonging to children; similarly children were buried at Ramshög (Lepiksaar 1971). Another possible interpretation could be provided by some of the chambers around Sarup, for example the dolmen of Damsbo Mark, which may have been a 'family' vault in the later TRB, since there are some indications of a genetic connection between the buried individuals (Andersen 1997, 125, note 87).

H. A. Nielsen's early-twentieth-century analysis of bones from about 30 Danish passage graves showed that children made up between 28 per cent and 46 per cent of all individuals and, for the whole of the Neolithic, Bennike quoted an average of 28 per cent (Bennike 1985, 473). This, interestingly enough, compares well with the recent figures suggested for the Rössberga chamber, where about 30 per cent of individuals died before the age of 20 (Ahlström 2001, Figure 10.6). Indeed it seems that at times children were given special treatment; the recently excavated children's cemetery at Borgeby in Scania, not far from the megalithic tomb of Gillhög, emphasises that children 'were blessed with a privileged position in society' (Runcis 2005, 39) although the criteria for such a distinction are not entirely clear.

Apart from human remains discussed so far, burnt bones are also occasionally found within the dolmen and passage grave chambers (as previously noted at Rheine, Westfalen). However, they are more often encountered outside, where they appear to have been associated, in a rather complex fashion, with votive deposits of pottery, flint tools and other items that result from activities conducted in front of the megalithic tombs (see **Votive deposits**, p. 148). With the possible exception of the deposit from the passage grave at Ostenwalde, the burnt bone can hardly be described as resulting from the process of cremation. At Ostenwalde, the cobbled floor paving had several depositions of cremated human bone, identified as remains of seven individuals, each placed in a different spot in the chamber. Tempel thought these to be secondary but, in Bakker's view, they could equally be later TRB interments (Bakker 1992, 50). The 394 TRB pots, identified primarily by their bases, came from this layer.

Finds of burnt bones have also been encountered in dolmen and passage grave chambers in Denmark and Sweden. Generally this seems to be a case of traces of burning: thus a few of the bones found in chamber 3 at Pærgaard dolmen showed traces of fire; individual bones from Ormshøj and Troldstuerne were burnt, and at Hjortegårdene burnt bones were found in the passage (Berg 1956, 115; Dehn *et al.* 2000, 125, 146, 218). A. P. Madsen (1896, 12) mentioned lightly scorched human bones from the southern chamber at Gundsølille, apparently mixed with secondarily burnt pottery, and burnt bone at Kyndeløse seems to have been associated with a fireplace that was set up inside the chamber (Kaul 1994, 20). The passage grave at Varpelev contained piles of charcoal and lightly burnt bones, mixed with burnt potsherds and flint tools. The burning obviously took place elsewhere, and prior to the deposition the remains were clearly selected, since the deposit lacked some of the long bones (ibid., 20). The Trollasten dolmen had two concentrations of very badly decayed burnt bone in the interior (Strömberg 1968, 154), and burnt remains of at least two individuals, possibly male and female, were found as part of the primary deposits at Gillhög (ibid., 197; see Tilley 1996, Table 5.1, for a list of further Scanian sites).

Grave goods in dolmens and passage graves

The vast majority of artefacts associated with the megalithic tombs derive from the votive layers outside the entrances to the chambers (see **Votive deposits**, p. 148). With the notable exception of the area west of the river Weser, the objects found within the chambers are, in comparison, relatively scanty and present us with a range of interpretative problems.

However, before we discuss the assortment of artefacts found within the megalithic chambers, we should perhaps consider what constitutes grave goods and how the items discovered in megaliths should be regarded. The term 'grave goods' is normally reserved for items that have been deposited with the dead during the burial ceremony. Thus grave goods will include personal items that may have belonged to the deceased in life, and objects that were regarded as essential for the appropriate conduct of the funerary ceremony by those who were performing the rituals. Personal effects could include garments or jewellery worn by the deceased in life, as well as some specific tools used regularly in daily tasks. The other set of items would have been selected by the community – that is, the immediate kin or the wider social group – as deemed necessary to the proper performance of the rite: items which formed the indispensable equipment for the transition from this life to the next.

However, the megalithic chambers provide circumstances where the interpretation of all items encountered in the interior as grave goods in the traditional sense of the word may be misleading. There are only a handful of chambers – predominantly those of the closed dolmen form – where items can reasonably be thought of as grave goods associated with the particular individuals. Elsewhere, the accessibility of the chamber, the lack of clear associations between human remains and accompanying artefacts, as well as secondary intrusions, seldom indicate any relationship between the burials and the accompanying objects.

Indeed, the question of grave goods within the open chambers needs to be considered against the background of the mode of interment. If we accept that complete bodies were buried in some of the chambers but then, after decomposition, the bones were sorted into piles and possibly removed to other locations, the artefacts found there can still conceivably be seen as grave goods accorded to the individuals but then becoming mixed up in the course of internal rearrangements.

If, on the other hand, we choose to interpret the skeletal remains in some of the open chambers as selections of bones following the process of the initial decomposition of the body elsewhere, then the interpretation of artefacts encountered inside the chambers is somewhat ambiguous. Were these selected at the time of death and kept elsewhere, for example at the deceased's house, in a cult house or some other appropriate location, until such time as the bones were interred inside the chamber (which could be quite a considerable time after death)? Or are these items 'symbolic' grave goods, following the established codes of funerary ritual without any reflection upon the life and death of particular individuals?

Indeed, are these grave goods at all, rather than objects placed within the chambers as offerings to the ancestors, spirits or even gods, perhaps being brought inside at ritually determined moments? As we shall see below, the ambiguity is not easy to resolve: some artefacts, such as pottery, large flint tools or caches of freshly struck flint blades, can easily fit into the category of 'offerings', and these are also items frequently employed in ceremonies outside the megaliths. Other objects, such as amber jewellery, arrow(head)s or small work tools, speak in favour of individual dead being buried with personal effects – the relationship being obliterated by subsequent reorganisations of the bones within.

The closed Danish dolmens provide some evidence of grave goods that can be attributed to specific burials. Such examples come from Grøfte, Ølstykke, Kellerød and Asnæs Skov, some of which contained undisturbed primary burials. Here we encounter a rather stereotypical set of goods – collared and/or lugged flasks, flint blades and flakes – which were placed according to a pattern: pottery by the feet of the deceased, and tools in the region of the upper body (Figures 4.2 and 4.3). The long dolmen from Bogø, published by A. P. Madsen in 1896, reveals similar arrangements: the dead individual was laid out on the back, remains of a collared flask and a sherd from another vessel stood by the feet, while nine large flint axes and chisels were distributed unevenly on both sides of the body; an arrowhead and two flint blades rested upon the left shoulder (A. P. Madsen 1896; Figure 4.15). Indeed, this manner of equipping the dead continues in many respects the earlier tradition seen within the long barrows, and also reflects a significant pattern of arranging grave goods around the individual dead, as evidenced in the contemporary flat graves (Kossian 2005, 112–13).

The undisturbed dolmen chambers from Mecklenburg also reveal the disposition of the grave goods in relation to the buried individuals: at Friedrichsruhe, each of

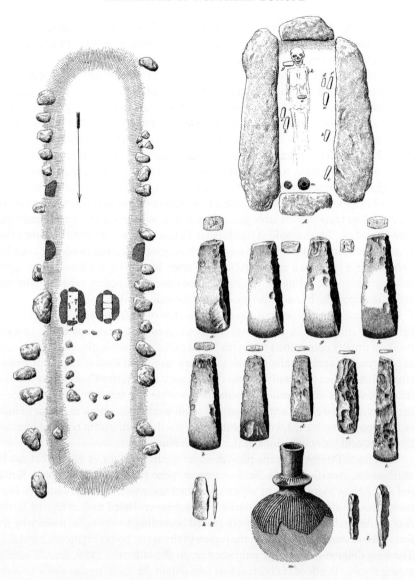

Figure 4.15 Burial and accompanying grave goods from the long dolmen at Bogø, south
Zealand

the two individuals (represented by a pile of selected bones and a skull) had
remains of a vessel close by, and a large amber piece lay next to one of the bone
assemblages. At Naschendorf 1, eight transverse arrowheads were scattered among
the fragmentary human remains, but the individual buried at Bavendorf 2 may well
have had a collared flask standing at the feet, although only fragments of a skull
survived at the opposite end of the chamber (Schuldt 1972, 71–2).

Grave goods from the open chambers, both dolmens and passage graves, are more difficult to interpret, as generally there is no relationship between them and any bones that may survive in the chamber. Only very rarely can the interior arrangement be thought to reflect the original placement of the grave goods, but even then such patterns may be local and not indicative of practices in other areas.

Although Klokkehøj was an accessible chamber, the primary deposit here does reflect the pattern typical of the closed dolmens. The decorated bone dagger lay close by the wrist of the adult, who lay in an extended position, and three vessels (two beakers and a lugged flask) stood at the feet. Since the primary deposit here also contained a single jaw of a child and lower and upper arm bones of another individual, the three pots could conceivably reflect each of these three burials (Thorsen 1981, Figures 7–9). With each of the primary double burials in the two chambers at one of the Frellesvig dolmens, there was one decorated bone wrist-guard (Skaarup 1985a, no. 73, 115), and in one of the Pæregård chambers an unusual find of a perforated plate made from wild boar's tusk accompanied flint axes, blades and a bone awl (Berg 1956, 110).

The evidence from the undisturbed chamber M1 at Kleinenkneten 2 is so far unique among the TRB megaliths. Here grave goods were found lying within small oval enclosures on the floor of the chamber (Michaelsen 1978, 242, Plates 32–4). From the available photographs these do not appear as standard compartments – of the type encountered, for instance, in Mecklenburg – and thus could conceivably reflect individual interments separated from one another by means of rather loose settings of stones.

The published arrangements from the megalithic chambers at Oldendorf, while perhaps somewhat idealised, do nevertheless offer the possibility of perceiving a relationship between the deceased and the grave goods that accompanied them (Laux 1980, 151–74). At Oldendorf I, two individuals may have been buried: at the eastern end of the chamber, near the surviving skull, sherds of a beaker and a shoul-dered pot were found; sherds of three other vessels further to the north – a high-handled cup, a shouldered vessel and a beaker – may have stood close to the head of the second individual, of whom only two long bones survive. The position of two transverse arrowheads suggests that two arrows were placed alongside the body, and a fragment of an axe appears to have been placed by the feet. At Oldendorf II, the grave goods were concentrated at the south-eastern end of the chamber, where two skulls and some other bones survived (Figure 4.16a). If these represent extended inhumations, then once again the grave goods seem to have been concentrated around the heads of the individuals although, curiously, such placements seem to be the reverse of those known from the Danish dolmens.

Human remains found at Oldendorf IV apparently involved six individuals, although the precise condition and location of these is not clear. Five separate assemblages were present: a shouldered bowl and an axe were found by the two skulls at the eastern end; a plain bowl, a clay drum and a pile of six flint chisels were placed by the south long wall, while opposite and further to the west another clay drum stood on its own. Seven arrowheads were apparently found, although

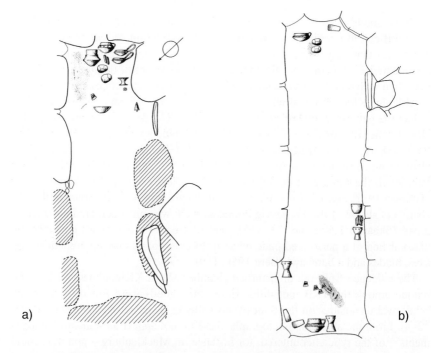

Figure 4.16 Burials and grave goods at the passage graves of Oldendorf, Lower Saxony:
(a) chamber II; (b) chamber IV

Laux's plan only shows the position of four; and, at the southern end of the
chamber, another group of grave goods included two axes, a shouldered pot and a
third drum (Figure 4.16b).

Similarly arranged assemblages are also known from the chamber at Mönchgut
on Rügen. Although this chamber was used over a long period of time and included
many secondary burials, the original deposits stood as separate assemblages. Such
were particularly clear along the walls of the relatively undisturbed northern half
of the chamber: a pot, a flint axe and a chisel, sometimes accompanied by transverse arrowheads and perforated amber beads – often in the vicinity of a definite
bone pile (Petzsch 1928, Plate IX).

The above examples, while not numerous, do nevertheless suggest that in some
chambers with multiple burials the grave goods may have accompanied individuals or groups of individuals. Analysis of the disposition of grave goods in some of
the Dutch chambers, albeit devoid of human remains, supports such an interpretation (see below).

Pottery is the commonest accompaniment of the dead in the accessible chambers,
although the number of vessels is generally small and any relationship between the
dead and the pots is difficult to estimate. The 59 chambers from north Jutland, analysed by Ebbesen, produced altogether 151 pots (an average of two and a half pots
per chamber; Ebbesen 1978, 122). However, from his earlier analysis of 1785 pots

from 264 megalithic graves in eastern Denmark (which is merely a selection of vessels in any case) it is simply impossible to say how many vessels come from the actual chambers and how many derive from the votive offerings in front of them; as these two forms of activity clearly fulfilled different purposes, chronological analysis of ceramic styles does not help us in our conundrum of interpreting the significance of pottery as grave goods.

Indeed, Skaarup's survey of the megalithic tombs from the southern Danish islands reveals how uneven that relationship may be: at the passage grave of Kragnæs, 29 TRB pots were found inside the chamber and at least 155 pots outside; at Hulbjerg there were 37 pots inside and 23 outside; at the long dolmen with three chambers at Nørreballe there were respectively 17, 12 and two pots inside and a minimum of 41, 100 and 44 vessels on the outside; and at the Frellesvig long dolmen the two chambers had respectively seven and three pots and there were at least 63 and 80 vessels on the outside. At Kinderballe, Raklev found remains of at least 24 to 25 individuals, but apparently only ten TRB vessels were placed inside (Skaarup 1985a, nos. 318, 260, 197, 74, 218).

Chambers from Scania and Västergötland on the whole contain only a small number of sherds, if any (Malmer 2002, 54). In Schleswig-Holstein there are usually one or more pots (Hoika 1990, 89), and in Mecklenburg at least 32 vessels were deposited inside the passage grave of Naschendorf, although generally the numbers are also small (Schuldt 1972, Table D).

The only region where massive ceramic deposits inside the chambers are encountered is west of the river Weser. Here the so-called 'service sets' sometimes run into hundreds of vessels: for example 160 pots in D26-Drouvenerveld, 536 pots in Wechte 1, at least 649 pots in D53-Havelte and a staggering 1200 vessels at Emmeln (Bakker 1992, 57; Knöll 1983, 7–12; Schlicht 1968, 21). As an example we may note that the Wechte 1 chamber contained between 30 and 40 collared flasks, over 40 beakers, 140 shouldered vessels and 230 bowls of various forms as well as other unidentified pots. Such quantities are quite exceptional in the context of the north European megalithic chambers and may reflect a specific regional tradition which, moreover, has to be seen alongside the prolonged period of use.

In her analysis of pottery from the chamber at Emmeln, E. Schlicht defined a 'service set' as an assemblage of several vessels, uniform in fabric and decoration style, possibly manufactured by one potter and then placed in the chamber on a single occasion (Schlicht 1968, 21). Since the dead in the contemporary flat graves were commonly given between five and six pots, it is reasonable to assume that assemblages of a similar scale would periodically be placed in a chamber, although they need not have been confined exclusively to burial ceremonies. In the *hunebed* G2-Glimmen, for example, about 400 pots were deposited over a period of at least 350 years. Since each service set may have included up to six vessels, such depositions need not have happened more than once every few years. Brindley (1986, 58) observed that at Glimmen the sherds of specific sets were close to one another, and this seems to reflect the arrangements noted at Oldendorf, where groups of vessels were assigned to individuals, although the burials were not numerous.

139

In the other Dutch and Lower Saxon chambers, where pottery is scattered all over the floor, the vessels are very fragmented and, where individual pots are often represented by a single sherd (for example the 100 or so bases identified by Fansa at Ostenwalde; Fansa 1978), we may perhaps see the results of trampling in the course of primary and, even more so, secondary use. Indeed the prolonged use of these chambers, as evidenced by the range of ceramics, provides an entirely practical explanation for the fragmentary state of the pottery; even once-a-year visits, if repeated over a hundred times, could have reduced most of the pottery to barely identifiable fragments. Deliberate clearances – if such ever took place – may have been undertaken more with a view to altering the nature of the chambers: pots may have been removed as a means of mediation in ancestral rites, or taken to be deposited elsewhere – scattered on settlements, thrown into the lakes and rivers as part of votive offerings or buried in the pits and ditches of enclosures – thus creating a physical as well as a symbolic link between the activities at megaliths and sites elsewhere in the landscape.

The pots are normally assumed to have contained food offerings to accompany the dead on their journey to the other world. Spectacular feasts, associated with funerary ceremonies or performed in honour of the ancestors, may be imagined – not least on account of pottery offerings left at the entrances to the chambers – although the meaning of such rituals could vary from region to region. As far as foods appropriate to the funerary ritual are concerned, the problems arise from the fact that there are hardly any analyses of food residues.

Some vessels appear to have contained a form of bread: chemical analysis of a pot from Kleinenkneten 1 revealed wheat bread with traces of fat (it is not certain if the analysed sherds came from the chamber or from outside), and another pot from the outside had food residue with a bone from a wild boar. A 'cooking' or 'roasting' spot was apparently found outside the mound (Michaelsen 1978, 236–7). Similarly a vessel from the passage grave at Emsen had traces of sour bread and, as Kossian reports (2005, 90), 'bread' was analysed in a couple of pots from the flat grave cemetery at Heek-Ammert, and plant oils and animal fat were found in vessels from Issendorf. Occasionally, the vessels reveal traces of repairs or of cooking – Koch noted that at least some of the funnel beakers recovered from Zealand's bogs had traces of fish meals, and that staining of the exterior walls suggested that foods had boiled over (Koch 1998, 151).

The presence of bread-like compounds should not be surprising, however mundane it appears to us today. Cereals, even if cultivated on any considerable scale, may well have been regarded as special. The pure emmer offering from Sarup and from other localities does emphasise the ritual importance of cereals and, as I have noted elsewhere, flat clay discs, which are commonly interpreted as bread baking plates, underlay the ancient bread-making traditions (Midgley 2005, 46).

The early dolmen ceramic assemblage of a lugged pot, a collared flask and/or beaker once again follows on from an older tradition, since such a combination is frequently associated with both graves and votive deposits at long barrows (Midgley 1985). This particular combination has been described by Sherratt as a classic 'drinking set' – equipment for handling liquids appropriate to ritual consumption (Sherratt 1991, 56). Indeed, he pondered whether reading the record upside down may not reveal a hidden iconography – whether an inverted collared flask did not look 'absurdly like a poppy-head' – and suggested the consumption of intoxicants in a liquid form. The opium poppy, *Papaver somniferum*, is known in north-west Europe from at least the second half of the sixth millennium BC (Midgley 2005, 29) but, attractive as this idea is in the context of ritual consumption – and ethnographic evidence does show the use of intoxicating substances during funerary ceremonies – its use needs to be tested through chemical analysis of such vessels. A tantalising glimpse of a possible intoxicating liquid is however offered by one of the tureens from Oldendorf IV, which, in view of the large amount of lime (*Tilia*) pollen adhering to the interior, may have contained honey or mead (Bakker 1992, 53).

Danish ceramics recovered from the megaliths display the widest range of forms during the time that passage graves were first used (MN I) and, although funnel-necked beakers are the commonest, various bowls, lugged beakers, pedestalled bowls and clay spoons were also deemed appropriate for inclusion; this pattern is also typical of chambers in Mecklenburg. Indeed, the two latter forms, which are among the most elaborately decorated ceramics, appear to be associated exclusively with funerary ceremonies, being found at tombs and in cult houses and rarely encountered elsewhere. The rather shallow and open format, with the high stand, implies solid rather than liquid food, and the highly decorated spoon emphasises the public mixing of ingredients. Thus, although ritual pottery depositions also take place elsewhere, the range of vessels is different: in the early stages of activities at Sarup I, beakers of various forms predominate, whereas later, at Sarup II, more open forms – bowls and shouldered vessels – are used (N. H. Andersen 1997, 58–9, 81–4). Foods consumed and disposed of at tombs and in other contexts, at enclosures as well as lakesides, may well have been different: ancestors needed different nourishment from that offered to gods and spirits.

With MN II the variety encountered inside the Danish chambers decreases dramatically. Shouldered bowls of various forms are typical, while hanging vessels, sometimes with their lids, are the hallmark of MN III forms; only rarely is later pottery put into the chambers. This may suggest that, in southern Scandinavia at least, the provision of a variety of foods gradually lost its ceremonial significance – although this does not appear to have been the case everywhere, as indicated by the large number of 'service sets' from the area west of the Weser.

Flint had an equally special meaning in the funerary rituals. We have already noted its use in the construction of chambers, as exterior protection or as paving on the floors, and this can further be seen in the importance of flint tools and flint coverings of votive deposits outside the megalithic chambers (see **Votive deposits**, p. 148). Flint tools also constituted important grave goods: large implements such as axes or chisels, flint blades, knives or scrapers are also placed in the megaliths, albeit in lesser quantities than pottery.

At Carlshögen the first burial placement in each of the compartments seems to have been accompanied by a pile of flints placed there concurrently, and similar assemblages (flakes and cores) are found as foundation deposits either beneath the floor (Carlshögen) or immediately outside at the base of the orthostats (for example at Carlshögen and Ramshög; Strömberg 1971, 310). Sometimes flint blades were manufactured specifically in connection with the burial ceremony; the 58 unused blades at the passage grave of Liepen, which were struck from a single nodule, are a good example. Similar blade caches have been found in a number of flat graves at Ostorf (Schuldt 1961, 173; Kossian 2005, 280–99). Moreover, the large quantities of flint debris in the vicinity of the kerbstones at Serrahn 2 indicated, according to Schuldt (1966a, 37–9), the residue of manufacture directly associated with burials.

Axes and chisels are not very numerous; in Denmark two or three axes are found in a chamber, and this contrasts strongly with the later TRB deposits outside the chambers. Ebbesen's analysis of flint axes from 259 megalithic chambers on the Danish islands accounts for 444 thick-butted examples (an average of 1.7 axes per grave; Ebbesen 1975, 153; he does state that these derive from the chambers), and apparently the assemblage from the passage grave at Hulbæk, comprising five flint axes, four chisels and at least 20 blades, is one of the richest in north Jutland (Ebbesen 1978, 127). The numbers are not much larger in other regions: Schlicht (1968, 17–18) commented on the general poverty of large flint tools as grave equipment in Emsland. In Mecklenburg, although some chambers have an impressive number of large flint tools – for example, 32 flint axes and chisels and two stone axes from Rerik 1 (Steinmann 2001, 88) or the 19 axes at Neu Gaarz – generally the numbers are smaller (Schuldt 1972, Table D). In Scania, modern excavations tend to recover small tools such as transverse arrowheads and small pieces of flint waste; axes are rare (Strömberg 1971; Malmer 2002, 55).

The significance of the axe, both as a working tool and as a symbol of a new way of life in northern Europe, is demonstrated in many ways. Indeed, the Ertebølle hunter-gatherers already procured stone axes from their southern farming neighbours and clearly regarded such exotica as highly prestigious and valuable status symbols, occasionally placing them in graves (Fischer 1982). During the Neolithic, axes are disposed of in massively consumptive hoards, coveted as prestigious items made of exotic materials (for example jade or copper axes) and, along the Atlantic façade, also seen in images decorating standing stones and some of the later chambers. Their incorporation in grave goods, albeit in smaller numbers than those recovered from votive offerings in front of the chambers, as well as the miniature imitations in amber (see below), demonstrate the importance of the axe not only as a tool – the wear on many of the axes found in the megaliths shows that they have been used – but also as a symbolic resource.

Transverse arrowheads are another ubiquitous item accompanying the dead. Generally the number is small, from a couple to a dozen or so, but occasionally the numbers are striking: 573 arrowheads come from the chamber at Emmeln (Schlicht 1979, 54) suggesting that every now and then massive caches of arrows were included. Arrows inside the chambers appear throughout the entire TRB province, but curiously enough they have played no role in the votive deposits outside the chambers. Arrows may thus have been among the items that indicated the status of the individual dead – as accomplished hunters or warriors – rather than being a requirement of the burial ceremony.

Dressing and adorning the dead

There is virtually no indication of any garments worn by the dead, although the various jewellery items found suggest that at least some of the dead may have been fully clothed and adorned with trinkets they coveted in life. Indeed, ethnographic evidence from different parts of the world suggests that dressing the dead is a very important aspect of the funerary ceremony. Elaborate garments, head dresses and other clothing paraphernalia are found in many cultures; some such items can be very costly, requiring contributions from many kin. Moreover, cloth can also be important in secondary burial practices, the best-known ethnographic example deriving from Madagascar, where the reopening of the Merina family tombs requires 'dressing' the ancestral bones in new, colourful and expensive cloth (Bloch 1971).

Items from Swedish chambers have been interpreted as some sort of clothing associated with the dead. According to Ahlström (2003, 261) the bodies in the Swedish chambers were seated, a position that was maintained during the decomposition process with the aid of strapping. Furthermore, phalanges of wild boar are known from the Swedish chambers, and 70 of these were found recently in the Frälsegården passage grave; they are interpreted as remains from hides, suggesting that the dead may have been wrapped in them.

Jewellery was an important aspect of everyday life in the Neolithic, and it is clear that individuals were equally adorned in death: necklaces and armbands were most commonly strung using amber beads, although slate, jet and bone were also used. Wild animal teeth, while not as common as during the Mesolithic, were occasionally fashioned into pendants and worn on account of their apotropaic qualities: examples of pendants made from the incisors and metapodials of pig, dog or wolf are known from Mecklenburg and from Lower Saxony (Lehmkuhl 1991, 373; Laux 1991, Figure 3). Copper trinkets, while rare, undoubtedly added greatly to the prestige of those individuals who were able to procure such exotic paraphernalia, and they may well have been included in composite jewellery items.

Amber has a very long tradition of use in northern Europe in the manufacture of jewellery and trinkets. Amber pieces, together with perforated wild animal teeth, were used by the Mesolithic hunter-gatherers to create composite necklaces and possibly to decorate garments. (Such were found at Skateholm cemetery, where a child was buried with an amber pendant and where another individual had a composite ornament of amber beads and red-deer teeth (Larsson 2001, 67, Figure 5).) However, the subsequent use of amber in the TRB culture shows interesting differences with the preceding period. While in the Mesolithic the amber fragments were hardly ever worked beyond the provision of a perforation to facilitate attachment, and were thus used in their natural form, the amber in the TRB is worked into culturally significant shapes of great symbolic significance. Amber beads found in the megalithic chambers are frequently miniatures of tools and weapons: axes, battleaxes and clubs. The somewhat less conspicuous forms include tubular, circular and discoidal shapes as well as elongated pendants. The perforations, as well as the presence of spacer beads, suggest that multi-strand necklaces, bracelets and other combinations of adornments decorated the dead bodies.

Ebbesen's study of the Danish amber hoards shows that the commonest form of bead is tubular (*c.* 90 per cent) and that these are also most common in Danish graves (Ebbesen 1995, 45). However, recent analysis of amber beads from the Swedish megaliths shows that here double axes and clubs were the most common forms, accounting for 52 per cent of all beads (Axelsson and Strinnholm 2003, 119), and that by far the largest proportion of these derives from Scania, where amber would have been easily available. Although generally the number of beads does not exceed a hundred, at least three Scanian graves, Storegård, Gillhög and Gantofta, had over 300 each.

The number of beads per single item, and indeed the form of jewellery, are difficult to determine, especially in the open chambers, although the distribution of 71 amber beads in three clear concentrations at Glimmen does suggest three separate necklaces (Brindley 1986, Figure 6). Ebbesen illustrates several reconstructions of necklaces from the Danish flat graves, for example from Hjørring Bjerge (Ebbesen 1995, Figure 13), which comprise fewer beads than those reconstructed from the hoards; the different contexts of depositions may be significant here. Kossian's flat grave inventories from Germany and the Netherlands give an interesting picture, as here normally only a few individual beads are found; these may be assumed to have been single pendants or decorations attached to garments (Kossian 2005, 107). Single beads close to the right or left hand of the dead at Ostorf suggest bracelets which, apart from amber, may have included other perishable materials (wooden beads are known from Sweden; Larsson 2001, 72).

That there are no strict rules, however, is seen from the 130 beads that were placed in a single flat grave at Hejnsvig (Ebbesen 1995, 54) and by the recent discovery, at Borgeby, Scania, of a flat grave cemetery with paired burials of young people (between 3 and 18 years of age); about 200 amber beads were found here, with at least a couple of graves having over 30. Among the beads, double axes and double-headed clubs are poignantly symbolic of double burials but other, somewhat unusual forms also appear, such as boat-shaped or half-moon-shaped pieces. The amber beads are found near the surviving teeth, suggesting that the dead youngsters were buried wearing necklaces (Runcis 2005, 25–6, Figure 4).

The natural gold or dark red colour also made amber an excellent medium for imitation of the rare metal items – such as copper discs and flat copper axes – which by now were reaching northern Europe. Flat copper axes were copied as miniatures either in bone or in amber, and two examples of the latter are known from the MN secondary grave no. 5 at Lindebjerg (Liversage 1981, Figure 33; Klassen 2000, Figure 119 also illustrates a bone imitation), where they were accompanied by three double-headed club beads; their position in a row suggested that they were sewn along the edge of a loosely hanging garment (Liversage 1981, 104). The destroyed dolmen at Handest, Jutland, had amber beads of various shapes as well as a copper spiral, suggesting that an individual's jewellery may have involved a combination of different raw materials (Klassen 2000, Plate 31).

E. Schlicht (1973) has analysed copper items from 21 megalithic chambers west of the Weser. She identified several forms, of which copper discs, various strips (some with rolled-up ends and perforations), beads, spirals and rings of various sizes are common. Discs may well have been worn as pendants (such as that round the neck of a male found in one of the Brześć Kujawski graves in Kujavia) or sewn prominently onto garments. Their imitations in amber – the so-called 'amber suns' – are known from early Danish TRB funerary contexts and from hoards; copper strips mixed with tubes and amber beads made up composite necklaces, and rings and armbands were also worn. Some of the western TRB flat copper sheets and strips could conceivably have been imitations of wild teeth pendants or even miniature axes (for example the well-known copper necklace from Preußlitz (Preuß 1966, Plate 11.3), or the finds of miniature copper sheet axes from Osłonki in Poland (P. Bogucki, pers. comm. 2006)). (While Brześć Kujawski and Osłonki belong to a different cultural complex, that of the Lengyel culture, the copper ornaments are instructive in providing possible forms also circulating within the TRB culture.)

An exceptional copper find comes from the Kosel passage grave in Schleswig-Holstein; here a wooden bowl decorated with copper sheets fixed by rivets was apparently found lying underneath the sherds of a similarly decorated clay pot (Hingst 1985, 79, Figure 19). While clearly not an item of personal adornment, such a vessel would undoubtedly have been a significant prestige item; its content may have been equally exceptional and its use as one of the grave goods could indicate an elevated social status of the individual concerned.

Interpretation of burials

The evidence for burials discussed so far offers a very complex scenario. The different patterns of deposition of human bodies found within the north European megalithic chambers do not speak in favour of one practice – be it single or communal, full inhumation or partial bone deposits – but rather of different ways of dealing with the dead. That these practices were neither uniform nor static is clearly seen in the changing traditions: initial emphasis on individual burials, albeit sometimes performed against the background of multiple presences within the confines of a single monument, slowly giving way to greater concern with the dead in their ancestral capacity. The original deposits within the passage graves, as well as contemporary deposits within the open dolmens, involve merely selected fragments of human remains; after a period of time some of the chambers may have become family vaults, with complete bodies being placed within them, although elements of secondary burial – bone rearrangements, skull displays and manipulation of other body parts – may well have continued. Such a sequence is now well documented on south-west Fyn, around Sarup. Evidence from Sweden also speaks in favour of some chambers being used to house complete bodies. On the other hand, the interpretation of megalithic burial practices in the remaining regions does not reveal such patterns; this may be on account of poor survival conditions or of different practices. While many scholars strive to arrive at one particular interpretation of megalithic burial practices, reality is not nearly as simple.

The ubiquitous presence of fragmented human bones on settlement sites suggests that some of the dead may have rested there temporarily, perhaps close to their house, in a settlement pit or in a building specifically devoted to such storage. Alternatively, the body may have been buried outside the settlement, in a flat grave, marked to enable subsequent retrieval. Exposure in a tree or upon a raised platform is another common way of allowing the body to reach a skeletal condition; indeed, Strömberg has raised the possibility of displaying bodies on stone platforms in the immediate vicinity of entrances to the chambers (Strömberg 1971). While regularly shaped platforms of stone and possibly timber components of the kind encountered at Ramshög and Hagestad are not commonly found, piles of stones are known from in front of many chambers, and some may well have been used to display bodies; stone cobbled courtyards, of the kind encountered at Nissehøj, could have served such a purpose well. Exposure platforms may also have been located within the enclosed sites of the Sarup type although, as Kaul (1994) suggested, the possibility that bones were moved in the opposite direction – from the chambers to the enclosures – should not be ignored; indeed, other activities are witnessed from the enclosures, and dealing with the dead need not have been the primary function (Chapter 5). The precise function of the cult house, known from Denmark and in smaller numbers from Germany, presents itself as another possibility, although such structures do not contain much evidence for any prolonged presence of the dead.

The concepts behind the need to engage in secondary burial rituals during the Neolithic were undoubtedly very complex, and combined a host of social, ideological and religious ideas. Ethnographic evidence suggests that different communities have different ideas with respect to the fate of the individual after death. Some do not believe in any form of afterlife: the Hadza's view, for example, seems to be that 'when one dies, one rots and that is that'; the Baka Pygmies, when asked what is the fate of the dead, say 'When you're dead, you're dead and that's the end of you' (Woodburn 1982, 193, 195).

On the other hand, there are many communities which, implicitly or explicitly, have views on afterlife, on the fate of the dead and, in particular, on the fate of the spirit or the soul of the departed. In fact, ethnographic evidence for dealing with bodies prior to secondary burial rites is so varied that any comparison of specific ethnographic and prehistoric circumstances is bound to be misleading, although general ideas can be enlightening. The use of selected human remains is generally interpreted as resulting from the practice of secondary burial, which may not just be related to the veneration of ancestors but may also reflect the beliefs of the living about the spiritual element of the dead – the soul.

The classic ethnographic exposition of this phenomenon by Hertz (1960) remains valuable to this day and helps us to broaden our interpretation. While ancestral rites may indeed have been gaining importance at the time when large dolmens and passage graves were being constructed, Hertz's analysis also emphasised the significance of the relationship between the body and the soul, particularly between the decomposition of the body and the journey its soul is making to the world of the dead. In an ethnographic context, the transit of the soul to the spirit world – as mirrored in the process of bodily decomposition – is often seen as difficult, fraught with trouble and danger, and the funerary practices are designed to facilitate this process.

However, as we have seen, there is little direct evidence for the manner in which the bodies were treated prior to their inclusion in the megalithic chambers. We know virtually nothing on the subject of preparing the body either immediately after death, when it may have been dressed and subject to public display to enable vigil by close kin, or indeed after it was reduced to bare bones, ready for secondary burial. The occasional presence of hides need not be related to the dressing of the body, but rather they could be a convenient container for the cadaver. The provision of grave goods, according to Gräslund (1994, 16), implies that they were actually meant to accompany the dead to the other world, but he also notes that grave goods (or their explicit lack) are an important clue to the understanding of beliefs about the soul.

Discussion of beliefs about the soul in the Neolithic is naturally fraught with difficulties, but there are some indications that religious beliefs may have been just as instrumental in the way the dead were buried as the more frequently invoked politics of social relationships and power. The emergence of ancestor cults may have had various origins at different stages, although many sociological studies show how the remains of important members, manipulated to serve the needs of a society, may lead to ancestral veneration.

We have already commented on the possible importance of ancestors in the emergence of the farming way of life in the north, where ancestors were responsible for its introduction and subsequently became guardians of this new way of life. But the ancestors were not merely instruments for the manipulation of relationships between the living. Kopytkoff has argued that there need not be a sharp distinction between the living and the dead: ancestors are merely 'extremely wise, dry and immobile persons' (Kopytkoff 1971). Moreover, in many contexts, notions about afterlife seem to be idealised versions of life on earth; the grave goods found in the megaliths suggest that tools and utensils would be important in the afterlife (even if only token items were provided) as well as favourite jewellery and dress (which would not have survived). Indeed, food offered to the dead was the valued food of the living.

At the other end of the scale, while we are not clear on religious beliefs held by the TRB communities, the ritual activities outside the burial contexts suggest some form of belief in gods and spirits who would have been in the sky, in the surrounding forests and, almost certainly, inhabiting the numerous waterlogged, boggy and marshy environments. While some of these spirits would have been appeased in their own right (as seen in the votive bog deposits) others may have been too powerful or too ambiguous to be approached directly; ancestral spirits may have been invoked for such dangerous communications. It is therefore necessary to explore the other aspects of the funerary practices, such as the conduct of rituals outwith the chambers themselves.

Votive deposits in front of megalithic tombs

Ceremonies outside the megaliths were an important component of the social, ritual and religious life of the TRB. That people came to the tombs at times other than during burials is shown by the intentional deposits of artefacts – pottery, stone and flint tools – placed at various times in the vicinity of entrances. Indeed, such activities formed part of a much wider practice that involved placing items in bogs, at the edges of lakes, at causewayed enclosures and possibly even on settlements – bringing the various sites into a relationship with one another, creating a network of ritual acts which, at different times, may have involved large communal gatherings, small groups of people or even individuals.

Pottery was placed at the entrances to the megalithic chambers from the later EN onwards, and this practice peaked at the time when passage graves were first constructed and used. The quantities of materials recovered from in front of megaliths, however, vary from region to region. The most intensive activity took place in southern Scandinavia during MN I and MN II, although in northern Jutland and Scania and on Bornholm this tradition persisted a little longer, as vessels decorated in styles typical of MN III are also known. After that, pottery was largely replaced by tools, among which flint axes and chisels were dominant.

Further south the chronological parameters are more difficult to ascertain and the practice is less well evidenced in the archaeological record, although this most probably reflects excavation techniques rather than a total lack of such activities. In Mecklenburg, Schleswig-Holstein or Lower Saxony there has been little investigation outside the chambers, and thus there is less information on such deposits. At the passage grave of Kleinenkneten 1, three beakers and a bowl found to the right of the chamber entrance may form a small votive deposit, and finds in front of the destroyed passage grave at Mehringen reveal a clear resemblance to patterns from southern Scandinavia: up to 25 kg of pottery in a layer up to 3 cm thick, associated with burnt unworked flint (Knöll 1959, 47). A similar find, of 9000 potsherds in association with burnt flint, is also known from Flintbek LA 40 in Schleswig-Holstein (B. Zich, pers. comm. 2005).

However, as noted in Chapter 1, the custom of placing vessels in the vicinity of a burial mound began much earlier, with the facades of the earthen long barrows providing the initial focus for such deposits. The Skogsdala long dolmen in Scania provides a remarkable example of continuity, before the accessibility of the chambers broke with the older tradition and created a different focus for votive depositions. The long mound had a small closed chamber designed for one burial, and there was no indication of any entrance in the rectangular kerb. The pottery, a relatively small amount by Scanian standards, was found to the east of the kerb; it was recovered from a gravelly sand and is considered to represent ceremonial offerings. Such a location, not associated with any clear entrance, reveals a similarity to placements of pottery at the façades of the earlier long barrows (Jacobsson 1986, 96, 112, Figures 3 and 7).

Similar scenarios can be envisaged at Onsved Mark, where an early long barrow had a couple of beakers standing by its timber façade, while the somewhat later dolmen had at least 13 beakers placed along the kerb, north of the presumed entrance (Kaul 1988, 35, Figures 7 and 12). At one of the early structures at Strandby Skovgrave, near Sarup, remains of a couple of pots were found at the small western end of the rectangular enclosure that preceded the construction of the dolmen; its construction may possibly have obliterated traces of an earlier grave (N. H. Andersen 1997, 96, Figure 125). Other examples of early dolmens with votive deposits are known from Langeland, for example at Pederstrup, where some sherds and flint tools have been found, covered with a stone pile, stretching all along the southern side, or the four pots – one beaker, one lugged beaker and two lugged jars – at the round dolmen of Fakkemose (Skaarup 1985a, 133, 206–10).

Although, as has already been noted, large numbers of pots are often identified inside the megalithic chambers west of the Elbe, the custom of votive deposits outside the chambers has been less well recognised. Nevertheless Bakker has stated that, when excavations extend sufficiently far beyond the chamber, pottery that does not match that from the chamber is indeed found; such was the case at D26-Drouwenerveld, where over 7700 sherds were recovered, mostly to the left of the entrance (Bakker 1992, 58, Figure 19). Equally, recent analysis of pottery from around the destroyed chamber at Fischbek revealed a deposit of about 200 vessels which ultimately had been covered with a stone pavement (Laux 2003, 46).

Schuldt's investigations in Mecklenburg hardly ever extended beyond the confines of the mounds, and he considered materials occasionally encountered in front of the chamber entrances as cleared-out primary deposits. This was, for example, the interpretation of the remains of about 50 pots and two flints found in front of the entrance to the passage grave at Naschendorf, although the differential depth, from near the surface to about 0.8 m below, cannot solely be explained in such terms. Equally the find of many flint flakes, distributed in several piles upon one of the semicircular stone rows at the back of Serrahn 2, may plausibly be interpreted as votive offerings, in this case placed high up on the visible kerb (Schuldt 1966a, 37; 1968, Figure 36).

In contrast, great quantities of pottery are known from southern Scandinavia, and the largest finds come from Scania: about 50,000 sherds from in front of the Västra Hoby chamber, 40,000 from Gillhög, and between 10,000 and 15,000 from several other Scanian chambers, although the estimates of the number of vessels vary according to the fragmentation of the ceramic material and the methods of analysis: a minimum of 1256 vessels ended up at Fjälkinge, and about 1000 pots at Hög (Hårdh 1989, 23). Fewer vessels are normally encountered in Denmark: from about 40 at Kong Svends Høj to about 350 pots recovered in front of the passage grave at Sarup Gamle Skole II, in the vicinity of the Sarup enclosure (Dehn *et al.* 1995, 96; N. H. Andersen 1997, 98).

The presence of pots in front of the megaliths was noted in Denmark as early as 1901, when large amounts of pottery were found at the passage grave at Mjels in south-west Jutland, and subsequent discoveries gave rise to numerous speculations. Nordman considered them as consecrations related to chamber construction, Sophus Müller thought such deposits were made each time a burial took place inside the chamber, while Rosenberg believed they represented clearings from the chambers to make room for new interments (Müller 1914; Rosenberg 1929). It was not until 1946 that Thorvildsen's investigations at Grønhøj unequivocally established that such vessels were found *in situ*, having originally been placed on the kerb and subsequently fallen down either in front of or behind the kerbstones (Thorvildsen 1946, 91). On the other hand, Kjærum's detailed analysis of stratigraphy at Jordhøj identified both the votive pottery placed on the kerbstones and some materials that clearly were removed at a later stage from the chamber (Kjærum 1969).

Although the general principle of placing vessels outside the chamber is the same, there were many ways in which this was done. The vessels could be placed either side of the entrance, as seen at the passage graves of Jordhøj, Kong Svends Høj, Vroue Hede; or directly in front of it, for example at the passage graves at Hulbjerg, Gillhög, Hagebrogård; or both, as seen at the long dolmens of Frellesvig and Ormstrup or at Kragnæs (Dehn *et al.* 1995, 112–19). Only rarely are vessels encountered at other places along the kerb: at Sarup Gamle Skole II the pots were spread out all the way around the kerb, while at Lønt there was an abundant layer of pottery sherds at the entrance, and nine vessels were placed equidistant all the way round the mound. At Fischbek, apart from being in front of and on both sides of the entrance, groups of pots were also found on the eastern and northern sides of the kerb (Laux 2003).

In many cases, vessels were placed on top of a shelf of flat slabs surmounting the kerb. At Jordhøj, pots were placed above the first five kerbstones either side of the entrance; the heaviest concentrations were around stones 2–3 on both sides. Eventually they had fallen down, or indeed might have been deliberately smashed (a large stone was used to smash a pot at Nørremarksgård; N. H. Andersen 2000, 23, Figure 4), ending up at the foot of the kerb, with some sherds falling behind it. Some of the shelf slabs had also slid down, as several of these covered the pottery layer (Kjærum 1969, Figures 11 and 12).

Similar arrangements have been envisaged at Grønhøj, where Thorvildsen identified about a hundred vessels that were thought to have stood on top and at the foot of the kerb (Thorvildsen 1946, 91). A continuous shelf of flat slabs either side of the entrance at the great dolmen at Vedsted supported numerous vessels whose sherds were found on and behind the kerbstones (Ebbesen 1979, 21), and at Tustrup the pots around one of the dolmens must have stood on the dry-stone walling slabs between the kerbstones (Kjærum 1957, 18). A more complex pattern was observed at Frelleswig, where the vessels seem to have been placed differently in front of each of the two dolmens. Remains of about 30 pots behind the kerb by the western chamber suggest that they originally must have stood on the kerb itself, and 33 more pots were found lying in front of the kerb, originally having been placed on a layer of burnt flint. The pots in front of the eastern chamber appear to have been placed in front of the kerb, and an individual vessel between the two entrances must also have stood high up on the kerb (Skaarup 1985a, 117).

Elsewhere pots were placed at the foot of the kerb or in niches between the kerb-stones, a practice best documented at Kong Svends Høj (Dehn *et al.* 1995, 87–101, Figures 105–8). Here, along the western façade of the mound, about 40 pots had been deposited, possibly in two separate events; several of them – beakers and, quite exceptionally, storage vessels – deep in the three niches. To the left of the entrance some of the other vessels rested on flat slabs that stood at the foot of the kerb. Moreover, the vessels were not placed at random, but formed specific sets: the ten beakers found to the right form an extraordinarily homogeneous group and are assumed to have been placed together on the same occasion; the beakers within the niches were much larger than those placed in front of the kerb and may repre-sent individual acts; to the left of the entrance, around stone no. 5, a group of three beakers and five shoulder bowls forms another group. However, the latter were placed later, as they are dated to MN II, while the beakers could not be younger than MN Ib; the bowls, moreover, are represented only by a few sherds – they may have been standing on the kerb or, indeed, been brought to the tomb in an already fragmentary condition. The whole ceramic deposit was ultimately covered with white burnt flint, another feature closely associated with such depositions.

Such groupings of vessels in clearly identifiable assemblages can also be observed elsewhere. Kjærum identified several sets at Jordhøj: for example four storage vessels were found to the right of the entrance, pedestalled bowls with their spoons to the left, and the four lugged bowls were placed in the later phase on the right, near stones 2–3 (Kjærum 1969, 49–52, Figure 29a). The discoveries at Fischbek not only provide a rare example of such votive deposits from the area south of the Elbe, but confirm the non-random deposition of clearly defined assem-blages. Here about 200 vessels had been deposited in five different episodes, distributed all around the mound except for its western end. The initial placement, of up to 140 pots, may have taken place at or soon after the construction of the chamber. As at Kong Svends Høj, the pots were placed as specific sets at several places round the foot of the kerb: for example a pedestalled bowl, a shouldered cup and a beaker were placed in front of the entrance, and a similar set consisting of two pedestalled bowls with a clay spoon, a beaker and a shouldered cup at the eastern end of the mound (Laux 2003, Figure 16).

This pattern of sets of vessels was repeated on subsequent occasions, and Laux compared such combinations to those observed elsewhere: at the flat grave at Issendorf, where a pedestalled bowl, a baking plate and a spoon originally stood on the roof of the grave, or at the destroyed megalith at Rahmstorf (ibid., 45) where pedestalled bowls, spoons and a baking plate may have formed a similar votive assemblage. The discovery of pedestalled bowls, while common in southern Scandinavia, is quite rare south of the river Elbe, and flat baking plates in ceremonial deposits are extremely rare, although they are known from the Danish cult houses of Tustrup or Søndermø (Kjærum 1955, 20, Figure 17; Becker 1996, Plate B IX:R).

Sometimes the votive offerings were placed on special stone pavements in front of entrances; those associated with the Scanian passage graves are quite elaborate and demonstrate that deposits were being made over a considerable period of time. Thus, at Gillhög, stone layers alternated with find layers; pottery was found predominantly in the lower levels, while flint tools were found mainly higher up, confirming the sequence of ceramic deposits being followed, at a later stage, by placements of tools. At Hög a semicircular stone pavement tells a similar story: the lowest level contained much pottery and was covered by a black sooty layer with pottery, flint tools and amber beads. This seems to have been covered by a layer of crushed flint upon which stones with more pottery were placed. A similar sooty layer was found in front of the Västra Hoby passage grave and since, in both cases, the pottery is not chronologically homogeneous, it is possible that this material was being accumulated elsewhere over a period of time and then deposited on a single occasion in front of the chambers (Hårdh 1989, 93–5). Trollasten seems to be the only Scanian dolmen where a stone platform was found in front of the entrance, containing not just the previously mentioned burnt human remains but also a large quantity of pottery and flint tools.

As noted, the most intensive period of pottery deposition in front of the megaliths is dated to the MN I–MN II period, although in certain regions the custom continued a little longer, with ceramic styles of MN III still deposited in Jutland and in Scania. After that, the custom switched towards the deposition of flint tools, among which axes and chisels predominate, although other tools are also encountered. The flint tools were very frequently damaged, either broken into fragments or quite commonly burnt. This destruction contrasts dramatically with flint tools from earlier votive deposits in waterlogged environments where tools were placed undamaged, frequently never even used. Axes and other implements placed in waterlogged environments were offered whole and were preserved, although there was no intention to retrieve them. They were not only taken out of circulation but, once offered to supernatural spirits and gods, became invisible. In contrast, the tools offered at the megaliths were destroyed in dramatically obvious fashions, the destruction rendering them not only functionally useless, but also visible to all.

We have no direct evidence that the actual destruction of flint tools took place at the megalithic graves themselves but, in a slightly different context, Larsson has expanded on the use of fire as an important element of sacred activities. His investigation of two sites in Scania, at the Early Neolithic Svartskylle and at the Late Neolithic Kverrestad, where flint tools seem to have been deliberately burnt in large quantities, suggests that such sacrificial burnings would have had dramatic visual as well as aural effects: '[F]lint explodes with a distinct bang and a cascade of shards' (Larsson 2000, 101). He moreover compared the visual transformation of flint – from natural black or grey, sometimes to red and finally to white – to changes similar to the cremation of a human body.

Once the votive activities ceased, the deposits were frequently sealed – clearly an important act signifying the end of use of a particular monument, or possibly creating conditions terminating the contact with ancestral remains within the chamber. Occasionally sand and/or stones were piled upon the broken pottery and flint tools: at Hagebrogård the votive layer was covered with stones and earth; at Nørrevangsgård, in east Jutland, the sterile sand was subsequently covered with stones; at Kragnæs, on Ærø, medium-sized water-rolled stones were used for this purpose, and similar arrangements have been observed at Hindby Mosse in Scania (Dehn *et al.* 1995, 112–19).

However, most often vast quantities of white burnt flint were spread over the votive deposits, and this pattern has now been recognised at many Danish megaliths. At Kong Svends Høj a 20-cm-thick layer of burnt flint (between four and five tonnes) covered the deposits all along the front of the south-western façade. At Sæby Skole, north Zealand, a band up to four metres in width encircled the entire mound, although here the sealing process was more elaborate, with the earlier pottery deposits initially covered by stones upon which flint artefacts, mainly axes and chisels, were placed; eventually, the whole was sealed by large amounts of burnt flint. At Jordhøj the burnt flint was found in front of the kerbstones, where it covered the pottery, as well as behind them, suggesting that some of it may have been placed over the mound (Kjærum 1969, 18, 54); and at the great dolmen at Vedsted the burnt flint appears to have covered part of the mound above the kerb, eventually sliding down during the process of decay (Ebbesen 1979, 20).

Evidence from Schleswig-Holstein, for example at Flintbek passage grave LA 40, suggests that a similar sealing process was practised there, and indeed Hoika noted that '[f]ired, crackled, chalk-white flint' frequently enables us to detect destroyed megalithic tombs in the field (Hoika 1990, 76). The presence of burnt unworked flint mixed with the votive deposits at the passage grave of Mehringen further supports such a practice (Knöll 1959, 47).

The frequency of votive deposits at tombs is difficult to determine, but the stylistic analysis of Danish pottery suggests that such events were relatively infrequent. Evidence from many sites – for example the dolmens of Borre Ål in west Jutland and Onsved Mark, north Zealand, or the passage graves at Kong Svends Høj, Jordhøj, Hagebrogård and Vroue Hede – suggests that most of the MN I pottery represents either one or, at most, a few large depositions. These could plausibly reflect large communal ceremonies; later vessels (dating to MN II, MN III and occasionally even later) offered as small assemblages or even as single pots may, on the other hand, reflect the activities of small groups of people or even individuals.

The Scanian deposits suggest a slightly different pattern. Here the tombs were used for votive offerings over a very long period of time (from MN I to MN IV) and the deposits, with their multi-layered structure, reflect this. Indeed, some of the layers contain chronologically mixed materials – for example those in layer II at

Hög – suggesting that such accumulations arose over a long time elsewhere and may have been deposited outside the megalith in one single event. Deposits at other Scanian tombs, for example at the passage graves of Västra Hoby and Annehill and at the dolmen of Trollasten, reveal a horizontal stratigraphy whereby the younger vessels appear to have been placed further away from the entrance to the chamber (Hårdh 1989, 98–9); thus those depositing pots at a later stage not only knew but respected the position of the earlier offerings.

It is clear that at most sites only parts of the vessels remain *in situ*. Holten's analysis of pottery from in front of the passage grave at Nissehøj implies that, in spite of good preservation of the ceramics, 80 per cent of the original weight of the pots has simply disappeared, and this is a pattern observed at many megalithic tombs. Moreover, the spatial distribution frequently suggests a wide scattering of surviving sherds (Holten 2000, 291, Figures 25.4–25.8). Holten has argued that the context of death was considered so anomalous within the TRB cosmology that it required formalised destruction so as to create new order through the reclassification of artefacts. The placement of damaged tools, burnt axes, chisels and other flint implements represents a different facet of the same phenomenon.

As Hertz argued a long time ago (Hertz 1960), sacrificed objects must be destroyed in this world if they are to pass to the next. Thus, if the votive deposits reflected food offerings left to be consumed – if only symbolically – by the ancestors, or as supplicatory offerings addressed to higher deities whose benefaction was sought through ancestral mediation, then destruction of the containers may have been necessary to make such offerings acceptable. Indeed, the destruction of flint tools, by either breakage or fire, reflects the same need to render them useless for everyday tasks.

However, pottery, as well as other items of material culture, is subject to symbolic concern on many different levels. While we do not know precisely what cosmological messages were embodied in TRB ceramics, their particularly rich decoration, while abstract and difficult to interpret, nevertheless emphasises other concerns than merely those of everyday practicalities. Ethnographic evidence suggests that pottery may be involved on many different symbolic levels. Paraphrasing Lévi-Strauss, Barley stated that pots are equally good 'to think with' and that they provide models for thinking about the human body, seasons or fertility; deliberate smashing of pots is a special ritual activity not to be undertaken lightly, as it heralds the irreversible process of transformation (Barley 1994, 112).

Thus the breaking of pots in association with megaliths may have expressed many different concepts: the broken pots outside may have symbolised the broken bones of the interior. Being made of earth, they may have emphasised concepts of fertility with respect to the agricultural cycle, already marked by the siting of megaliths on ploughed fields. The breaking of pots, and by implication other material items, in connection with the dead also ruptures time and effectively separates the dead from the living. It may have been an effective way of 'marking off' the ancestral time from all other times.

5

ARCHITECTS OF
STONE AND SYMBOLS

Symbolic use of raw materials

In the middle of the nineteenth century, the Mecklenburg antiquarian Friedrich Lisch described the grey of the granite boulders, the red of the sandstone slabs and the white of the burnt flint scattered on the chamber floors as 'sound colour composition … in the world of few colours' (quoted from Steinmann 2001, 15). This extraordinary consideration was, alas, not followed up for at least a century and a half. The idea that the megalith builders consciously employed certain raw materials, not only for practical purposes but also with consideration for the mystical and symbolic meaning of certain textures and colours, has recently been experiencing something of a revival in British archaeological literature (Jones 1999; Jones and MacGregor 2002). Little discussion of such matters has taken place elsewhere, although the results of recent work in Denmark in relation to the restoring of passage graves are beginning to encourage a similar debate (Dehn *et al*. 1995).

Modern ideas on aesthetics, which have developed mainly since the Renaissance, may not be entirely appropriate for the analysis of colour, texture and design in the Neolithic. Although we should not assume that aspects of beauty would not be pleasing and appreciated, it is more likely that they provided a medium through which one could symbolise the mysteries of the world and the powers of the supernatural. Certain raw materials were indeed employed in a quite dramatic fashion, although detailed geological and petrographic analysis of stones used in the north European megaliths has hardly begun. Since most of the orthostats and capstones were of glacial origin, it is reasonable to assume that building materials would not have come from afar.

The petrographic work carried out at the passage grave of Kong Svends Høj and two neighbouring mounds on Lolland suggests that granite boulders were dominant, with gneiss and other rocks used in lesser quantity. The restorers noted that, in relation to its present natural availability on Lolland, gneiss was over-represented in construction and was most likely chosen for its good working qualities. On the other hand, the desire to create a red-coloured south-east façade at Kong Svends Høj is shown in the fact that three different types of rock – granite, porphyry and pegmatite – were used; clearly the colour of this façade was significant, and may well have contrasted with the grey character of the kerbstones at the opposite end (Dehn *et al*. 1995, 142). Such deliberate choices can occasionally be documented at other sites. The western façade of one of the longest Danish dolmens, Grønjægers Høj on Møn, also displays a tall kerb of red stones, as does the long dolmen at Nobbin on Rügen, with its massive red *Wächtersteine* flanking both sides of the south-west façade (Figures 3.10, 3.13). One may envisage such coloured stones creating particularly dramatic effects at certain times of the day, such as at sunrise or sunset.

Martha Strömberg's researches at the tombs in the Hagestad region of Scania have demonstrated that the different stones used in construction were all available within a radius of between 1.5 and 3 km from the monuments (Strömberg 1971), and Hårdh's investigations of tombs in the valleys of the Saxån and Råån rivers suggest that local Kågeröd sandstone – which, in contrast to the Cambrian sandstone, displays sharp edges – must have been quarried from the nearby outcrops (Hårdh and Bergström 1988). There can be little doubt that red sandstone, used in dry-stone walling within and outside the chambers, was used not merely for its good splitting quality but also to provide a contrast through the highly aesthetic juxtaposition of different shapes and colours.

Similarly, the rocks used in the construction of the passage graves on the Falbygden plateau reflect locally available raw materials. Here, as we noted before, the sedimentary rocks were used mainly for uprights of the chamber and passage, while igneous rocks provided capstones and keystones. As Tilley suggested, the tombs' structure was embedded – in more senses than one – in the local geology (Tilley, 1996). However, even here the relationship between the raw materials and their employment can be perceived only in very general terms; there is little to point to specific referents in the landscape.

The spatial relationship between the sources of raw materials and their employment in the monuments is argued to structure the way in which such monuments are experienced in the landscape (Jones 1999; Scarre 2003, 2006). Unfortunately the lack of precise knowledge on the distribution of erratics within the Neolithic landscape of northern Europe makes it difficult to ascertain any spatial relationships, although one might venture to suggest that the visible dolmen capstones were intended to replicate the random strewing of glacial boulders. Indeed, the employment of certain exotic building materials does raise the question of the visibility or, at least, partial visibility of chambers.

As noted previously, many megaliths today are dramatic ruins, completely devoid of any covering materials. However, the principles of construction of passage graves (Figures 3.34 and 3.38), especially the various packing materials outside the chambers and the great efforts to ensure the chambers were stable and dry, suggest that most north European passage graves were intended to be hidden within their mounds. However, passage grave chambers on the Falbygden plateau may have been partly exposed, and Swedish archaeologists commonly assume that, because of the relatively low two-tier construction of the mounds, the massive capstones covering the passage graves remained visible on the surface. From the area of the Weser estuary, megalithic tombs are known which, during the later part of the Neolithic, were covered by a rising bog. Several of these did not have any covering mound prior to their being swallowed up by the bog, suggesting that here also certain chambers may have been left uncovered (Behre 2005, 215, Figures 4 and 5). Interestingly this may be precisely what was being portrayed in the early eighteenth-century engraving from Nunningh's *Sepulchretum gentile*, discussed previously (Chapter 3), in which indeed only the 'inner skeleton' of the chamber is illustrated.

Moreover, some exotic materials further suggest that certain parts of dolmens may well have remained exposed. Thus the quartzite capstones, such as the one covering a dolmen chamber at Grønjægers Høj on Møn (Figure 3.10), or the one atop the Bakkebølle dolmen on south-east Zealand (Figure 3.18c), must have been chosen deliberately. Such boulders would have been selected for their dramatic impact; it seems unlikely that such visually impressive capstones were not intended to be seen, and in both cases the shape of the mound and the size of the kerbstones make it improbable that these spectacular gleaming capstones would have been covered. Another example may be provided by the chamber at Werpeloch 1, where the keystone was impressively red in colour. (I thank Ute Bartelt for drawing my attention to this site.) In other instances, as illustrated in Figure 3.18, the deliberately massive shapes of the capstones – far in excess of what was needed to cover the chamber – are a further testimony to the importance of shape and texture in creating particular visual effects.

Indeed, some Danish scholars have recently argued that the simpler dolmens could have been either free-standing structures or only partly covered. Thus Eriksen has suggested at least five possible stages of construction: some dolmens within the stone kerb only having a very light fill around the chamber (such as Ormslev, Tustrup 1, or Damsbo); dolmens with a slight mound between the chamber and kerb (such as Poskær Stenhus or Tustrup 2); others covered with a mound up to the capstones (such as the round dolmen at Tårup), with the mound then being raised over the capstones and finally even covering parts of the kerb (Eriksen 2004, 59–61).

The excavations at Ormslev revealed only slight packing around the dolmen chamber: a 1-m-wide zone of up to two layers of stones, covered by a layer up to 30 cm thick of crushed flint, capped with another stone layer (N. Nielsen 2003, 128). Moreover, a curved stone platform found 3 to 4 m from the entrance may originally have surrounded the entire dolmen and, on the old land surface before the entrance, there was a large concentration of pottery dating to MN I–II and some even later MN IV–V sherds. Normally, votive deposits were placed at the foot of the kerb, but this evidently was not the case here. Indeed, N. Nielsen argued that this demonstrated the area in front of the entrance was always free, and that Ormslev was probably never covered by a mound. Similarly to Eriksen, she noted a number of free-standing dolmens, especially on the Djursland peninsula, for example at Stenhuset, whose positioning on a steep elevation and within the small stone kerb creates angles impossible to allow for a mound (ibid., Figure 6).

Andersen's recent investigations of megaliths around Sarup also suggest that some of the dolmens in that area may well never have been hidden within mounds. Sarup Gamle Skole X was enclosed in a palisade but did not seem to have a mound; among the dolmens at Strandby Skovgrave several may not have had any substantial mounds either (N. H. Andersen 1997, 96), as pottery was found outside the entrances. Finally, an interesting case is offered by the recent reconstruction of one of the dolmens at Tustrup (Figure 3.19a–d). The polygonal dolmen is surrounded by a kerb of boulders about 8 m in diameter and up to 2 m tall, and the space in between them was partially filled with dry-stone walling. A slight stone layer was found in the space between the kerb and chamber, and similar stones were found outside the kerb, with a considerable mixture of pottery either side of the entrance. Kjærum did not think the dolmens at Tustrup were covered by mounds (Kjærum 1955, 28), and the present reconstruction, with dry-stone walling up to the top of the kerbstones and a mound between the chamber and the kerb, has not been accepted by all (N. Nielsen 2003, 144).

Another important structural component was flint. It is evident that a distinction was made between the use of crushed flint in its raw and in its burnt states. Crushed flint, as we have already seen, was used as a construction material around the chamber where, once the mound was completed, it would no longer be visible. Burnt white flint, on the other hand, was commonly placed where it would be seen – even if only by a handful of individuals – on the floor of dolmens and passage graves and outside the chambers themselves, either by the entrance where it often covered votive deposits or, indeed, sometimes surrounding the entire mound on the outside.

Hansen has suggested that burnt flint may have been gathered from the surface of the surrounding fields after the vegetation cover had been burnt, but the evidence from outside the passage grave at Liepen in Mecklenburg suggests that, in some cases at least, the burning of flint was carried out specifically for the purpose of inclusion in a tomb. Indeed, while the protective and draining qualities of crushed flint were important, there is no particular practical need for it to be burnt, so this activity may well reflect some symbolic requirement.

The burning of flint must have been a spectacular affair associated with the construction of the tomb or, indeed, preceding an initial funerary ceremony. Hoika has argued that if flint was present in chambers when fires were lit 'the process would have involved the production of powerful explosive noises. It would have sounded like fireworks. Indeed various cultures use loud noises to chase away ghosts in a sort of magical clamour' (1990, 90). These comments were treated rather cautiously by Bakker, who noted that the burning of granite – used as flooring in the western TRB – does not produce a noise louder than that of burning wood; indeed, he wondered: 'Why should the North Group have preferred more noise than the West Group, and would not the need for a grit layer provide a simpler and better explanation?' (Bakker 1992, 29). Be that as it may, even if the flint was initially burnt for purely practical reasons of providing a well-drained chamber floor, it still made a lot of noise in the process, and this may have created symbolic meanings where it was practised. Indeed, we already noted Larsson's comments (2000) on the symbolic meaning of the burning of flint (Chapter 4).

While there is some evidence that burnt human bones were incorporated within megaliths, the metaphor of transformation – transforming the 'living' usable flint into a 'dead' matter – is certainly apt in the context of burial ritual. Andersson has argued that, in the TRB culture, the notion of objects being animated – passing from birth (production), through life (consumption), death (destruction) and burial (deposition) – was important, as it brought objects and people into close relation with one another (Andersson 2004, 160). Thus deposition of burnt flint on a chamber floor rendered an important raw material obsolete in terms of consumption, while the presence of grinding and polishing stones in the chambers' structure, and the destruction of pottery and tools in front of megalithic tombs, marked the cessation of quotidian functions for useful artefacts, irrespective of whether they were offered to the gods or the ancestors.

The significance of colours in the Neolithic is difficult to ascertain, but clearly there was a mystical and symbolic relationship between the colour and the architecture of the tombs. White, most obviously, would have created special visual effects upon entering the chamber – with the light of a few flickering torches dramatically reflected against the white floor. Indeed other visible construction elements suggest that a white colour was far from accidental. Keystones frequently have a substantial component of white flecks and, as already noted, there are examples of passage graves in Denmark where birch bark sheets have survived (Dehn and Hansen 2006b). These were folded in between the slabs of dry-stone walling, filling the gaps between the orthostats, and in well-preserved cases are easily seen to this day (for example at Maglehøj, Ubby Dysselod and Rævehøj; Figure 5.1). We know that bark survives only when the chamber had remained completely dry and had never been filled with earth, so the present-day rarity of this feature is not an indication of its rarity in construction. In other passage graves, instead of sheets of bark, the slabs of the dry-stone walling have been set within a sort of chalky mortar, which stands out clearly from between the red sandstones. Apart from the practical cushioning function, which protected the fragile slabs from the enormous pressure of the capstones, these raw materials may well have been chosen for their aesthetic effect – the white standing out sharply against the red sandstone slabs, adding to the effect of white on the floor.

Certain colours – the famous triad of red, white and black – appear universally in many cultures past and present. These have been argued to be among the earliest and most emphatic symbols, perhaps related to vivid interpretations of life on earth and in the hereafter (Birren 1978). The view commonly endorsed by archaeologists follows the work of Turner on the metaphorical significance of these basic colours related to the products of the body: white symbolising semen or mother's milk; red symbolising blood, bloodshed and animal food preparation; and black associated with excreta and thus being symbolic of death and fertility (Turner 1967). Indeed, in his discussion of the south Scandinavian tombs Tilley has argued that the 'blood' of amber and ochre, mingled with the 'semen-milk' of the ancestral

Figure 5.1 Maglehøj passage grave, east Zealand, with birch bark surviving *in situ* between the dry-stone walling slabs

bones, were powerful metaphors for linking monuments and artefacts (Tilley 1996, 322).

In contrast to Turner's analysis, Wierzbicka (1990) has suggested a scheme based on the universal human experience, in which white may denote day, black denote night, red signify fire, yellow the sun, etc. While such symbolic meanings of colours will naturally be embedded within specific historical contexts, they offer a wider range of possible interpretations. Indeed, they permit us to consider colours that have not been translated from nature to culture. Green and blue, for example, were present everywhere: the various shades of green represented through vegetation, and multiple blues – be it of the sky or of water in the lakes, rivers and sea. These colours normally do not feature in material contexts, as green or blue dyes are not known to have been used in the Neolithic, but they must have been part of the general cosmology of Neolithic communities and therefore important and imbued with symbolism, possibly related to the gods in the sky and to the spirits of the forests and fields, and most certainly those inhabiting bogs and mires. The latter locales, with the spontaneous combustion of marsh gas, were ideal abodes for supernatural creatures (see below).

Amber – a raw material of the Neolithic *par excellence* – varies in colour from white, through yellow-green, light brown and orange to very dark red. Rather than representing blood, as suggested by Tilley, it may well have been a symbol of the sun. The various shades could reflect the sun at different times of day, as amber discs would suggest; sunlight sustains all life and, without it, there is death. In historical times amber has been known to be used against certain ailments, such as fever, rheumatism, toothache or headache (Birren 1978, 85). Amber beads may have been worn as amulets, protecting against illness or other misfortunes, becoming mere ornaments in modern times. On the other hand, as I argued before (Midgley 1992, 292), amber jewellery in the form of axes and battleaxes accompanying the dead may be early symbols of a male deity associated with thunder, rain and water; this is precisely the context in which amber is washed up on shore, and such symbolism – while it cannot be proven – appears at least as likely as that of blood.

Figurative representations in the TRB context are extremely rare, although amber axes and examples of face or sun motifs on ceramics from the MN period can plausibly be interpreted as such. The distinct lack of 'megalithic art' in northern Europe, which contrasts so dramatically with its profusion along the Atlantic coast, is rarely commented upon in literature. Kaul's interpretation of a number of tiny decorated stone slabs, which are known from the south Scandinavian early and middle MN period as art – decorated with motifs familiar from contemporary pottery – need not be questioned (Kaul 1997), but this can hardly be 'megalithic art' as understood elsewhere. Indeed, the lack of true 'megalithic art' may well be related to what went on before the megalithic tombs were constructed. Much of the figurative Armorican art pre-dates the construction of the chambered tombs, as it is very intimately associated with standing stones whose use in the megaliths is secondary. However, the profuse decoration of TRB ceramics everywhere – from the Netherlands to Poland – and, especially, the rich geometric designs of ceremonial wares, speak clearly in favour of highly developed, abstract cognition. Moreover, such designs are frequently highlighted with white paste, adding another dimension to the symbolic use of different colours.

Thus, in simple terms the megalithic architecture appears full of contrasts and contradictions: it has visible and hidden aspects, it emphasises light and dark (exterior/interior), juxtaposes horizontal and vertical (boulders and dry-stone walling) with colour play (dark grey, red and white), hard and soft (hard boulders within softer mounds), and so on. On a more profound level, the numerous raw materials used in the construction of megalithic tombs – some exotic and others extremely common – suggest that we may think in terms of culture and nature being merged within the structure of a megalith. Not only was the natural landscape being transformed through new agricultural practices, but new structures were being placed upon it. Natural and man-made forms and notions were put together: land was ploughed, ancient rocks – gathered from the surface and excavated from quarries – were moulded into new shapes, and life, death and rebirth became incorporated into one never-ending cycle.

Concepts of duality in the megaliths

In Chapter 3, while discussing the construction of the megalithic chambers, we have alluded briefly to the concept of twin stones and twin passage graves; this now requires further consideration. Like so many features that are currently attracting scholarly attention, the splitting of the stones was also noted in the nineteenth century. The Revd William Lukis, who investigated Dutch megaliths in 1878, thought some of the orthostats and capstones in the Drenthe *hunebeds* had been split (Bakker 1979), but there was little consideration given to this matter. The phenomenon of splitting building blocks from a larger stone is not, of course, unique to northern Europe. The most evocative examples are the previously mentioned capstones on some of the Locmariaquer chambers, notably at Gavrinis and at La Table des Marchands (Figure 6.3), where massive menhirs, once forming independent alignments, were broken up and reused in the construction of the chambers (L'Helgouac'h 1983, 1998; Bailloud *et al.* 1995). However, one hardly thinks in terms of the shortage of building materials, but rather of the significance – symbolic or religious – which the incorporation of old monuments into new ones must have had for the communities living along the Atlantic coastline.

Split stones have been noted in some of the north German megaliths, but this was considered a purely technological matter, of creating suitable shapes and sizes of building components. However, recent research in Denmark has shown that just under half of the Danish chambers contain such stones, mainly of granite and gneiss, which were split from a single erratic, and that their employment in construction is far from random (Dehn and Hansen 2006a, 57). In simple dolmens, such twin stones are most commonly placed opposite each other, for example at Grønjægers Høj on Møn or at Stokkebjerg Skov, north-west Zealand (Figure 3.15c), but in the more complex chambers they stand in a specific relationship: most often either next to or opposite each other. Thus they are side by side in the north-west corner at Grøfte (Ebbesen 1990, 55) and opposite each other at the east end of the great dolmen chamber at Groß Labenz 1 (Schuldt 1967, notes). At the Grovlegård dolmen not only are the two halves standing opposite each other but the capstone's twin can be found on another dolmen, the famous Poskær Stenhus, 2 km away (Eriksen 1999, 58–60; Figure 3.18b): two communities clearly sharing similar practices and ideas.

In passage graves the twin stones are arranged in several ways. They may serve as cornerstones, for example at Jattehøj on Bornholm, or as a cornerstone and a neighbouring passage stone, as at Frejlev Skov, where they create a small niche. Sometimes they stand side by side opposite the entrance, for example at Knudshoved Odde or, most impressively, in the 2.6-m-tall chamber at Ubby Dysselod. In passages they normally serve as opposing door casing stones, as at Nissehøj or Jordehøj. They may be placed as capstones, where they tend to lie side by side, for example at Lähden, Kleinenkneten 2, Sieben Steinhaüser E, or separated by another capstone, as at Olshøj. An exceptional arrangement has been observed at the twin passage grave at Troldstuerne, where the two halves of the stone were each placed over an entrance to the chambers (Bakker 1992, 25–6; Dehn *et al.* 1995, 59–61; Schirnig 1982, 24).

At Frejlev Skov two pairs may originally have been intended, but only three stones are present, the fourth not used in the construction in the end. Finally, at

Kong Svends Høj there are, most exceptionally, five pairs of twin stones, three pairs of split granite and two of gneiss, all clearly arranged: one pair forms the south-west end of the chamber; next there are two opposing pairs – the innermost standing on the narrow ends – and another pair, this time standing side by side in the north wall; the final pair are side by side along the north wall of the passage (Dehn *et al.* 1995, 55, Figure 57; Dehn and Hansen 2006a, 57–8).

Since, as is evident from the above description, the twin stones are never randomly placed, the practice of splitting boulders is not likely to reflect a lack of suitable shapes or sizes. Rather it seems to be a matter of intentional splitting of stones to create relationships of pairing or duality. The most dramatic example of such a concept of duality is found in the construction of a twin passage grave – a construction which, at present, seems unique to Denmark, although Hårdh (1989) mentions three double passage graves in Scania. About thirty twin passage graves are still preserved, mostly in north-west Zealand, with a few examples scattered on the islands and in north Jutland (Dehn and Hansen 2000, Figure 18.3). The surviving examples are all very complex architectural constructions, which were conceived and executed as a single building project. The twin passage graves were either built as one long chamber (with two passages) divided by two orthostats (of which two slightly different versions exist) or, in the most complicated version, built around one common orthostat. In the latter the main axis of each chamber runs differently and, in ground plan, it creates a V-pattern; the passages diverge outwards from the chambers.

The twin chambers have interesting architectural features which cannot be regarded as essential from the constructional point of view, and thus must express symbolic requirements that must have pervaded the social process of construction. Thus, one of the twin chambers (normally the one to the left looking from the entrance) is generally larger and better built than the other: the orthostats may be taller, more regular in shape; the common orthostat is better integrated towards the larger chamber; the dry-stone walling is of better quality, as are the keystone, the capstones and intermediary layers. Although it could be argued that, as the chambers may have been built in succession, the better building materials had been used up, this does not seem to be the case, since all the materials would have been prepared before the building process began. The reason for one chamber being better built than the other must be socially significant. In one twin passage grave, that of Troldstuerne, the two chambers are in fact mirror images in shape and ground plan, making it clear that existing differences were by design and not mere accidents of construction (Figure 5.2).

A principle similar to that at Troldstuerne also seems to have been applied in the construction of single chambers, with an interesting example offered by the western Zealand chambers at Grønnehøj and Ubby Dysselod, which stand 70 m apart. Grønnehøj is a traditional, average chamber 1.7 m tall, while Ubby Dysselod was built of carefully selected orthostats reaching 2.6 m in height. However, both chambers have a peculiarly white casing stone, and they also display identical, mirror-image ground plans (Dehn and Hansen 2006a, 59–60; Figure 5.3).

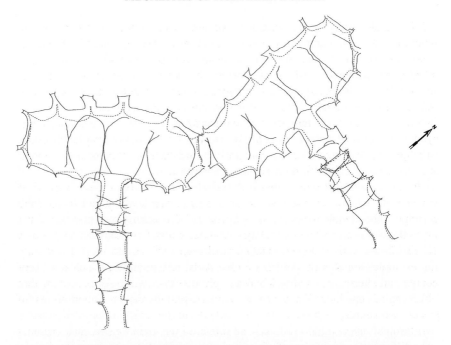

Figure 5.2 Ground plan of the twin passage grave at Troldstuerne: the two chambers are mirror images of each other, rotated along the main axis which runs through the common orthostat, north-west Zealand

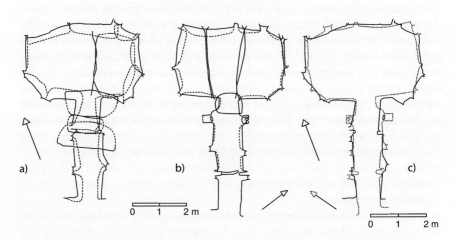

Figure 5.3 Ground plans of passage graves at (a) Ubby Dysselod and (b) Grønnehøj; (c) superimposition of both plans with (b) reversed from left to right, and Ubby Dysselod shown with a continuous line

Such forms of duality are difficult to account for but, since they clearly are not functional, they must be related to the social or religious aspects of life among the local communities. Just as there was a conscious choice to set up twin stones in relation to one another, even in places where this created architectural difficulties, so the construction of twin passage graves must reflect a deliberate enterprise. In the simplest terms it could represent the coming together of two separate groups, forming an alliance through marriage or other form of partnership which was then symbolised in such a joint venture. By erecting a truly demanding architectural structure, the communities could gain prestige and, through the veneration of joint ancestors, express their commitment to one another.

But there are other exciting possibilities. In their discussion of the cosmological structure of Nordic Bronze Age society, Kristiansen and Larsson discuss the concept of the Divine Twins – a pair of principal divinities in the pantheon of the Proto-Indo-European religion, ruling the upper realm (Kristiansen and Larsson 2005). They tentatively suggest that some elements of twin rituals may well date further back to the third millennium BC. Although they note the examples of double male burials of the Corded Ware culture, they nevertheless conclude that 'there is nothing else in the material culture to suggest anything about the more precise nature and role of this twin male ritual' (ibid., 265).

Although we know virtually nothing of the religion of the Neolithic communities, simple duality pervades all life and would have played an important role in the Neolithic European cosmology: the duality of nature and culture, day and night, right and left, men and women, kin and strangers, life and death. The concept of twins ruling the upper realm, as known in the Pre-Indo-European religions, may have arisen independently in several areas – initially reflecting normal life experiences of day and night, sun and moon, the agricultural cycle – and found expression in a variety of different forms.

In this sense the duality present in the megalithic tombs – initially as twin stones and later as twin passage graves – may well reflect the emergence of new cosmological views which, eventually, crystallised into the Bronze Age idea of the Divine Twins. While detailed discussion of this topic is clearly outside the scope of the present work, we may quite pertinently remind ourselves that examples of duality are present in northern Europe from the earliest Neolithic onwards. One of the earliest manifestations may be the pair of long barrows at Barkær, and the burial of four individuals, laid out in pairs inside the wooden chamber of Bygholm Nørremark long barrow, offers another roughly contemporary example.

Duality in the juxtaposition of building materials may also have been symbolic. Parker Pearson and Ramilisonina (1998) have considered the symbolism of stone, in contrast to perishable materials such as timber, within the historical context of tomb building on Madagascar, as a metaphor for durability and endurance. Their ethnographic analogy is well known and requires no elaboration here. Nevertheless it is pertinent to note that within the TRB, after the initial reliance on timber in burial structures, followed by a certain period of overlap in the use of both, stone becomes a dominant material precisely at a point when temporal cosmological concepts revolving around the ancestors may have been elaborated. The contemporary use of timber in the causewayed enclosures may further emphasise the cognitive notions linking and separating the paired spheres: those of the living and the dead.

The already-mentioned double burials of children at the cemetery of Borgeby, in Scania, are a further example of pairings. While the excavators' idea of at least one burial being that of twins cannot be proved, the accompaniments of amber beads, in the shape of miniature double battleaxes and two-headed clubs, provide a very poignant instance of paired symbolism. Indeed, ethnographically, twins are frequently regarded as anomalies, sometimes thought to possess special powers, and at other times thought to be dangerous; they may also stand for symmetry and balance (Runcis 2002).

Finally, a quite dramatic example of pairing in the Danish TRB is provided by the so-called stone-packing graves, which appear in north Jutland from the MN II onwards and to date are known from 47 localities (Fabricius and Becker 1996). These linear cemeteries, sometimes stretching over a distance of up to 2 km, are typically double rows of stone-filled pits of human length, arranged in up to three pairs and interspersed with single rectangular mortuary houses. They are in a close spatial relationship with local megaliths, for example in the area of Vroue Hede, and may be a local, individual expression of important structural changes in later TRB society. Owing to the high acidity of the soil, human remains do not survive, and thus the nature of these burials is highly conjectural. While groups of graves may reflect families or some other filial arrangements, it is difficult to provide a rational explanation for the consistent pairing of the graves; equally there is nothing within the grave goods to provide an explanation. However, against the background of twin symbolism, as we see it crystallising in different ways throughout southern Scandinavia, the stone-packing graves are among the strongest expressions of this idea, irrespective of whether it reflects a religious or a social concept.

Whaling has drawn attention to several notions of dualism that seem to be a feature of many primal religions – dualisms that are realities with which human nature must come to terms. Thus he distinguishes dualism at the level of nature, where notions are complementary, based on harmony of opposites, and cannot exist without one another. Examples could include black/white, light/dark, male/female, right/left, sun/moon, winter/summer, etc. A different form of dualism is related to the world as a created order, which is characterised by a cosmic conflict between opposing forces, involving spiritual forces of right and goodness as well as those of wrong and evil. The third and most common duality is that which represents the difference between spirit and matter as expressed through a conflict between body and soul (Whaling 1985, 46–7).

Thus, duality in the context of the north European Neolithic TRB burials may reflect several different notions brought together. The relationship between spirit and matter (body and soul, as already discussed in the chapter on burials) is especially pertinent in the context of funerary monuments, but complementary pairings such as light/dark, male/female, sun/moon, fleeting/permanent may also have played an important role. The ultimate translation of such notions, through oral traditions and symbolic meanings of objects and structures, into the concept of Divine Twins as proposed by Kristiansen and Larsson (2005) naturally requires further attention in the future, not only within the area of northern Europe but across Neolithic Europe as a whole.

Megaliths and the wider north European ceremonial landscape

While megaliths were undoubtedly the most enduring and visible structures of their time, the investment in the ceremonial landscape of northern Europe extended well beyond their construction and maintenance. Indeed, life in general – in addition to quotidian activities – appears to have been punctuated by a vast range of ritual and ceremonial acts at different places, in which individuals would participate either singly or as members of larger groups, be it at a village or a greater communal level. Some sites, such as cult houses, appear to be intimately associated with the megaliths while others, although related through a range of activities, were more distant and may have fulfilled different roles. Here we may include sites in bogs, mires and waterlogged places, where votive offerings were placed, or enclosed ceremonial sites that offered venues for larger public gatherings, bringing several communities together for thanksgiving, worship, pilgrimage and possibly even facilitating social and economic encounters with strangers.

At these sites material culture – pottery, stone and flint tools, jewellery – was deposited in various combinations, sometimes accompanied by animal and human remains. While utilitarian, the various items of material culture were thus important symbolic resources employed in different aspects of ritual and religious life. While the precise meaning in each context may have been slightly different, such items also expressed relationships between nature and culture within the wider cosmological system of the TRB. Thus, in order to understand the complex framework of socio-ritual interactions within which the megaliths were but one element, we now need to turn our attention, however briefly, to other manifestations of ritual activities.

Megaliths and cult houses

In 1955 the first so-called cult house was discovered at Tustrup, Djurland Peninsula, clearly forming part of a larger contemporary ceremonial setting comprising two dolmens and a passage grave (Kjærum 1955; Figure 3.19). Since then there have been about a dozen such structures recognised, so far all of them in north Jutland (Becker 1996). Some are in close spatial relationship with megalithic tombs (for example Ferslev, Trandum Skovby II and Engedal) while others have later stone-packing graves superimposed upon them (for example Foulum, Engedal or Herrup XXVI; indeed the latter also appears to have overlain an early TRB grave). We cannot be certain whether megalithic tombs were associated with all of them and are no longer traceable on account of destruction. None appear to have contained contemporary burials.

The buildings are of a fairly standard format: they are either a single rectangular room opened at one end or supplied with an additional open-ended vestibule. Walls were made of timber posts with planks slotted in between; two central posts supported a gable roof that seems to have been covered with birch bark and a mixture of grass and turf sods. The Tustrup house was somewhat more substantial, its timber walls additionally supported by lines of orthostats and dry-stone walling, replicating elements of the neighbouring megalithic constructions.

Since the finds within the houses consist predominantly of discrete sets of pots, which in style and in nature of the deposition resemble the votive pottery offerings in front of the megalithic chambers, the buildings have been interpreted as ceremonial cult houses connected with ceremonies carried out at the tombs. Their subsequent deliberate destruction, through either dismantling or fire, levelling and covering with a layer of small stones and cobbles, entirely supports such an interpretation. The votive deposits within the buildings date from the same time as ceramics in front of tombs, mainly from MN I (pedestalled bowls and ornamented spoons are particularly well represented, followed by bowls and beakers) although at Ferslev such activity may have extended up to the time when MN III style was in vogue.

Although Kjærum rightly rejected the idea that these structures were mortuary houses or ossuaries, their interpretation as places of offering has understandably been rather vague, and not very much more can be inferred from the available evidence. Ceramics placed in the interior do demonstrate that votive depositions occurred, but the occasions for such ceremonies are more difficult to determine. On the one hand, these may represent a local variant of division within a ceramic deposition ceremony – with the pots intended for the ancestors being put in front of the tomb, while those offered to spirits and supernatural beings were physically separated from the former.

Alternatively, it is possible that the buildings served to display the body or the exhumed bones prior to interment within the chamber, where preparatory ceremonies may have taken place. Such could have included washing and dressing of the body or wrapping of the bones; feasting, dancing, chanting relevant songs and retelling of myths appropriate to burial ritual may also have taken place. Indeed, individuals not required to attend the actual interment inside the chamber may have gathered in and around the cult houses to remember and pay their final respects. Evidence for cult buildings associated with the burial area exists from a period pre-dating the megalithic tombs: the rectangular, ochre-coloured structure at the Mesolithic cemetery of Skateholm may have fulfilled such a role (Larsson 1988a), as could some of the timber structures that did not contain burials from within the confines of the long barrows (Midgley 2005).

Until such structures are encountered elsewhere, it is difficult to ascertain whether the use of cult houses in association with megaliths represents a continuation of earlier tradition, or whether it is a specifically regional short-lived phenomenon, developed and practised exclusively in north Jutland. Suggestions for other possible cult houses within the TRB culture, for example at Troldebjerg on Langeland or at Klein-Meinsdorf in Schleswig, have not won general acceptance.

Places with votive offerings

The tradition of votive offerings in waterlogged environments – at the edges of lakes, in boggy or marshy areas or rivers – began during the late Mesolithic and continued in use throughout the TRB culture. Thus wet areas appear to have been considered sacred locales before the Neolithic and to have continued as places of permanent importance and interest to individuals and communities. This tradition is well documented in southern Scandinavia, especially on Zealand and in Scania; it has been less studied in other areas of the north European plain, although sporadic evidence suggests that similar activities were taking place over the whole area of the TRB culture. Many so-called 'stray' early amphorae from Mecklenburg may well belong to this category, and finds from Brandenburg – either pottery or else pottery in association with stone tools – from boggy areas, such as Niederlandin, Malchow, Rittgarten or Sternhagen, or in association with large boulders, for example at Koblentz (Kirsch 1994), confirm the widespread occurrence of votive practices.

A significant aspect is the spatial relationship between votive sites, megalithic tombs and, where ascertained, settlements. Spatial analysis undertaken in some regions has for long suggested that deposits of axe hoards in waterlogged environments were in close proximity to megalithic tombs (Ebbesen 1982). Koch's analysis of the votive bog deposits on Zealand revealed that the majority are within a radius of one kilometre from known settlement sites and megalithic tombs (Koch 1998, 139–140, Figures 108–11). The circumstances at Sigersdal, north Zealand, provide a good illustration: apart from two human skeletons (see below), within an area of a few hundred square metres there were several other votive deposits, three long dolmens, a passage grave, four destroyed megalithic graves, and a hoard of 13 flint axes (Bennike and Ebbesen 1987, Figure 2). The votive site at Hindby Mosse, in Scania, was less than 500 m to the north-east of the settlement, and a megalithic grave was roughly the same distance to the east; similar circumstances appear to have prevailed around the settlement of Dagstorp (Andersson 2004, figure on p. 173; Svensson 2004, figure on p. 198).

Koch's study of the Neolithic bog pots from Zealand shows that the most intensive votive deposits date from the period between 3500 and 2950 BC, coinciding precisely with the construction of megaliths and the ceremonial use of causewayed enclosures (Koch 1998, 172). Karsten's (1994) work on the Scanian Neolithic votive deposits supports this well: not only is there a great increase in the frequency of deposits during the period from ENC until MN II, but this is also the time when specific locations begin to be used time and again, leading to cumulative deposits (60 per cent of all Scanian Neolithic cumulative deposits date to that period) and when, simultaneously, votive activities in settlements and at mega-lithic tombs increased. Such activities were much less common during MN III–V, at the time when axes – replacing pots – tended to be placed in visible locations, notably at the megalithic tombs.

The votive deposits can comprise just one category of items, such as axes or amber beads, or a combination of artefacts: pottery, flint and stone tools, together with animal bones or human remains. At some sites, offerings were made in the same locations over a long period of time: at Gammellung bog on Langeland, Skaarup noted 24 different deposits (Skaarup 1985a, 71–2) and long-term activi-ties have been documented at Lille Åmose, Sørbylille and Sigerslev Mose on Zealand (Koch 1998, 354–70, 376–9, 389–91), Hindby Mosse and Röekillorna in Scania (Svensson 2004, 211), and at Gingst on Rügen (Baier 1896).

While there are similarities with offerings at the tombs, there are also significant differences which may be of general or regional significance. Thus, pottery from Zealand bogs is represented mostly by domestic forms, among which the beaker is commonest (89 per cent of vessels), whereas types encountered outside the mega-liths, such as various decorated bowls, pedestalled bowls, or the richly decorated so-called *Prachtbecher* which are known in megalithic contexts throughout north-ern Europe, are rare; no clay spoons or discs are known from Zealand bogs at all (Koch 1998, Figures 117–19). Interestingly, vessels of period MN III–V are rare, corresponding to the demise of votive offerings observed by Karsten in Scania, although Koch notes that some flint axes and chisels continued to be deposited on Zealand. An important contrast is also seen in the treatment of the artefacts: while items deposited in front of the megaliths were normally destroyed, many of the vessels from the votive bog offerings are complete or nearly complete, and many of the axes are in pristine condition, apparently never having been used.

The bog vessels may represent leftovers from communal meals; some reveal staining from foods which have boiled over. In this context the presence of animal remains is significant, as over half of the Zealand wetland sites contained animal bones, although these are rare in Scania. These include wild animals, such as red and roe deer or fish, and domesticated species. Among the latter, cattle are com-monest, with sheep and goat interestingly also providing important sacrifice animals – in contrast to pigs, which were consumed at causewayed enclosures but less so during meals whose residues ended up in lakes. Very exceptional finds include complete skeletons of domesticated cattle, such as those found at Store Åmose and at Jordløse Mose XXII, where a clearly arranged and stone-covered deposit was found, consisting of the bones of six cattle together with remains of sheep, goats, red and roe deer, birds, fish and domesticated dogs (Koch 1998, 305–54, 363).

The votive fen not far from the settlement at Hindby Mosse, in Scania, provides an interesting insight into the variety of items that could be deposited (Svensson 2004, 211–17). The finds, apart from the usual association of pottery and large tools, also include other, less commonly encountered categories. Notable are the 13.5 tonnes of stone (much of it burnt) which is thought to derive from cooking places along the edges of the fen, butchered animal bones representing the remains of meals which were prepared there; mortar and grinding stones used in the preparation of food, as well as the vessels that served the meals, were all disposed of in the fen. Bone and antler tools, small flint implements such as scrapers, sickles, arrowheads and cores may also have been used at various stages of food procurement and meal preparation; all these items were thought to be too highly charged to be used in quotidian activities and, consequently, were disposed of after the feasts.

In addition, wet areas in southern Scandinavia commonly yield human remains, either in association with votive deposits or on their own. While only a few examples can be quoted from Sweden, mainly in Scania (Tilley 1996), remains of at least 150 individuals with votive deposits have been recovered from over 50 areas in Denmark (Bennike *et al.* 1986; Bennike 1999; Koch 1998, 155–157). While dating these remains can be problematic, there are 17 skeletons that have been dated to the period from EN I to MN II; and altogether there are at least 35 skeletons from this period deriving from bogs (Bennike 1999, Figure 6.4).

The contexts of deposition vary from individual finds (in some instances merely skulls, of which 71 examples are known from Denmark) to pairs of skeletons (for example at Sigersdal or Bolkilde) and multiple depositions (for example at Myrebjerg and Sludegårds Sømose). In contrast to evidence available from contemporary graves, a large number of bog bodies are those of young individuals aged between sixteen and twenty years, that is those on the verge of adulthood.

Among the multiple finds we may note the five individuals (two children, two juveniles and one female adult) from Myrebjerg at Magleby, whose broken-up remains were placed together with pottery and tools and covered with a sort of stone pavement (Skaarup 1985a, 76–7), and a find of TRB materials and partial remains of four individuals (one with clear traces of a blow to the head) at Sludegårds Sømose, near Frørup (Bennike and Ebbesen 1987, 101). At Hindby Mosse votive site, remains from two adults and a child (skull fragments being twice as common as the long bones) were also found (Svensson 2004, 215). The presence of such fragmentary human remains is commonly considered in terms of extended funerary practices, whereby parts of individuals that were not interred in a traditional manner within the megalithic chambers formed a part of the overall votive ritual.

However, some finds of complete human bodies recovered from the bogs can hardly reflect traditional burial rites. While some of the bog bodies found in northern Europe may conceivably be considered as individuals who had lost their way in the bog (Pieper 2003), several Danish finds of human skeletons dating to the TRB culture period clearly suggest that such individuals did not end up in their watery graves accidentally, but were sacrificed and deposited deliberately.

The two individuals from Sigersdal, north Zealand, are both young women, found lying 5 m apart – one 16 years old and the other, who was strangled with a rope, aged between 18 and 20 years; certain facial skull features suggest that the two women may have been related (Bennike and Ebbesen 1987, 92). A lugged flask and animal bones (fragments of skulls from cattle, goat, roe deer) and a carapace of a pond tortoise were found near the younger skeleton; more deposits of animal bones (skulls of goats, and an aurochs) and three polished axes were found some distance away, and a hoard of 13 early TRB thin-butted axes was found about 300 m away from the bodies (ibid., 86, Figure 2).

The Bolkilde bog, on Als, has yielded substantial remains of two male skeletons, a young male of about 16 years of age and an older individual, of about 35 years old, who also appears to have been strangled. The latter had been seriously injured some time in his life, and the damage to his left hip had most certainly crippled him, causing permanent limb dislocation and difficulties in walking (Bennike *et al.* 1986, Figure 2). Indeed, it was suggested that such a serious injury must have taken place through heavy work, possibly moving boulders during construction of a megalithic chamber; three other Danish skeletons display a similar condition (ibid., 202).

Two other skeletons, of male individuals from the Døjringe bog, near Søro, both had a shorter upper arm – one left, the other right; either they may have been crippled or, as Strassburg suggested (2000, 361), they could have been accomplished left- and right-handed archers who suffered shortening of the arm on account of repetitive bow action. Both men underwent skull trepanation, and in one case this may have been following a blow to the head with an axe; Bennike notes that many known Danish examples from different periods in prehistory show such treatment on the left side of the skulls, consistent with injuries in battle or other conflicts (Bennike 1999, 32). Indeed, the individual from Rolfsåker, Halland, suffered devastating blows with an axe to his head, arm and leg, and the 35–40-year-old man recovered from Porsmose bog, south Zealand, was killed with lethal arrow shots, one to the head, the other to the chest – although whether this was a result of some incident or a ritual killing cannot be ascertained (Strassburg 2000, 361; Bennike 1999, 29).

The interpretation of such finds within the Scandinavian archaeological literature has centred on human sacrifices. The number of crippled and young individuals tends to support this idea, although it is not clear why such persons were chosen for sacrifice. In contrast to the human remains from most of the megalithic chambers, as well as votive offerings which incorporate fragments of human bodies, the bodies of sacrificed individuals appear to have been preserved to the point that today we can still identify some of their infirmities. Since many date to the Early Neolithic, the idea of fertility rites – ensuring a plentiful supply of novel food and ample harvests – may be relevant, but there could have been other reasons. The appeasement of the spirits thought to reside in lakes and other watery places is a possibility, as are some transgressions or socially unacceptable behaviour of the individuals concerned. The latter explanation tends to be invoked in the context of the much later prehistoric bog bodies (Taylor 2002), but the wide range of votive activities associated with waterlogged environments in the Neolithic speaks against this interpretation. While they may have been liminal and numinous environments, they were also places in which to deposit goods (food, tools and ornaments) beneficial to communities. It is against this background that fertility rites are a preferred interpretation for the Neolithic human sacrifices.

Causewayed enclosures

While votive depositions in waterlogged environments were acts most probably performed by individuals and small family groups, other activities clearly demanded the participation of a large number of people – close kin and neighbours as well as strangers, some possibly coming from afar. These required different, more formal settings and, in the TRB culture as in much of contemporary Europe, they were facilitated by enclosures. Enclosed sites have a long ancestry and are a feature of many Neolithic cultures throughout Europe. They vary in form and in preserved materials, and it would be naive to assume that they were functionally identical; in fact, various surveys available in the literature clearly emphasise chronological, regional and functional differences. Indeed, the enclosures known from the TRB itself and from neighbouring contemporary cultures demonstrate the individuality of sites, even if certain characteristics are recurrent.

TRB enclosures have only been known for the past 30 years, and although they have fired scholarly imagination and feature in archaeological literature quite prominently, hardly any sites have been fully published and the interpretations, of necessity, are somewhat speculative in nature. In the context of the present discussion it is not necessary to describe the TRB enclosures in detail; the interested reader may refer to my earlier consideration of this type of site (Midgley 1992) and, indeed, to a much more comprehensive exposé provided by N. H. Andersen (1997). However, we may briefly highlight some recurrent features as well as draw attention to features peculiar to specific regions or individual sites.

TRB causewayed enclosures may be defined as sites encircled by one or more parallel lines of ditches of varying lengths, interrupted by numerous causeways. Sometimes timber palisades were erected on the inside of the ditch-marked perimeter; the palisade at Sarup I may have stood between 2 and 3 m tall, and if so it must have been quite impressive and undoubtedly visible from a considerable distance. Offerings were placed inside the ditches; pits containing deposits are encountered in the interior; and, in some cases, there are additional small fenced enclosures outside the palisades, sometimes associated with short ditch segments – such being well documented in both phases at Sarup and also known from Büdelsdorf (N. H. Andersen 1997, Hingst 1971).

The majority of sites are found in conspicuous locations, on hilltops and promontories – positions further accentuated by the presence of river valleys or low-lying marshy ground. They vary in size from as little as 1.6 ha (Bjerggård) to over 20 ha (Lokes Hede). On present evidence the use of enclosures dates to between later EN and MN I; thus they are contemporary with the period during which megalithic tombs were being built on a massive scale. Whereas the enclosures fall out of use after that, the localities are by no means abandoned, as substantial occupational debris testifies to their use as settlements. Some sites, however, may have retained their largely non-domestic character into the later TRB period, when they were refashioned into simple palisaded enclosures, as seen for example at Vasgård and Rispebjerg on Bornholm, or Dösjebro in Scania – sites which apparently continued in use during the Battle Axe culture (Kaul *et al.* 2002, 136; Svensson 2004, 221–3).

The evidence from causewayed enclosures reaffirms that a wide range of activities took place there and that these sites offered venues which, at different times, catered for specific rituals, from deposition of human remains to exchanges of goods, some coming from distant locations. However, although the finds are important, we should perhaps remind ourselves that the numerous re-cuttings of ditches and alterations to the architectural layout at some sites suggest that the process of construction of enclosures may have been just as significant as what went on within them. Creation of enclosures, of necessity, involved a considerable number of individuals who may have come together only rarely in their lives, and their involvement in the process would have created bonds that emphasised engagement with a wider community than that offered by daily encounters within the close neighbourhood. Indeed, some may have come from far away and, apart from meeting strangers, the building of an enclosure, like all other non-domestic activities, would have provided a spiritual experience not available in the context of quotidian life.

Human remains, while not numerous, have been encountered in the ditches at several sites. They create an obvious link to megalithic graves and form an element within the extended burial tradition; indeed, the previously mentioned miniature dolmen found within a ditch at Sarup Gamle Skole enclosure strengthens this link further. From Sarup I, two sets of human jaws, one from a child and another from an adult, are known, and may be all that remains from the skulls. At Hygind a human skull was found lying between those of a sheep and an ox; a burnt human tooth and a thigh bone were found at Åsum Enggård, and human skulls have been known for quite some time from Bundsø (P. O. Nielsen 2004, 22). Fragmentary remains are also known from several other Danish enclosures.

Such small quantities of human bone most probably reflect the very poor preservation conditions, but the fact that they derive from ditches does point to a degree of consistency. Andersen has argued that the system ditches reflected individual units – families, clans, etc. – and that the dead, temporarily placed in them, were brought to the enclosures to participate in the wider community and then, after a suitable interval, returned to a local burial place in a megalith (N. H. Andersen 1997, 307–9). Thus causewayed enclosures might have provided one of the places in which the bodies of the dead could be left until the flesh had rotted away, so as to permit the soul to undertake its long journey to the other world and to allow the necessary time for the dead to be incorporated into the world of the ancestors.

However, even if the enclosures acted as temporary resting places for some of the dead, the available evidence demonstrates that people gathered there for other purposes as well. Thus enclosures appear to have combined a range of functions which, at other places, might have been conducted separately. While some of the cultural material could represent domestic debris, perhaps from the time of the construction of the enclosures, other items were more formally disposed of. Pottery – mainly beakers and various forms of bowl – was placed in ditches as well

174

as in the interior pits. At Sarup I, pots were displayed at the foot of the palisade (altogether 278 pots) in a manner reminiscent of vessel placement at the megalithic tombs, and we may assume that similar arrangements were made at other sites. From a number of sites there are suggestions that pottery used in ceremonial contexts may have been manufactured at enclosures (Store Brokhøj and Büdels-dorf) and, indeed, communication among large numbers of individuals coming together for rituals may have contributed to a degree of uniformity in contemporary ceramics and their decoration over large areas. Axes, battleaxes and small tools were also formally disposed of, as were other items such as grinding stones or amber beads. Animal bones in the ditches and caches of burnt cereals suggest feasts; these could have been held to venerate ancestors, to affirm alliances with more distant groups or to celebrate harvests and seek continued prosperity.

Summary

The types of site discussed above, with evidence of ritual activities – the cult houses, votive places in waterlogged environments and causewayed enclosures – define a network of ceremonial locales that provided venues for individual and public engagements. While the cult houses – which on present evidence appear to be a rather local north Jutland feature – seem to be associated intimately with burial ceremonies at megaliths, the activities performed at waterlogged votive sites and causewayed enclosures testify to a broader range of ceremonies, some of which relate to burial, while others express symbolic relationships between the real or imagined natural forces, as well as between communities living near and far.

Although our knowledge of the religion and beliefs of the TRB folk is limited, the lure of the bog areas must have been very powerful. Indeed, Karsten (1994) suggested that there must have been an oral tradition, maintained for many generations, that passed on both the information on these votive places and the forms of ritual required, since too much time passed before the renewal of offerings in certain places. While the precise significance of these locales may have altered with changing cosmologies, it has persisted not just in the Neolithic but throughout subsequent periods of prehistory and through the historical periods. People need not necessarily have been afraid of waterlogged environments, and the fact that they traversed them regularly is amply documented by the Neolithic trackways that we discussed earlier. However, this does not preclude the bogs and mires being thought of as providing access to the supernatural world via sacred ritual. Historical sources, from Tacitus' *Germania* onwards, have provided us with a rich folklore which clearly demonstrates that such localities were also thought to be the abodes of supernatural beings – gods, water spirits, ghosts and restless ancestral souls – who had to be appeased through offerings ranging from utilitarian objects to human sacrifices.

The flint axes and related hoards have, in the past, been interpreted as evidence of conspicuous consumption, ensuring that the demand for such items continued and that they retained their prestige. However, since the objects from votive bog offerings, as well as those placed in the interior pits of causewayed enclosures, are by and large undamaged, a further dimension to votive offerings could be to consider them as acts of ritual carried out by or on behalf of skilled craftsmen. Mary Helms (1993), in a fascinating work on this subject based on wide-ranging ethnographic discussion, demonstrated how skilled craftsmen in non-industrial communities are frequently at the interface of different cosmological worlds and form a link with the 'original' ancestral master craftsmen, with the source and origin of a particular craft or skill. If the cosmology of the TRB communities carried over some of the concepts, even if transformed, prevailing in the Meso-lithic, the waterlogged places may also have been considered as temporally distant ancestral locales – associated with the original, distant ancestors of TRB commu-nities, those who provided the initial skills.

Helms considers skilled crafting – be it manufacture of objects or performance of acts such as oratory, dance, myth-telling, body painting, navigation, to name but a few – as the ordering of nature for cultural purposes. Accordingly, acts of crafting were necessary social transformations, just as the objects themselves were trans-formations of raw materials into things beneficial to the community: amber into amulets, raw flint into useful tools, wet clay into containers, tree trunks into canoes, stone and timber into massive structures, plants and animals into food; the outside realm provided raw materials that were transformed into social good. The practical aspects of axe or pot manufacture can be expressed pragmatically in terms of time, capacity and size, but the spiritual force behind creating an axe or a vessel may have formed an interface between society and the outer world. Return-ing some of these back to where they metaphorically belonged, into the world from which they originally ('ancestrally') came, may have been at the very core of such votive acts.

Similarly, while enclosures were undoubtedly places at which burial rites and ancestor worship took place, other activities brought the world of human existence into a relationship with the outside realm. Vernacular traditions of the time are not known to us, but there can be little doubt that dance, music, song, telling of myths and recounting of heroic exploits featured prominently in ceremonies (the clay drums from the southern regions of the TRB are a tantalising example of the importance of music and sound) and, in conjunction with the provision of food for feasts and the disposing of precious items as votive offerings, may have constituted elements through which prominent members of the communities strove to acquire or retain their prestige and importance.

While the evidence is not overwhelming, there are indications that enclosures may also have served as places of exchange, where strangers arrived with desirable exotic items to exchange them for locally available goods. Alpine jade axes, copper axes and trinkets are an early if infrequent example, and the copper and amber hoard found at the enclosure of Årupgård supports this idea. We have already discussed the possibility that some of the sites were strategically placed along long-distance routes of passage and communication, although the lack of full publication of excavated sites makes this difficult to prove. Nevertheless,

Büdelsdorf is close by a ford across the river Eider, and the large amount of non-local flint suggests that imported materials were coming to this site, although their dating is uncertain (Haßmann 2000). Similarly, a boat from Jutland or one of the southern Danish islands could have arrived at Helnæs Bay, with the Sarup enclosure easily accessed by river or on foot; the very fine battleaxe recovered there (N. H. Andersen 1997, Figure 106) may be an example of a gift from outside the local area.

Transactions and relationships with strangers demanded behaviour and attitudes different from those that operated among kith and kin, and causewayed enclosures may have provided suitable places where such formal encounters were made possible. Indeed, Mary Helms has argued that dealings with foreigners involved a 'ritualized, therefore sacralized or at least honor-associated atmosphere' (1993, 98). Not only did causewayed enclosures provide such an environment, but the presence of the dead in the ditches (in the process of transition to becoming ancestors), as well as the world of the ancestors symbolised through the surrounding megaliths, may further have aided the undertaking of exchanges and the formation of alliances with strangers.

6

THE WIDER EUROPEAN
MEGALITHIC CONTEXT

Megaliths in north-western Europe

The megaliths of northern Europe that are the principal subject of this work do not, of course, represent an isolated development, but belong to a much wider north-west European phenomenon, which stretches all the way to the Atlantic along the continental coastline and to the British Isles, with further enclaves along the Mediterranean and across to the North African coast.

The search in the later nineteenth and early twentieth centuries for a common historical origin of European megaliths was set within the then prevailing framework of morphology, typology and diffusion. The subsequent dramatic impact of radiocarbon dating, together with the processualist approach, emphasising economic, social and cultural change, led Renfrew and others to question the validity of a single-source theory and to pose the possibility of independent nuclear areas for the emergence of megaliths in different regions of Europe (Renfrew 1973, 1976, 1980; Chapman et al. 1981). This proposition substantially freed scholars from the typo-chronological straitjacket and permitted them to consider the megaliths within their regional cultural settings, concentrating on local characteristics of both the structures and the funerary practices associated with them. Nevertheless some scholars, notably those of the French and German schools, remained sceptical of an independent development model which, at its extreme, placed the emergence of the megalithic tradition within local Mesolithic milieux (Burenhult 1984).

However, an even more significant development within the past two decades or so has been the recognition of the enormous diversity of burial monument forms and accompanying ritual practices present in all the regions from the earliest Neolithic onwards (see the various papers presented in Beinhauer et al. 1999, Burenhult 2003, and Joussaume et al. 2006). This diversity suggests that the emergence of monumentality, and by implication that of the megalithic structures, was intricately interwoven with the process of the establishment of farming communities. The question of crystallisation of the Neolithic within the broad coastal zone, from Scandinavia in the north to the Iberian peninsula in the south-west, need not concern us in detail, but it is important to note that new researches have shed better light upon the cultural circumstances immediately prior to the adoption of agriculture. Thus we can now better evaluate the relationship between the indigenous hunter-gatherers and the incoming farmers – whether of Danubian or Mediterranean extraction – groups of which, even if small in numbers and perhaps trickling in rather than invading, undoubtedly were making themselves felt within the various regions.

This process was neither synchronous nor identical along its broad coastal front, since varied local conditions demanded different responses; the plethora of monuments confirms this beyond any doubt. Indeed we may also note that, while in certain regions monumentality was given an enthusiastic expression early on – for example in the long mound cemeteries of the Paris basin (Midgley 2005) – the resistance to converting this phenomenon into 'megalithic' forms was quite pronounced (Leclerc and Tarrête 2006). Elsewhere, most notably along the Atlantic façade, monumentality and 'megaliths' seem to have appealed more or less simultaneously (Cassen *et al.* 2000; Joussaume and Laporte 2006; Le Roux 2006).

The scope of the present survey has of necessity to be brief and geographically limited, but it is pertinent at this point to consider some of the most important features of the megalithic phenomenon in areas of relative proximity to northern Europe. Thus, while along the extensive north-west boundary of the Danubian cultural world veritable long mound cemeteries offer the locally earliest examples of monumentality (Chapter 1 and Midgley 2005), the long mound form features equally prominently along the western Atlantic façade and eastern Britain. Indeed, over one hundred long mounds are known from Brittany, and more than fifty from the Poitou-Charente region. While they were built over a long period of time, the earliest available dates place some of the western French long mounds in the middle of the fifth millennium BC (Joussaume 1997; Laporte and Le Roux 2004; Joussaume and Laporte 2006), with those of eastern Britain most probably following upon the beginning of the fourth millennium BC (Scarre 2005; Bradley 2007). Thus, irrespective of regional dynamic and diversity, the long mound idea was an important element structuring the burial practices of these early farming communities.

Naturally, the long mounds vary in shape and form and in the structures that they cover. Some are very large, although some of the extreme developments are a result of successive extensions and aggrandisements. Cleaven Dyke, in Perthshire, began as a simple long mound, although in its final stage it measured over 2 kilometres (Barclay and Maxwell 1998). Equally, many of the Atlantic *tertres* are multi-period structures resulting from an addition to, or extension of, initially small round mounds or cairns covering closed cists or small chambers. Thus, at Er Grah in Locmariaquer, a chamber set within a small circular cairn about 10 m in diameter was soon engulfed within a trapezoidal structure about 43 m long, and eventually the monument was extended to about 140 m in length (Le Roux 2006). La Motte des Justices, Deux-Sèvres, was 180 m long (Joussaume 1997; Laporte and Le Roux 2004) and Prissé-la-Charrière – which expanded from a mound 23 m long to 100 m – was extended at least three times, each stage involving its own complicated series of modifications (Laporte *et al.* 2002; Scarre *et al.* 2003). A different form of aggrandisement is offered by the huge Carnac mounds (*tumulus carnacéens*) such as the tumulus of Saint-Michel, Le Manio 2 or Mané Lud at Carnac (Bailloud *et al.* 1995; L'Helgouac'h 1998).

Some mounds have undergone transformation from mainly timber to stone. At Lochhill, Kirkcudbright, once the timber chamber and the adjacent façade were burnt, the whole structure was enveloped in a cairn with the original façade replicated by means of orthostats (Masters 1983), and at Wayland's Smithy an early mound was completely sealed beneath a much larger structure with a transepted megalithic chamber built at the eastern end (Atkinson 1965). Importantly, such a transformation has a wider European provenance – a principle also witnessed in northern Europe, most emphatically in the previously mentioned Bygholm Nørremark in Jutland.

Some mounds reveal no traces of burial structures beneath them. British examples, most notably around Avebury, at Horslip, South Street and Beckhampton Road, apparently covered neither a burial structure nor human remains (Ashbee 1970). Equally, no burial arrangements have been found, for example, under the first oval phase at Le Petit Mont, Morbihan, mound D at Champs-Châlon, Charente-Maritime, or at Mondreau, Deux-Sèvres (Lecornec 1994; Joussaume 1997, 2003). It is entirely possible that inner structures either did not survive or were removed in advance of the mound construction; however, such mounds could also have been raised in response to some specific social or religious commemoration requirement.

Timber structures do, however, exist, perhaps better known from Britain than along the Atlantic façade. British timber chambers (commonly referred to by the relatively neutral term 'mortuary structure') vary from massive, oak-plank rectangular chambers – as found at Haddenham, Cambridgeshire – to lighter structures defined at each end by a large timber post, with walls built of thin planks or wattlework, of the kind postulated at Street House, Cleveland, at Pitnacree, Perthshire, or at Dalladies, Kincardineshire (Hodder and Shand 1988; Vyner 1984; Coles and Simpson 1965; Piggott 1974). The reconstruction of the first phase at Wayland's Smithy (Atkinson 1965), with its tent-like shape and a small flint cairn, reveals a certain similarity with the northern Konens Høj type chamber, although the variety of other contemporary forms in both areas argues for formal rather than direct similarity.

At Er Grah, there were traces of post holes that may be remnants of a timber palisade, aligned towards the base of the Grand Menhir Brisé and subsequently covered by the southern cairn extension. The evidence was not sufficient to reconstruct the original form of this structure, although Le Roux wondered about the possibility of a vast 'house of the dead' (Le Roux 2006, 248, Figures 61–4). Other timber structures are also known from western France, as observed around the grave pit at Croix-Saint-Pierre at Saint-Just, Ille-et-Vilaine (Laporte and Le Roux 2004), or possibly at Sarceaux in Normandy, where a secondary burial of several young individuals may have been placed within a wooden chamber (Chancerel and Desloges 1998).

That other forms of burial were also practised is tantalisingly revealed by accidental discoveries such as the very early Neolithic double pit burial at Ger-mignac, Charente, whose inventory of over 3000 discoidal shell beads is perhaps linked to the preceding Mesolithic tradition (Laporte and Le Roux 2004, 12–13). The so-called *sépultures sous dalle*, in the vicinity of Malesherbes on the Essonne plateau, Loiret (Verjux *et al.* 1998), provide an interesting variant of individual graves simply covered at ground level by a massive prostrate megalithic slab – an example of 'succinct megalithism' as it was recently referred to by Leclerc and Tarrête (2006, 385). Some of the covering slabs have been used as axe polishers and sometimes, as at Chaise, the grave is further marked by the presence of a small menhir.

Emerging around the mid-fifth millennium BC, the Chamblandes cist burials, predominantly from the Valais, Lausanne and the Leman basin, Switzerland, with possible extension to eastern and central France (for example at Monéteau, Yonne), present a 'light' megalithic form: cists, built of thin slabs and covered by a capstone, initially contain single inhumations but subsequently become collective graves (Lausanne 'Vidy' with remains of an adult male, female and three children; Leclerc and Tarrête 2006, 391, Figure 5).

The early presence of passage graves along the Atlantic façade has been the subject of considerable discussion. Joussaume (2003) once again raised the impor-tant question of whether the earliest megalithic chambers were simple open struc-tures – as seen in the first chamber at Prissé-la-Charrière, Deux-Sèvres – or whether passage graves (that is chambers with a contemporary passage allowing access to the interior) belong to the same period of construction. The earliest chamber at Prissé-la-Charrière was a small structure with a funnel-like entrance, closed with a slab that permitted repeated depositions, and set within a little circu-lar cairn (Figure 6.1); the area in front of it remained free for some time, not only facilitating access but also providing a setting for rituals. This early phase was in itself a rather complicated series of modifications, resulting in a closure of the chamber within the first long mound. The two passage graves further to the east – one rectangular with an offset passage, and the other circular – clearly belong to the later stages of construction (Laporte *et al.* 2002; Scarre *et al.* 2003).

Similarly, the largest tumulus at Bougon, Deux-Sèvres, is a multi-period con-struction, although the relationship between the circular passage grave in its round setting to the south (F0) and the chamberless long mound extending north of it (F1) has not been clearly established (Figure 6.2a and b). The passage grave may be one of the very early examples of this form, as the bones recovered inside it date to the middle of the fifth millennium BC; equally it may have provided a secondary resting place for bones derived from an earlier structure (Mohen and Scarre 2002).

Passage graves in western and central France display a wide range of forms and placements within the mounds. Chambers are commonly circular or quadrangular with an offset passage (the so-called *dolmens angoumoisins*), built of dry-stone walling, orthostats or a combination of both, frequently with a corbelled roof. In round mounds, for example at La Hogue and La Hoguette, Calvados, dry-stone cir-cular chambers are arranged with their passages radiating towards the exterior

Figure 6.1 The small chamber of the first phase at Prissé-la-Charrière long mound,
Deux-Sèvres

(Caillaud and Lagnel 1972), while in rectangular and trapezoidal mounds the
chambers may be found opening onto the long sides, for example Champ-Châlon
A and B, or towards one of the ends, for example Champ-Châlon C (Joussaume
1998, 58–9). Very long mounds, created through successive extensions, may have
many chambers arranged along the long axis, for example Availles-sur-Chizé,
Deux-Sèvres, with its ten chambers (Bouin and Joussaume 1998, 79) or the famous
Barnenez covering eleven chambers (Giot 1987; L'Helgouac'h 1998).

It is this latter monument, in fact, which has been at the forefront of the polemic
on the early presence of passage graves in western France, although the original
two-period construction suggested by Giot clearly underestimated the complexity
of the monument. Irrespective of the controversy surrounding the early radiocarbon
dates from this site, it now seems that chambers F and G are the earliest and that
their passages were extended several centuries after the original construction, possibly when other chambers were being built. The extensions prominently employ
large slabs, which could derive from menhirs originally standing in the vicinity of
the cairn. This practice is reflected at a number of other later passage graves, spectacularly located around the Morbihan gulf and most famously documented by the
decorated broken stele, part of which was used at La Table des Marchands (Figure
6.3), and the other at Gavrinis (Bailloud *et al.* 1995; L'Helgouac'h 1998). Passage
graves of Charente-Maritime also document such usage.

Indeed, the erection of decorated or plain menhirs, either singly, in pairs or
forming alignments, was an important early manifestation of monumentality

Figure 6.2 Bougon long tumulus F, Deux-Sèvres: (a) passage grave F0 at the south end of the monument; (b) chamberless long mound F1 extending north from F0

Figure 6.3 Passage grave at La Table des Marchands with a broken menhir for its capstone, Locmariaquer

within the western French Neolithic. To what extent this feature could be said to have been rooted in the preceding traditions is a matter for discussion. Early, albeit unspectacular menhirs have been noted at the Hoëdic Mesolithic cemetery (Péquart and Péquart 1954); an anthropomorphically shaped stone may have stood in the vicinity of the eastern end of a Villeneuve-Saint-Germain long house at Le Haut Mée in eastern Brittany, perhaps accompanied by timber equivalents (Cassen *et al.* 1998); indeed, timber equivalents of western menhirs have been suggested within the context of the monumental cemeteries of the mid-fifth millennium BC in Burgundy (Midgley 2005, 97–8). There is, however, a dramatic difference in scale between these early markers and the subsequent Neolithic menhirs; simple derivation from the Mesolithic prototypes may not be a sufficient explanation, as clearly the menhirs symbolise a very different cosmology.

Standing stones also accompanied mid-fifth-millennium BC Breton mounds, for example at the western end of Le Petit Mont (Lecornec 1994); small menhirs of uncertain chronological age were sealed under the mound of Lannec er Gadouer (Cassen *et al.* 2000); and a conspicuous decorated menhir marked the mound of Le Manio 2 (Bailloud *et al.* 1995). While the subsequent usage of fragments of standing stones within the passage graves is not in doubt, opinion differs as to whether the collapse of some of the large stelae was caused by deliberate destruction – perhaps a result of some cosmological crisis, or instigated by new settlers with a different set of beliefs – or whether natural disasters, such as earthquakes, were responsible (Joussaume 2003, 39–40).

Standing stones have been reused in some of the chambers in the British Isles, although the situation there is less clear. The bi-facially decorated stone at Bryn Celli Ddu on Anglesey, hidden behind the chamber, is a good candidate for a standing menhir prior to its incorporation in the mound; indeed it may have belonged to a small circle of stones that subsequently had a mound imposed upon it (Scarre 2005, 67–8). Equally the reuse of certain decorated stones in the Irish passage graves, where some of the decoration is hidden from view, suggests that they were, at least, carved in a free-standing form, and Eogan's work at Knowth indicates that the stones used in the principal chamber were initially part of a different structure (Eogan 1997).

Moreover, free-standing timber elements, in the form of timber façades, or as posts arranged in association with stone-built chambers, are known from both western France and Britain. Timber façades at the British long mounds – usually at right angles to the burial chamber – are very common, either as veritable timber walls effectively separating the mortuary structure from the outside, for example at Street House or Haddenham, or as rather more freestanding arrangements of posts, for example at Nutbane.

We have already mentioned the presence of timber posts at Er Grah. Timber posts, with votive ceramic offerings at the foot, have also been found in front of the first megalithic chamber at Prissé-la-Charrière (Joussaume 2003, 25; Scarre *et al.* 2003) and a line of timber posts in front of a chamber has also been reported from Mané-Lud (Joussaume 2003, 26). The already-noted small menhirs, of the kind found sealed at Erdeven or the large decorated stone forming part of the arrangements at Le Manio 2, offer more tangible examples of the possible use of organic counterparts (Bailloud *et al.* 1995; Cassen *et al.* 2000). Equivalents of the timber façade may well be represented by alignments of stones in a gable-like format, as known for example from Bois de Fourgon, Vendée, or in other arrangements, although these date rather late and do not appear to be associated with a tomb but rather provide an independent ceremonial setting (Benéteau-Douillard 2006).

Subsequent developments along the broad Atlantic zone in western France, from the mid-fourth millennium BC onwards, involve the appearance of transepted chambers – a form also well represented in the British Isles – found either side of the Loire estuary as far north as Brittany, and of the chambers known as *dolmens angevins*, which are centred on the middle Loire with extensions to both the north and the south. Some of the latter are truly gigantic, such as the Bagneaux dolmen near Saumur, with a floor surface of 85 square metres (Figure 6.4), or the chamber of Roche-aux-Fées at Essé, Ille-et-Vilaine (Laporte and Le Roux 2004).

Megalithic chambers of the British Isles demonstrate a comparable variety of forms. Thus, the so-called portal dolmens – possibly the oldest megalithic chambers, beginning around 4000 BC – with a formal entrance, and often a massive precariously inclined capstone, are common in south-west Britain; local equivalents are known from Ireland and along the western coast of Scotland. True passage graves are found primarily in Wales and in Ireland; in the latter region they often form spectacular cemeteries (for example at Brú na Bóinne or Loughcrew;

Figure 6.4 The massive chamber at Bagneaux, near Saumur, Maine-et-Loire

Cooney 2000). Local versions of passage graves, such as the Cotswold-Severn tombs – trapezoidal cairns with a deep concave façade allowing access to a transepted chamber – are known in western England; the Clyde cairns, with tele-scopically arranged chambers, are common in western Scotland, and the so-called Orkney-Cromarty and Maes Howe chambers are known in northern Scotland, the latter most spectacularly on Orkney (Henshall 1963).

Hand in hand with the variety of funerary architecture goes the manner in which the living dealt with their dead, ranging from a disposal that leaves no visible archaeological trace (this may well have been the fate of the majority of Neolithic populations) to a prolonged series of funerary acts which, at the end, leave merely a handful of bones. The argument as to whether complete bodies or merely selected bone fragments were brought into the chambers was raised previously (Chapter 4), and the same applies to the burial chambers in other areas of north-western Europe. Indeed, the recent study of human remains from a selection of the French Neolithic tombs by Philippe Chambon has once again highlighted the difficulties of distin-guishing between these practices (Chambon 2003b). Most probably both were in use concurrently, and the choice may have depended on a range of considerations, not necessarily related directly to the time of deposition. Moreover, once reduced to bones, human remains were treated by the living in a variety of ways: either the skeletons could be left untouched, preserving the identity of the dead, or the living would manipulate the bones, sometimes through rearrangements or removal of selected skeletal parts, or by the creation of anonymous groups of ancestral bones.

British monuments in which human remains have been found – the long barrows and megalithic chambers – tell a similar story of inhumations, although the quantities and precise arrangements vary considerably. Some, over a period of time, have accumulated remains of many individuals – for example the remains of about 57 persons at Fussell's Lodge, 341 at Isbister and the estimated 400 at Quanterness, on Orkney (Ashbee 1966; Hedges 1984; Renfrew 1979) – although many retain only a handful of individuals.

The disarticulated remains found in many timber mortuary houses of the British long barrows can hardly result from taphonomic processes or be due to a prolonged period of use of such chambers. Some do contain articulated bodies, albeit in different stages of preservation; this is best seen at Nutbane, where complete bodies were introduced to the timber chamber at different times (Morgan 1959, 24). Elsewhere, bones could be arranged in piles: at Wayland's Smithy I the level of disarticulation was most pronounced in lower levels, while at Fussell's Lodge the division of the timber chamber and the composition of different bone piles along the longitudinal axis suggest periodic moving of selected bones further inwards – here primary and secondary forms of burial both appear to have been practised, a pattern also suggested for the massive timber chamber of the Haddenham long barrow (Atkinson 1965; Ashbee 1966; Hodder and Shand 1988). That bones circulated more widely within the ceremonial landscape of southern Britain is clearly demonstrated by the incompleteness of skeletons within some of the timber chambers, as well as by the contemporary presence of human remains on settlements and within causewayed enclosures; not all chambers need represent final resting places.

While the lifespan of the timber chambers was not likely to extend beyond a couple of generations at the most, the megalithic chambers could be used over much longer periods of time, although estimates vary from as little as 150 years before the closure of Hazleton North to as long as 800 years before the final sealing of the Isbister chamber. The architecture of the stone chambers and their accessibility created circumstances of even more complex processes in attending to the dead. Although most human remains are found in disarticulated condition, there is evidence that complete bodies were placed in some chambers; such are encountered in the Cotswold-Severn lateral and transepted chambers, such as at Hazleton North, Lanhill or West Kennet (Saville 1990; Keiller and Piggott 1938; Piggott 1962) as well as in some of the Orcadian tombs, for example at Midhowe or Rowiegar (Davidson and Henshall 1989). It is the subsequent history of such deposits, and the different activities engaged in by the living, that create the complex palimpsest of funerary practices.

There is some evidence of bodies in a skeletal state being pushed aside to make room for new interments, but such rearrangements do not appear to be principally a matter of creating extra burial space, as often the bones have been arranged in specific, albeit variable patterns. Thus skulls were frequently grouped against chamber walls – for example at Ascott-under-Wychwood, Penywyrlod, Knowe of Yarso – or deposited inside cells as at Isbister, and in many chambers the long bones rest in bundles along the side walls.

Sometimes representative samples from all parts of a skeleton are arranged in discrete piles, although such bones need not derive from one particular individual; this was observed at Pipton and Penywyrlod (Wysocki and Whittle 2000, 598), and apparently the skulls at Lanhill were composed of fragments of two separate individuals (Keiller and Piggott 1938, 125). Once the flesh disintegrated, some bones were clearly removed to other localities: Hazleton North, for example, had a clear deficit of skulls and long bones in relation to the number of individuals interred (Saville 1990, 251), and it remains a matter of discussion whether at least some of the bones within the ditches of southern English causewayed enclosures may initially have been de-fleshed in the burial chambers, rather than the transfer being in the opposite direction. Furthermore, bones may have also circulated among different chambers: a recent suggestion, for some of the Orkney stalled cairns on Rousay, has raised the possibility that bodies may have been allowed to decay in one chamber and then been removed in a partially disarticulated state to another with skulls, finally finding a resting place in a yet different chamber (Reilly 2003).

Age and sex, moreover, while clearly not criteria excluding burial in a chamber, were emphasised among some groups. Men and women appear to have been separated at Lanhill, and children interred at Nympsfield were buried in a separate cist (Clifford 1938). The arrangements of human remains in the West Kennet transepted chamber reveal that younger individuals, whose skeletons were also subject to greater disarticulation, were placed in segments to the left of the passage, while skeletons of older members were less disturbed and placed on the opposite side (Piggott 1962); similar arrangements are known from other chambers.

Turning now to the area of north-western France, we note that inhumation of complete human bodies appears to have been quite common, although there were many expressions of this practice. Those buried in *sépultures sous dalle* (of the Malesherbes type) were simply placed crouched in grave pits, and at Orville an additional twenty individual graves surrounded such a *sépulture sous dalle*, only one individual being placed in extended position (Simonin *et al.* 1997). The Chamblandes cists, appearing around the middle of the fifth millennium BC, illustrate an interesting transition from initially single (occasionally double) inhumations to a collective practice over a period of about 1000 years (Leclerc and Tarrête 2006).

Complete bodies were also interred in some passage graves, for which the Normandy monuments of La Hoguette, La Hogue and Condé-sur-Ifs provide very interesting data, although some of them were excavated in the nineteenth century and thus the information is of a somewhat general nature. We noted previously that some of these mounds – La Hogue, La Hoguette and La Bruyère du Hamel at Condé-sur-Ifs – each comprising several passage graves, were conceived as a single architectural and structural project. Their plan and the layout of the chambers, as well as the nature of burials in each of them, strongly suggest that the number of persons to be interred may well have been projected at the time of construction (Chambon 2003b, 68). Indeed, the dental studies carried out with respect to the La Hoguette chambers present the possibility that these were designed for specific family groups (Piera 2003), although the mitochondrial DNA pattern of the bones from chamber C at Condé-sur-Ifs did not show any genetic connection among the ten individuals analysed (Chambon 2003b, 71).

In at least half of these chambers, complete bodies were deposited and allowed to decompose without any subsequent interference, with adults and children placed in a crouched position on either their left or their right side, although it is not possible to determine whether these represent simultaneous or successive placements. Chamber I at La Hoguette displays an interesting spatial arrangement in relation to sex and location: females were placed to the west and males to the east; those buried lying on their right side were mainly towards the back of the chamber, aligned with their backs to the wall (Figure 6.5). In chamber II the dead were roughly equidistant from one another, and in chamber C at Condé-sur-Ifs there was a bipartite division of burial space, with a sort of 'corridor' leaving the central zone of the chamber free (Figure 6.6).

The coherence of these individual burials contrasts with evidence from other chambers, either within the confines of the same monument (chambers IV and V at La Hoguette) or at its close neighbour La Hogue; a similar pattern was observed at several chambers at Condé-sur-Ifs. These chambers reveal a more complex funerary practice, which may have included primary as well as secondary burials, and which most certainly involved a rearrangement of skeletal fragments. Some of the skulls in Condé-sur-Ifs (chambers A2, B and C) are found at a considerable distance from the actual skeleton, lacking mandibles or facial parts; small slabs 'protect' skull fragments in chamber IV at La Hoguette, and long bones also show displacement. The most dramatic evidence of manipulation comes from Vierville B, where three layers of human remains are separated by slab pavements.

La Hoguette is particularly interesting in this context, as both forms of burial seem to have been practised, albeit within different chambers. This is one monument at which division of sex seems to have been of some concern to the community that used it, and it is possible that other considerations were also expressed through the differential treatment of the dead – in this case leaving some bodies to rest in peace and rearranging the bones of others.

Burial customs in other French passage graves are more difficult to evaluate. The almost total lack of human remains from the Breton open chambers precludes any consideration of the possible mode of burial, and the recently proposed evolutionary scheme for the development of the architectural sequence, which encompasses a hypothetical burial sequence (Boujot and Cassen 1993), has not met with overall approval. Although human bones survive in other western French passage graves, for example in chambers at Bougon, Champ-Châlon and Montiou, interpretation is also fraught with difficulties, as in some cases the long use of the chambers and disturbances created by subsequent depositions have obliterated the original arrangements. Thus at Montiou, in spite of the fact that the two surviving chambers had remains of 14 and 22 individuals respectively, no initial arrangements could be identified with any certainty. However, there was an interesting difference in the presence of young individuals: 64 per cent in chamber I and

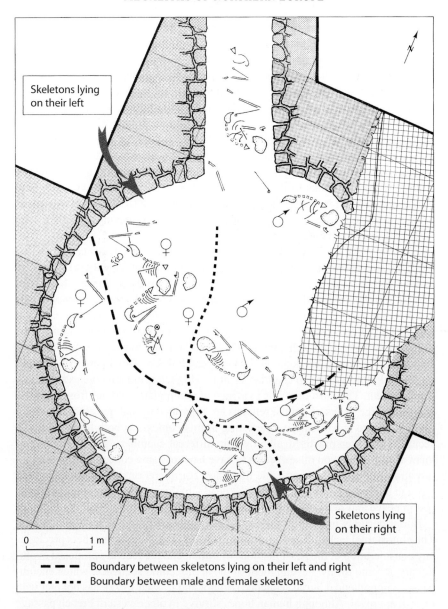

Skeletons lying
on their left

Skeletons lying
on their right

0   1 m

− − − Boundary between skeletons lying on their left and right
• • • • • Boundary between male and female skeletons

Figure 6.5 Position of burials in chamber I at La Hoguette (Fontenay-le-Marmion),
Calvados, displaying spatial arrangements according to sex

23 per cent in chamber II, so some differential deposition may have taken place
(Chambon 2003b, 104).

The Bougon F0 chamber, with its minimum number of 11 individuals, has been
interpreted by Chambon as either receiving a simultaneous deposit of individuals

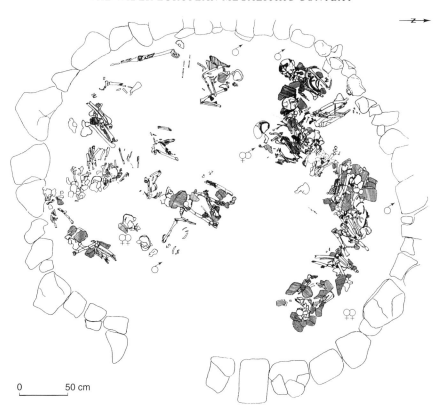

0   50 cm

Figure 6.6 Position of burials in chamber C at Condé-sur-Ifs, Calvados

who died at different times and whose bodies were thus at different stages of decomposition, or as a simultaneous deposit with differential manipulation of skeletons; or, possibly, as the result of a collective practice with bone displacement resulting from successive interments (ibid., 78). Another chamber from Bougon, B2, as well as chambers A and C at Champ-Châlon, appear to have been emptied at some stage. At Bougon B2 most of the long bones have been removed, although the presence of carpals suggests that complete bodies were buried here; 16 fragmentary skulls were left, either belonging to those buried in the chamber or brought in from elsewhere in the cemetery. At Champ-Châlon, similarly, the removal of the bones was not motivated by the need to create space for subsequent interments (ibid., 157, 163).

Although this review of the megaliths outside northern Europe has been extremely brief, the most important point emerging from the discussion is that of the immense regional diversity of burial structures from the early Neolithic onwards. Therefore, seeking precise equivalents of chamber forms among different regions of north-western Europe is a vain exercise. Our previous discussion of the north

European passage grave forms, for example, indicates little architectural relationship with passage graves from Britain or western France beyond the common idea of an accessible chamber. A comparison of ground plans of three-dimensional structures, so common to the older typological approaches, only obfuscates the issue. Indeed, there are only a limited number of ways in which to build a stone chamber and to assure its accessibility; for that reason alone we may encounter a degree of similarity which should be seen as functional rather than implying a particularly close genetic connection.

Seeking explanations for the emergence of megalithic structures in north-western Europe requires looking well beyond the architecture of the stone chambers, into the local preceding traditions and historical contexts of contemporary cultural developments. That the study of megalithic architecture in north-west Europe cannot be separated from the circumstances of the living communities responsible for its creation is a common-sense proposition, and this point has been made many times even if individual research projects have followed more specific trajectories. This approach may, for instance, take into consideration the relationship between the funerary and domestic architecture, although other aspects are equally relevant. A particularly poignant example may be the relationship between the principal forms of domestic dwellings and tombs found on the islands of Orkney, which was noted a long time ago and where recent research has emphasised the very strong symbolism of general as well as specific aspects of both tombs and dwellings, setting this relationship firmly within the local context (Richards 2005).

Laporte and Tinévez (2004) have explored a similar theme in the very complex scenario along the Atlantic façade. In brief, their argument encompasses the notion that here both the Danubian and the western Mediterranean currents may have played an important role, with some groups choosing to emphasise the domestic features, such as the elongated shape of the Danubian house, in the external appearance of the long mounds, while others may have concentrated on the symbolism of circular house forms or domestic storage structures in the internal arrangements, with emphasis placed upon the circular and quadrangular chambers, which were less visible but not necessarily less important.

On the other hand, evidence for contacts of both a short- and a long-distance nature between communities, seen through the dispersal of domesticated resources and the wide range of raw materials and finished artefacts, suggests that past models for indigenous regional developments need to be balanced against inter-cultural contacts. The intensity of such contacts may have fluctuated over space and time, but nevertheless they must have contributed greatly to the exchange of world views, ideas and practices over vast swathes of north-western Europe. Indeed, in this context, the widespread similarities in the treatment of the dead, ranging from full inhumations to selections of bone deposits, may be indicative of the emergence of a core of cosmologies which shared common principles and cognitive structures.

Conclusions

Now that we have reviewed the general context of the north-west European mega-liths, it is time to offer some concluding thoughts. Although they relate principally to the monuments of northern Europe which form the subject of this work, it is hoped that some of the conclusions discussed here may also have a wider, pan-European significance.

The various north European architectural forms – the closed and open dolmens and passage graves, with a plethora of regional variants – were discussed in detail in Chapter 3, and the evidence is by now familiar. While typological approaches, especially those relying heavily on two-dimensional plans of three-dimensional structures, are no longer in vogue, the general sequence of development of the north European megaliths, as established through the twentieth century, is sup-ported by the evidence available in terms of both architectural detail and chronol-ogy. The sequence commences with timber chambers, followed by a period of overlap when both timber and stone were used concurrently to create burial cham-bers, sometimes within the confines of the same monument. However, closed dolmens soon gave way to a variety of open forms, with permanent access to the chamber, and finally the complex open dolmens led to the highly sophisticated form of the passage grave. The precise details of the sequence, the coexistence and the variety of forms, as well as the popularity of particular architectural styles that emerged in different regions of northern Europe, naturally vary from one area to the next, but the general principle still holds good.

The monumental sequence in northern Europe thus begins in the middle of the fifth millennium BC, with the earthen long barrows forming veritable cemeteries across the north European plain, and slightly later expanding further north, where the barrows tend to be found singly or in pairs. They clearly were burial monuments, as fully attested by the presence of the dead, whose remains are found within a variety of timber chambers. However, as I and others have argued before, there is a further dimension to these sites, a commemorative element that links the emergence of monumentality with the ancestral past as seen through the prism of the Danubian communities, the first farmers across the vast swathes of central Europe. The arguments for the abandoned Danubian villages providing models for monumental long barrow cemeteries in Europe have been rehearsed many times, are briefly reiterated in Chapter 1, and require no repeti-tion here.

We may nevertheless consider the idea that knowledge of the Danubian past had an 'origin' value that contributed to the emergence of the new world views. Such knowledge most probably originated with the north European hunter-gatherers, some of whom may even have had a rare but direct contact with their southerly farming neighbours, and then passed from one generation to the next. While the Danubian ancestors were distant in both time and space, they were thought of as the originators and bringers of agriculture – of domesticated plants and animals, as well as of farming practices – and thus of a different way of life. In this sense the emergence of monumentality created a mythological link between the distant past and the newly developing farming communities in northern Europe.

However, we might also suggest that the commemorative, ancestral significance of the long barrow cemeteries – and, indeed, of early long mounds across the whole of north-western Europe – was only the first stage in the long process of evolving Neolithic world views. Irrespective of the social importance of the individuals interred within the timber chambers of the long barrows, their dead bones were not truly accessible, becoming, over the course of several generations, a distant memory of an even more distant past. But the Neolithic world view was evolving fast, and the changes following the time of the long barrows are indicative of the truly dynamic nature of Neolithic cosmologies.

In northern Europe, the various megalithic chamber forms that follow upon the timber barrow structures are best seen as local architectural developments. This is not to deny the contacts and influences that were reaching northern Europe from other regions, but these were most probably ideological and cosmological in nature rather than providing templates for specific structural forms. As noted earlier, the closed and early open dolmens can be regarded as replicas of the earlier timber chambers, whose own architectural variety was considerably greater than their surviving vestiges would suggest. Curiously, the practice of using twin stones in the construction of dolmens and passage graves may derive from the tradition of building timber chambers using split tree trunks, this carpentry technique being subsequently translated into a new medium, sometimes creating considerable constructional challenges. Initially it symbolically linked the stone and timber forms but, over time, the twin stones may have acquired their own symbolic meanings, being one of many expressions of duality that pervaded all levels of life.

The abundance of stone, in the form of glacial erratics, red sandstone and other rocks, provided an opportunity for the creation of architectural styles that reflected the constructional potential of the local building materials; the transformation of these natural materials into cultural forms firmly linked the communities with their natural environments. On the one hand, the change from timber to stone may have been related to a very practical aspect of land clearance, namely the need to provide areas suitable for agricultural activities that involved not only cutting down the forests but also the removal of large stones. On the other hand, the temporal qualities of stone must have been apparent, its natural properties providing permanence and longevity – the 'Tangible Durability' of Mary Helms's elegant phrase (Helms 1998).

As our discussion in Chapter 3 demonstrated, the building of megalithic tombs – the chambers and their covering mounds – was a considerable engineering feat, requiring great skill and expertise as well as profound knowledge of the different properties of building materials. Some monuments were substantial, requiring many months of work, a large workforce and skilled individuals – foremen and master builders – to oversee the building projects. Others demanded particular skills, such as making boulders stand on end, creating exceptionally wide chambers, manoeuvring huge capstones onto loose intermediary stone layers, or constructing complicated entrances.

While one would not wish to return to former ideas of either zealous megalithic missionaries or an exclusive priestly order within Neolithic society, it is clear that megalith building, in northern Europe as elsewhere, must have been one of the great Neolithic crafts, which not only called for exceptional technical skills but may also have been regarded as a power deriving from a privileged connection with the spiritual world. Such craftsmen – the master builders and their apprentices – combined technological expertise with an equally important symbolic knowledge. Not only could they design complex structures and find solutions to architectural problems but, at the same time, they would have understood the symbolic requirements of structures and possessed the esoteric knowledge of rituals needed for the megaliths to function within the cosmological order of the Neolithic world. It is not inconceivable that some of them were highly regarded and were sought after in different regions, providing skilled services to many communities. Indeed, some of the subtleties and intricacies of construction, such as are especially demonstrable in the Danish passage graves, clearly point to particular master builders, who may have been responsible for the construction of several different monuments (S. Hansen, pers. comm. 2004).

The transition from a closed to an accessible chamber, taking place some time after the first dolmens were built, was not only an architectural but an important functional change, which moreover was accompanied by a profound change in dealing with the dead and by a range of new rituals that were performed in the vicinity of tombs. Equally, the emergence of the passage grave form was a significant change that must have been related, at least in part, to a different way of using the chambers, perhaps ensuring greater seclusion of the interior while, at the same time, facilitating different ways of moving inside the chamber during interment ceremonies.

The existence of open chambers is not a purely north European characteristic. Accessibility of the chamber interior over time was, as we noted earlier, an important feature in all regions of north-west Europe where megaliths were constructed. Indeed in some areas, such as western France, such passages were extended by the addition of massive orthostats at a later stage of the monument's use, to create even more imposing means of access, while elsewhere they were emphasised by forecourts, decorated stones or elaborate kerb sections. This feature was not synchronous over the entire megalithic province, being clearly a later development in the north than along the Atlantic façade; together with other aspects of burial practices, it may well reflect the wider ideological aspect of the Neolithic view of the world, where contacts between different regions were conducive to the transmission and subsequent local elaboration of certain fundamental cosmological principles.

In her study of cosmology in low-technology societies, Mary Helms suggested that the adoption of an increasingly sedentary lifestyle and agriculture was accompanied by an important cosmological restructuring, in which a temporal dimension was added to the already existing spatial dimension, and that this addition required 'reconfigurations of the world of Others'. Within this framework the human dead, and their physical remains in the form of bones, held a very high potential for the elaboration of the temporal cosmological dimension and of ideas of duration and durability (Helms 1998, 48–9). This concept offers an interesting avenue to explore the phenomenon of accessibility of chambers, with the accompanying changes in the treatment of the dead.

New images and metaphors had to be developed to transform the dead into a temporal category of 'ancestors', and burial within a durable and accessible chamber – together with the elaboration of funerary rituals within and outside the chamber – offered an appropriate means to accomplish such a cosmological restructuring. Thus open chambers became the visible abodes of the dead members of households, shrines in which their bones, after the ritual cleaning, were brought and preserved. That such transition was further accompanied by a series of elaborate rituals has been demonstrated earlier in our discussion of the different treatments of the dead (Chapter 4). While burial practices across the north-west European megalithic province were diverse, there were also certain similarities: the most significant and recurrent acts performed during such prolonged funerary rituals involved the temporary storage of bodies, permitting the purification as well as the separation of body and soul, and the secondary (often fragmentary) burial in the megalithic chambers.

That the placement of the dead in a chamber was not the culmination of a protracted ritual is further evidenced by the periodic visitations that involved the sorting, display, and possible removal of ancestral remains, either to be circulated as relics among the living or deposited elsewhere. Thus the dead became an important symbolic resource. In Helms's phrase (ibid., 50), 'the most enduring portions of the physical remains of the dead themselves – long bones and skulls' became the most commonly encountered and most frequently rearranged fragments of human bodies in chambers across the whole of the north-west European megalithic province.

It was therefore the presence of ancestors in their accessible and durable chambers, and the elaborate burial rituals ultimately conferring that status, rather than the architectural form of the megalithic chambers themselves, that expressed the fundamental principles of Neolithic cosmologies. The precise sequence and form of the rituals naturally depended upon local circumstances, but it is through this symbolic treatment of the dead that a shared set of values within the Neolithic world became disseminated and formed part of the wider cosmology encountered across this vast area.

Naturally not all community members qualified to become 'ancestors'. The human remains surviving within the megalithic chambers – even if we account for the normal taphonomic processes, disturbances in subsequent periods of prehistory, and modern destruction – make it clear that only some community members were interred in the megaliths. Indeed, the evidence for other, non-megalithic burial in all regions suggests that many of the dead – placed in flat graves or in settlement pits, or obscured from view by the superimposition of megalithic chambers upon earlier graves – were relegated to future oblivion and are known only through accidents of archaeological discovery.

Ethnographic evidence from past and present communities demonstrates that only some individuals will achieve the status of ancestors who deserve to be remembered, are placed in ancestral shrines and serve the living community as models on account of their particular accomplishments. The criteria for achieving such a status within the Neolithic are difficult to judge, but they undoubtedly included a whole range of achievements in the social, economic and political life of communities, contributions to the communal well-being, and perhaps special relations with the outside world, however that was perceived.

The status of ancestor may thus have been bestowed variously upon a particularly charismatic or successful farmer, hunter, warrior or peacemaker. Special qualities, such as skilled craftsmanship, artistic prowess, ability to establish and maintain alliances, procurement of exotic and desirable goods from outside the home range, or esoteric knowledge acquired in the course of travel to distant places, may also have been important criteria for 'ancestorship'. It should therefore not be very surprising that the remains of the dead that we encounter within some megalithic chambers account for only a relatively small proportion of the contemporary population. Some chambers housing ancestral remains may have been sealed soon after the initial depositions, while others continued in use; community members deemed worthy of joining the 'original ancestors' may have been interred in such tombs over successive generations.

Against the background of these ancestral concepts, the burials of children offer an interesting case. Borgeby in Scania is a rather exceptional example of a cemetery devoted exclusively to non-adult burials, although such practices may have been more common than is attested in archaeological evidence. However, children's status in the megalithic burials is ambivalent. While some scholars are keen to see the Neolithic communities as hierarchical societies, in which the presence of children could be attributed to the social position of a family within such a system, there are other possibilities to account for the presence of children within the megaliths. Clearly, such young individuals could not have distinguished themselves sufficiently in their short lives in the social, political or economic spheres. On the one hand, it may be precisely because their life experience had been so short that they were buried under the protection of ancestors, to be guided along the difficult path to the afterworld. On the other hand, ethnographic evidence suggests that, in some societies, children are not fully integrated into the community and are sometimes regarded as personifications of the dead, more closely related to the world of the dead ancestors than to that of the living adults (Helms 1998, 24–5). Either of these factors may have played a role in placing children in the megalithic chambers.

Apart from the role the dead may have played in the cosmological dimension of time, creating tangible links with the past, present and future, other religious factors may have been symbolised in the elaborate process of burial ritual. In stark contrast to modern Western ideologies, many non-industrial societies have strong ideas about, and beliefs in, the afterlife. The prolonged process of transition from the world of the living to the world of the dead, and the importance of the separation of body and soul as expressed through secondary burial, were discussed previously (Chapter 4). It is important, however, to emphasise again that Neolithic burial practices, as witnessed in the context of the megaliths, may have embodied a wide range of world views in which the transition from one world to the next was also given particular expression. The dead were not necessarily thought dead, but just departed to a different world, and still a part of life. In the guise of their dry, hard, white bones, they continued to influence life – from small, individual benefactions, through crop fertility, to the general prosperity of the living communities on many levels.

Communication with the dead – be it in their ancestral or other capacities – was clearly important. While single acts of communication between the living and the dead are archaeologically virtually unidentifiable, we need not assume that such did not take place. Ethnographic evidence from many parts of the world suggests that conversation between individuals and their dead relatives, taking place outside the formal ritual framework, is an almost daily occurrence, that it forms an important element in the life of individuals and offers a medium through which personal requests and solicitations can be made. In times of particular need the tombs may have served as oracles and places of divination.

Public forms of communication that involved larger numbers of participants, on the other hand, are attested not only in the accessibility of the chambers and the manipulation of the bones of the deceased, but also in the numerous ritual acts that took place in the vicinity of the megalithic chambers, among which votive deposits – principally pottery, stone and flint tools – around the entrances are the clearest archaeological indicator. Apart from the depositing and destruction of objects, there would have been feasting, dancing, singing, recounting of myths, initiations and other activities. The scenarios associated with such activities may have been festivals of the dead, vigils designed for the ancestors or even for higher-order deities, access to whom was mediated by the dead resting inside the tomb. The relative rarity of such events may reflect the times when chambers were formally opened to rearrange or remove the bones within them; such occasions would only occur at ritually determined times, perhaps only once or twice for each particular megalith.

The belief that ancestors were involved in the well-being of a farming community was also given clear expression, as the marvel of the new human–plant–animal relationship became firmly associated with the regenerative powers of the ancestral bones. The offerings to the dead and, through their agency, to higher-level deities and spirits included various forms of agricultural produce: domesticated animals, caches of selected cereal grain or morsels of humble bread placed in front of megalithic tombs, as well as disposed of during formal ceremonies at causewayed enclosures, lakes, bogs and other locations.

More significantly, we noted earlier that many of the long barrows were located in previously cultivated fields, and that this practice continued throughout the

TRB, with many megalithic chambers similarly constructed upon ploughed land. Interpretation of this phenomenon requires more of an explanation than arguments about the introduction of the plough, or the simple opposition between ritual ploughing and accidental survival. Indeed, against the background of the 'distant origins' of agriculture, the relationship between cultivation and the dead clearly assumed an important dimension. In the early TRB, when farming in northern Europe began to be practised for the first time, it may itself have been as much a practical as a symbolic activity – ploughing the cleared land with the domesticated and treasured oxen in order to create conditions for the growing of recently acquired cereals. If ancestors were thought to have played an important role – as instigators of agriculture, as guardians of previously cleared land and as a medium through which good harvests could be ensured – then placing the dead in the midst of that for which they were responsible must have been an entirely logical act.

The Falbygden plateau in Sweden, with its linear arrangement of tombs and the complementary use of igneous and metamorphic rocks, constitutes one of the most evocative expressions of the juxtaposition of the importance of ancestors within the agricultural context with other factors within the life of local communities, which may have involved accommodating strangers. Recent isotope analyses of human remains suggest that between 20 and 25 per cent of the population buried there were incomers, most probably from western Sweden; cattle found in the region also appear to have come from outside (K.-G. Sjögren, pers. comm. 2007). These analyses have only just begun, but they offer an interesting possibility for the future interpretation of the extraordinary formality of this funerary landscape against the background of the circulation of domestic stock and of agricultural produce as well as other commodities, which may have come about as a result of population movement, whether on a temporary, seasonal or permanent basis.

The idea that megaliths served as signalling devices has been suggested many times within different interpretative paradigms: from the processual view of tombs as territorial markers within heavily populated regions, to the metaphorical relationship between the megaliths and natural landscape features of the phenomenological approaches (Renfrew 1976; Chapman 1981; Tilley 1994, 2004). That the location of the megaliths expressed concepts other than only the relationship between ancestors and agriculture was suggested in our discussion of the distribution of the megaliths (Chapter 2). Indeed, in certain regions of northern Europe the employment of locally available raw materials, as well as the siting of the monuments, does lend itself to phenomenological interpretations.

Several regions do offer evidence for the deliberate siting of tombs in relation to islands, coastlines, rivers, slopes and other natural landscape features, although over such a vast area there are no simple patterns. Random scatters, variations between the clustered and dispersed distributions, as well as striking linear arrangements across some of the landscapes, must have embodied a whole range of expression intended to convey a wide range of meanings, from cultural liminality of the abodes for the dead to the signalling of ancestral presence to strangers. The fact that so many megaliths are found along the much later, historically attested communication routes supports the idea that they also played a role in the overall network of contacts and communication between different regions.

Indeed, ancestors are frequently associated with long-distance travel, either through myths of origin and migration, or through blessings before and protection during a journey. Thus, under certain conditions, the megaliths may also have been protective and instructive devices placed along frequently traversed routes. Moreover, ethnographic evidence further demonstrates that transactions – exchanges – between strangers are frequently formal occasions that are structured and follow certain patterns. They have profound consequences on the social life of individuals as well as communities; often, existence and survival (in social rather than economic terms) depends on the successful establishment and subsequent maintenance of allegiances and obligations. Such processes require appropriate formal settings, and megaliths – perhaps in conjunction with other types of site such as causewayed enclosures – may have created a network of places at which encounters with strangers *en route* could be conducted in safety, under the protective watch of the ancestors.

The north European megaliths not only rank among the most enduring structures built in prehistory but, imbued with numerous symbolic meanings which we have tried to interpret throughout the pages of this work, they reflected the various levels of Neolithic life. They bridged the gap between immediate, quotidian and local realities and the anomalous entities of the multi-dimensional universe in which past, present and future were given the tangible permanence that fascinates us today and will continue to do so in the future. In the cosmological model of the Neolithic world – in so far as it can be elucidated by the archaeological evidence from this remote period – the megaliths thus appear as the physical and conceptual expressions of the very core of Neolithic ideas about the nature of the world inhabited by the first northern farmers.

BIBLIOGRAPHY

Ahlström, T. (2001), 'Det döda kollektivet Skelettmaterialet från Rössbergagånggriften', in P. Persson and K.-G. Sjögren, *Falbygdens gånggrifter, Del 1. Undersökningar 1985–1998*, Göteborg: Göteborgs universitet, 301–57.

Ahlström, T. (2003), 'Grave or ossuary? Osteological finds from a recently excavated passage tomb in Falbygden, Sweden', in G. Burenhult (ed.), *Stones and Bones, Formal disposal of the dead in Atlantic Europe during the Mesolithic-Neolithic interface 6000–3000 BC*, 253–69, Oxford: British Archaeological Reports, International Series 1201.

Albrethsen, S. E. and Brinch Petersen, E. (1977), 'Excavation of a Mesolithic cemetery at Vedbæk, Denmark', *Acta Archaeologica* 47, 1–28.

Andersen, N. H. (1997), *Sarup Vol. 1: The Sarup Enclosures*, Moesgaard: Jutland Archaeological Society Publications XXXIII:1.

Andersen, N. H. (2000), 'Kult og ritualer i den ældre bondestenalder', *Kuml 2000*, 13–57.

Andersen, S. H. and Johansen, E. (1992), 'An Early Neolithic Grave at Bjørnsholm, North Jutland', *Journal of Danish Archaeology* 9 (1990), 38–58.

Andersen, S. Th. (1988), 'Pollen Spectra from the Double Passage-Grave, Klekkendehøj, on Møn. Evidence of Swidden Cultivation in the Neolithic of Denmark', *Journal of Danish Archaeology* 7, 77–92.

Andersen, S. Th. (1995), 'Pollen analytical investigations of barrows from the Funnel Beaker and Single Grave Cultures in the Vroue area, West Jutland, Denmark', *Journal of Danish Archaeology* 12 (1994–5), 107–32.

Andersson, M. (2004), 'Domestication and the first Neolithic concept 4800–3000 BC', in M. Andersson, P. Karsten, B. Knarrström and M. Svensson (eds), *Stone Age Scania, Significant places dug and read by contract archaeology*, Malmö: Riksantikvarieämbetets Förlag, Skrifter No 52, 143–90.

Aner, E. (1963), 'Die Stellung der Dolmen Schleswig-Holsteins in der nordischen Megalithkultur,' *Offa* 20, 9–38.

Ashbee, P. (1966), 'The Fussell's Lodge Long Barrow Excavations 1957', *Archaeologia* 100, 1–80.

Ashbee, P. (1970), *The Earthen Long Barrow in Britain,* London: J. M. Dent.

Asmus, G. (1987), 'Menschliche Schädelfragmente aus der Grabung Bundsø-Flintholm', in J. Hoika (1987) *Das Mittelneolithikum zur Zeit der Trichterbecherkultur in Nordostholstein*, Offa-Bücher 61, Neumünster: Wachholtz, 265–7.

Assendorp, J. J. (2004a), 'Archäologie der Geest', in M. Fansa, F. Both and H. Haßmann (eds), *Archäologie, Land, Niedersachsen. 25 Jahre Denkmalschutzgesetz – 400 000 Jahre Geschichte*, Oldenburg: Theiss, 337–46.

Assendorp, J. J. (2004b), 'Die TBK Siedlung von Pennigbüttel, Ldkr. Osterholz', in M. Fansa, F. Both and H. Haßmann (eds), *Archäologie, Land, Niedersachsen. 25 Jahre Denkmalschutzgesetz – 400 000 Jahre Geschichte*, Oldenburg: Theiss, 366–8.

Atkinson, R. J. C. (1965), 'Wayland's Smithy', *Antiquity* 39, 126–33.

Axelsson, T. and Sjögren, K.-G. (2001), 'Gånggriften vid Frälsegården i Gökhem: fortsatta undersökningar 2001', *Falbygden Årsbok* 55, 73–81.

Axelsson, T. and Strinnholm, A. (2003), 'Beads of Belonging and Tokens of Trust. Neolithic Amber Beads from Megaliths in Sweden', in C. W. Beck, I. B. Loze and J. M. Todd (eds), *Amber in Archaeology. Proceedings of the Fourth International Conference on Amber in Archaeology, Talsi, 2001*, Riga: Institute of the History of Latvia Publishers, 116–25.

Axelsson, T., Heimann, C. and Sjögren, K.-G. (2003), *Falbygdens gånggrifter – bevarande och kunskapsförmedling*, Göteborg: Göteborgs universitet.

Bagge, A. and Kaelas, L. (1950/1952), *Die Funde aus Dolmen und Ganggräbern in Schonen, Schweden*, Stockholm: Wahlström & Wildstrand (Vol. I, 1950; Vol. II, 1952).

Baier, R. (1896), 'Tongefässe aus der Steinzeit auf der Insel Rügen', *Verhandlungen der Berliner Gesellschaft für Anthropologie, Ethnologie und Urgeschichte*, 350–61.

Bailloud, G., Boujot, C., Cassen, S. and Le Roux, C.-T. (1995), *Carnac. Les premières architectures de pierre*, Paris: CNRS Éditions.

Bakker, J. A. (1976), 'On the Possibility of Reconstructing Roads from the TRB Period', *Berichten van de Rijksdienst voor het Oudheidkundig Bodemonderzoek* 26, 63–91.

Bakker, J. A. (1979), 'July 1878: Lukis and Dryden in Drenthe', *The Antiquaries Journal* 59, 9–18.

Bakker, J. A. (1988), 'A list of the extant and formerly present *hunebedden* in the Netherlands', *Palaeohistoria* 30, 63–72.

Bakker, J. A. (1991), 'Prehistoric long-distance roads in North-West Europe', in J. Lichardus (ed.), *Die Kupferzeit als historische Epoche*, Symposium Saarbrücken und Otzenhausen 6–13 Nov. 1988, Bonn: Dr. Rudolf Habelt GmbH, 505–28.

Bakker, J. A. (1992), *The Dutch Hunebedden, Megalithic Tombs of the Funnel Beaker Culture*, International Monographs in Prehistory, Archaeological Series 2, Michigan: Ann Arbor.

Bakker, J. A. (1999), 'The Dutch megalithic tombs, with a glance at those of north-west Germany', in K. W. Beinhauer, G. Cooney, C. Guksch and S. Kus (eds), *Studien zur Megalithik: Forschungsstand und ethnoarchäologische Perspektiven*, Weissbach: Verlag Beier & Beran, 145–62.

Bakker, J. A., Kruk, J., Lanting, A. E. and Milisauskas, S. (1999), 'The earliest evidence of wheeled vehicles in Europe and the Near East', *Antiquity* 73, 778–90.

Barclay, G. J. and Maxwell, G. S. (1998), *The Cleaven Dyke and Littleour: Monuments in the Neolithic of Tayside*, Edinburgh: Society of Antiquaries of Scotland.

Barley, N. (1994), *Smashing Pots: Feats of Clay from Africa*, London: British Museum Press.

Barley, N. (1995), *Dancing on the Grave: Encounters with Death*, London: John Murray.

Barrett, J. C. (1988), 'The Living, the Dead and the Ancestors: Neolithic and Early Bronze Age Mortuary Practices', in J. C. Barrett and I. A. Kinnes (eds), *The Archaeology of Context in the Neolithic and Bronze Age: Recent Trends*, Sheffield: Department of Archaeology and Prehistory, 30–41.

Becker, C. J. (1996), 'Tragtbægerkulturens mellemneolitiske kulthuse', in K. Fabricius and C. J. Becker, *Stendyngegrave og Kulthuse. Studier over Tragtbægerkulturen i Nord- og Vestjylland*, Arkæologiske Studier XI, Copenhagen: Akademisk Forlag, 277–362.

Behre, K.-E. (2005), 'Die Einengung des neolithischen Lebensraumes in Nordwestdeutschland durch klimabedingte Faktoren: Meeresspiegelanstieg und großflächige Ausbreitung von Mooren', in D. Gronenborg (ed.), *Klimaveränderung und Kulturwandel in neolithischen*

Gesellschaften Mitteleuropas, 6700–2200 v. Chr., Mainz: Verlag des Römisch-Germanischen Zentralmuseums, 209–20.

Beier, H.-J. (1995), 'Die hercynische Megalithik. Gedanken aus mitteldeutscher Sicht', *Jahresschrift für mitteldeutsche Vorgeschichte* 77, 89–120.

Beinhauer, K. W., Cooney, G., Guksch, C. E. and Kus, S. (eds) (1999), *Studien zur Megalithik*, Weissbach: Beier & Beran.

Beltz, R. (1899), 'Die steinzeitlichen Fundstellen in Mecklenburg', *Jahrbuch des Vereins für Mecklenburgische Geschichte und Alterthumskunde* 64, 78–192.

Beltz, R. (1910), *Die vorgeschichtlichen Altertümer des Großherzogtums Mecklenburg*, Berlin: Reimer.

Bénéteau-Douillard, G. (2006), 'Les alignements de menhirs anthropomorphes du sud de la Vendée. Architectonique, iconographie et art pariétal', in R. Joussaume, L. Laporte and C. Scarre (eds), *Origine et développement du mégalithisme de l'ouest de l'Europe*, Colloque international du 26 au 30 octobre 2002, Musée des Tumulus de Bougon (Deux-Sèvres), Vols 1 and 2, Niort: Conseil Général des Deux-Sèvres, 567–75.

Bennike, P. (1985), 'Stenalderbefolkningen på øerne syd for Fyn', in J. Skaarup, *Yngre Stenalder på øerne syd for Fyn*, Rudkøbing: Langelands Museum, 467–91.

Bennike, P. (1990), 'Human Remains from the Grøfte Dolmen', *Journal of Danish Archaeology* 7 (1988), 70–6.

Bennike, P. (1999), 'The Early Neolithic Danish bog finds: a strange group of people!', in B. Coles, J. Coles and M. S. Jørgensen (eds), *Bog Bodies, Sacred Sites and Wetland Archaeology*, Exeter: WARP Occasional Paper 12, 27–32.

Bennike, P., Ebbesen, K. and Jørgensen, L. B. (1986), 'Early neolithic skeletons from Bolkilde bog, Denmark', *Antiquity* 60, 199–209.

Bennike, P. and Ebbesen, K. (1987), 'The Bog Find from Sigersdal. Human sacrifice in the Early Neolithic', *Journal of Danish Archaeology* 5 (1986), 85–115.

Berg, H. (1956), 'Langdolmen bei Pæregaard, Langeland', *Acta Archaeologica* 27, 108–27.

Binford, L. R. (1971), 'Mortuary practices: Their study and their potential', in J. A. Brown (ed.), *Approaches to the social dimensions of mortuary practices,* Memoirs of the Society for American Archaeology no. 25, Washington: Society for American Archaeology, 6–29.

Birren, F. (1978), *Colour and Human Response*, New York: Van Nostrand Reinhold.

Bloch, M. (1971), *Placing the Dead: Tombs, Ancestral Villages and Kinship Organisation in Madagascar*, London: Seminar.

Bock, H., Fritsch, B. and Mittag, L. (2006), *Großsteingräber der Altmark*, Halle: Landesamt für Denkmalpflege und Archäologie Sachsen-Anhalt.

Bogucki, P. (2003), 'Transegalitarian Societies in Mid-Neolithic Europe, 5000–3000 B.C.', paper presented at *Heterarchy and Hierarchy in European Prehistory*, a symposium in honour of Bernard Wailes on the occasion of his retirement at the University Museum, University of Pennsylvania, 5 April 2000 (unpublished manuscript).

Bouin, F. and Joussaume, R. (1998), 'Le tumulus du Planti à Availles-sur-Chizé', in R. Joussaume (ed.) *Les premiers paysans du Golfe. Le Néolithique dans le Marais poitevin*, Chauray: Éditions Patrimoines et Médias, 79.

Boujot, C. and Cassen, S. (1993), 'A pattern of evolution for the Neolithic funerary structures of the west of France', *Antiquity* 67, 477–91.

Bradley, R. (1998a), *The Passage of Arms. An archaeological analysis of prehistoric hoard and votive deposits*, Oxford: Oxbow Books (2nd edn).

Bradley, R. (1998b), *The Significance of Monuments. On the Shaping of Human Experience in Neolithic and Bronze Age Europe*, London: Routledge.

Bradley, R. (2000), *An Archaeology of Natural Places*, London: Routledge.

Bradley, R. (2002), *The Past in Prehistoric Societies*, London: Routledge.

Bradley, R. (2005), *Ritual and Domestic Life in Prehistoric Europe*, London: Routledge.

Bradley, R. (2007), *The Prehistory of Britain and Ireland*, Cambridge: Cambridge University Press.

Bradley, R. and Phillips, T. (2004), 'The high-water mark: the siting of megalithic tombs on the Swedish island of Tjörn', *Oxford Journal of Archaeology* 23, 123–33.

Brindley, A. (1986), 'Hunebed G2: excavation and finds', *Palaeohistoria* 28, 27–92.

Brøndsted, J. (1957), *Danmarks Oldtid: I. Stenalderen*, Copenhagen: Gyldendal.

Burchard, B. (1998), 'Badania grobowców typu megalitycznego w Zagaju Stradowskim w południowej Polsce', *Sprawozdania Archeologiczne* 50, 149–56.

Burenhult, G. (ed.) (1984), *The Archaeology of Carrowmore, Co. Sligo*, Theses and Papers in North-European Archaeology 14, Stockholm: Institute of Archaeology.

Burenhult, G. (ed.) (2003), *Stones and Bones. Formal disposal of the dead in Atlantic Europe during the Mesolithic-Neolithic interface 6000–3000 BC*, BAR International Series 1201, Oxford: Archaeopress.

Caillaud, R. and Lagnel, É. (1972), 'Le cairn et le crématoire néolithiques de La Hoguette à Fontenay-le-Marmion', *Gallia Préhistoire* 15, 137–97.

Carr, C. (1995), 'Mortuary Practices: Their Social, Philosophical-Religious, Circumstantial, and Physical Determinants', *Journal of Archaeological Method and Theory* 2, 105–200.

Casparie, W. A. and Groenman-van Waateringe, W. (1980), 'Palynological analysis of Dutch barrows', *Palaeohistoria* 22, 7–65.

Caspers, G., Elbracht, J., Schwarz, C. and Streif, H. (2005), 'Lebensraum Niedersachsen: Geologie und Landschaftsgeschichte', in M. Fansa, F. Both and H. Haßmann (eds), *Archäologie, Land, Niedersachsen. 25 Jahre Denkmalschutzgesetz – 400 000 Jahre Geschichte*, Oldenburg: Theiss, 41–53.

Cassen, S., Audren, C., Hinguant, S., Lannuzel, G. and Marchand, G. (1998), 'L'Habitat Villeneuve-St-Germain du Haut Mée (Saint-Étienne-en-Coglès, Ille-et-Vilaine)', *Bulletin de la Société Préhistorique Française* 95, 41–76.

Cassen, S., Boujot, C. and Vaquero, J. (2000), *Éléments d'architecture. Exploration d'un tertre funéraire à Lannec er Gadouer (Erdeven, Morbihan). Constructions et reconstructions dans le Néolithique morbihannais. Propositions pour une lecture symbolique.* Chauvigny: Association des Publications Chauvinoises.

Chambon, P. (1997), 'La nécropole de Balloy «Les Réaudins»: approche archéo-anthropologique', in C. Constantin, D. Mordant and D. Simonin (eds), *La culture de Cerny. Nouvelle économie, nouvelle société au Néolithique*, Actes du Colloque international de Nemours, 9–10–11 mai 1994, Mémoires du Musée de Préhistoire d'Île-de-France, no. 6, 489–98.

Chambon, P. (2003a), 'Revoir Passy à la lumière de Balloy: les nécropoles monumentales Cerny du bassin Seine-Yonne', *Bulletin de la Société Préhistorique Française* 100, 505–15.

Chambon, P. (2003b), *Les Morts dans les Sépultures Collectives Néolithiques en France. Du Cadavre aux Restes Ultimes*, XXXVe supplément à Gallia Préhistoire, Paris: CNRS Éditions.

Chancerel, A. and Desloges, J. (1998), 'Les sépultures pré-mégalithiques de Basse-Normandie', in J. Guilaine (ed.), *Sépultures d'Occident et genèses des mégalithismes (9000–3500 avant notre ère), Séminaire du Collège de France*, Paris: Éditions Errance, 91–106.

Chapman, R., (1981), 'The emergence of formal disposal areas and the "problem" of megalithic tombs in prehistoric Europe', in R. Chapman, I. Kinnes and K. Randsborg (eds), *The Archaeology of Death*, New Directions in Archaeology, Cambridge: Cambridge University Press, 71–81.

Chapman, R., Kinnes, I. and Randsborg, K. (eds) (1981), *The Archaeology of Death*, New Directions in Archaeology, Cambridge: Cambridge University Press.

Clark, G. (1977), 'The Economic Context of Dolmens and Passage Graves in Sweden', in V. Markotic (ed.), *Ancient Europe and the Mediterranean*, Warminster: Aris and Phillips, 35–49.

Clifford, E. M. (1938), 'The excavation of Nympsfield long barrow', *Proceedings of the Prehistoric Society* 4, 188–213.

Coles, J. M. and Simpson, D. D. A. (1965), 'The Excavation of a Neolithic Round Barrow at Pitnacree, Perthshire, Scotland', *Proceedings of the Prehistoric Society* 31, 34–57.

Cooney, G. (2000), *Landscapes of Neolithic Ireland*, London: Routledge.

Coye, N. (1997), *La Préhistoire en Parole et en Acte. Méthodes et enjeux de la pratique archéologique 1830–1950*, Collection Histoire des Sciences Humaines, Paris: L'Harmattan.

Cummings, V. and Whittle, A. (2004), *Places of Special Virtue. Megaliths in the Neolithic Landscape of Wales*, Oxford: Oxbow Books.

Cummings, V. and Pannett, A. (2005), *Set in Stone. New Approaches to Neolithic Monuments in Scotland*, Oxford: Oxbow Books.

Davidson, J. L. and Henshall, A. S. (1989), *The Chambered Cairns of Orkney: an inventory of the structures and their contents*, Edinburgh: Edinburgh University Press.

Dehn, T. and Hansen, S. (2000), 'Doubleness in the Construction of Danish Passage Graves', in A. Ritchie (ed.), *Neolithic Orkney in its European Context*, Cambridge: McDonald Institute for Archaeological Research, 215–21.

Dehn, T. and Hansen, S. (2006a), 'Megalithic architecture in Scandinavia', in R. Joussaume, L. Laporte and C. Scarre (eds), *Origine et développement du mégalithisme de l'ouest de l'Europe*, Colloque international du 26 au 30 octobre 2002, Musée des Tumulus de Bougon (Deux-Sèvres), Vols 1 and 2, Niort: Conseil Général des Deux-Sèvres, 39–61.

Dehn, T. and Hansen, S. (2006b), 'Birch bark in Danish passage graves', *Journal of Danish Archaeology* 14, 23–44.

Dehn, T. and Hansen, S. (2007), 'Examples of megalithic technology and architecture in Denmark', in J. H. F. Bloemers (ed.), *Tussen D26 en P14: Jan Albert Bakker 65 jaar*, Amsterdam: Amsterdams Archeologisch Centrum, 17–31.

Dehn, T., Hansen, S. and Kaul, F. (1995), *Kong Svends Høj. Restaureringer og undersøgelser på Lolland 1991*, Stenaldergrave i Danmark, Bind 1, Copenhagen: Skov- og Naturstyrelsen.

Dehn, T., Hansen, S. and Kaul, F. (2000), *Klekkendehøj og Jordehøj. Restaureringer og undersøgelser 1985–90*, Stenaldergrave i Danmark, Bind 2, Copenhagen: Skov- og Naturstyrelsen.

Dehn, T., Hansen, S. and Westphal, J. (2004), 'Jættestuen Birkehøj. Restaureringen af en 5000 år gammel storstensgrav', *Nationalmuseets Arbejdsmark* 2004, 153–73.

Ebbesen, K. (1975), *Die jüngere Trichterbecherkultur auf den dänischen Inseln*, Copenhagen: Akademisk Forlag.

Ebbesen, K. (1978), *Tragtbægerkultur i Nordjylland, Studier over Jættestuetiden*, Copenhagen: Det Kongelige Nordiske Oldskriftselskab.

Ebbesen, K. (1979), *Stordyssen i Vedsted, Studier over tragtbægerkulturen i Sønderjylland*, Copenhagen: Akademisk Forlag.

Ebbesen, K. (1982), 'Yngre stenalders depotfund som bebyggelseshistorisk kildemateriale', in H. Thrane (ed.), *Om Yngre Stenalders Bebyggelseshistorie*, Odense: Skrifter fra Historisk Institut, 60–79.

Ebbesen, K. (1985), *Fortidsminderegistering i Danmark*, Copenhagen: Fredningsstyrelsen.

Ebbesen, K. (1986a), 'Megalithic Graves in Schleswig-Holstein', *Acta Archaeologica* 55, 117–42.

Ebbesen, K. (1986b), 'Bornholms dysser og jættestuer', *Særtryk af Bornholmske Samlinger 1985*, 175–211.

Ebbesen, K. (1990), 'The Long Dolmen at Grøfte, South-West Zealand', *Journal of Danish Archaeology* 7 (1988), 53–69.

Ebbesen, K. (1995), 'Die nordischen Bernsteinhorte der Trichterbecherkultur', *Praehistorische Zeitschrift* 70, 32–89.

Eckert, J. (1999), 'Das Großsteingrab in Rheine', *Rheine gestern – heute – morgen. Expedition in die Vergangenheit, Archäologische Bodenschätze aus Rheine* 1999, Rheine: Greven, 96–105.

Eogan, G. (1997), 'Overlays and underlays: Aspects of megalithic art succession at Burgh na Bóinne, Ireland', in J. M. Bello Diéguez (ed.), *III Coloquio internacional de arte megalítico: Actas*, La Coruña, Brigantium 10, 217–34.

Eriksen, P. (1999), *Poskær Stenhus, Myter og Virkelighed*, Moesgård: Moesgård Museum.

Eriksen, P. (2002), 'Ramper og stilladser. Løft af store sten i oldtiden', *Kuml 2002*, 65–106.

Eriksen, P. (2004), 'Newgrange og den hvide mur', *Kuml 2004*, 45–76.

Estorff, G. O. C. von (1846), *Heidnische Alterthümer: der Gegend von Uelzen im ehemaligen Bardengaue*, Hannover: Hahn'sche Hof-Buchhandlung.

Fabricius, K. and Becker, C. J. (1996), *Stendyngegrave og Kulthuse. Studier over Tragtbægerkulturen i Nord- og Vestjylland*, Copenhagen: Akademisk Forlag.

Fansa, M. (1978), 'Die Keramik der Trichterbecherkultur aus dem Megalithgrab I von Ostenwalde, Kreis Aschendorf-Hümmling', *Neue Ausgrabungen und Forschungen in Niedersachsen* 12, 33–77.

Fergusson, J. (1872), *Rude Stone Monuments in All Countries: Their Age and Uses*, London: John Murray.

Fischer, A. (1982), 'Trade in Danubian shaft-hole axes and the introduction of Neolithic economy in Denmark', *Journal of Danish Archaeology* 1, 7–12.

Fischer, U. (1956), *Die Gräber der Steinzeit im Saalegebiet*, Berlin: Walter de Gruyter & Co.

Frederik VII (1862), *Om Bygningsmaaden af Oldtidens Jættestuer*, Copenhagen: Berlingske Bogtrykkeri ved L. N. Kalckar. (English version 'On the construction of "giants' Houses", or "Cromlechs"', reprinted from *Archaeologia Cambrensis*, January 1862.)

Fritsch, B. and Müller, J. (2002), 'Die Megalithgräber in der Altmark', in B. Fritsch (ed.), *Hünengräber – Siedlungen – Gräberfelder*, Archäologie in der Altmark, Band 1: Von der Altsteinzeit bis zum Frühmittelalter, Oschersleben: Dr. Ziethen Verlag, 63–73.

Gabriel, I. (1966), 'Das Megalithgrab zu Tannenhausen, Kreis Aurich', *Neue Ausgrabungen und Forschungen in Niedersachsen* 3, 82–101.

Gandert, O.-F. (1964), 'Zur Frage der Rinderanschirrung im Neolithikum', *Jahrbuch des Römisch-Germanischen Zentralmuseums Mainz* 11, 34–56.

Gebauer, A. B. (1990), 'The Long Dolmen at Asnæs Forskov, West Zealand', *Journal of Danish Archaeology* 7 (1988), 40–52.

Gehl, O. (1972), 'Das Baumaterial der Megalithgräber in Mecklenburg', in E. Schuldt, *Die mecklenburgischen Megalithgräber*, Berlin: Deutscher Verlag der Wissenschaften, 109–15.

Giot, P.-R. (1981), 'The Megaliths of France', in C. Renfrew (ed.) *The Megalithic Monuments of Western Europe*, London: Thames and Hudson, 18–20.

Giot, P.-R. (1987), *Barnenez, Carn, Guennoc*, Rennes: Travaux du Laboratoire d'Anthropologie, Préhistoire, Protohistoire et Quaternaire Armoricains.

Glob, P. V. (1949), 'Barkær. Danmarks ældste landsby', *Nationalmuseets Arbejdsmark* 1949, 5–16.

Gräslund, B. (1994), 'Prehistoric Soul Beliefs in Northern Europe', *Proceedings of the Prehistoric Society* 60, 15–26.

Hansen, S. (1993), *Jættestuer i Danmark, Konstruktion og restaurering*, Copenhagen: Skovog Naturstyrelsen.

Hårdh, B. (1982), 'The Megalithic Grave Area around the Lödde-Kävlinge River', *Meddelanden från Lunds universitets historiska museum 1987–1988*, New Series 4, 29–47.

Hårdh, B. (1986), *Ceramic Decoration and Social Organisation: Regional Variation Seen in Material from South Swedish Passage-Graves*, Scripta Minora 1985–1986:1, Lund: CWK Gleerup.

Hårdh, B. (1989), *Patterns of Deposition and Settlement: Studies on the Megalithic Tombs of West Scania*, Scripta Minora 1988–1989:2, Stockholm: Almqvist & Wiksell International.

Hårdh, B. and Bergström, J. (1988), 'Red Walling in Passage-tombs', *Meddelanden från Lunds universitets historiska museum 1987–1988*, New Series 7, 40–52.

Haßmann, H. (2000), *Die Steinartefakte der befestigten neolithischen Siedlung von Büdelsdorf, Kreis Rendsburg-Eckernförde*, Universitätsforschungen zur prähistorischen Archäologie, Band 62, Bonn: Dr. Rudolf Habelt GmbH.

Hayen, H. (1987), 'Peatbog Archaeology in Lower Saxony, West Germany', in J. M. Coles and A. J. Lawson (eds), *European Wetlands in Prehistory*, Oxford: Clarendon, 117–226.

Hedges, J. (1984), *Tomb of the Eagles*, London: John Murray.

Helms, M. (1988), *Ulysses' Sail. An Ethnographic Odyssey of Power, Knowledge, and Geographical Distance*, Princeton: Princeton University Press.

Helms, M. (1993), *Craft and the Kingly Ideal. Art, Trade, and Power*, Austin: University of Texas Press.

Helms, M. (1998), *Access to Origins. Affines, Ancestors and Aristocrats*, Austin: University of Texas Press.

Henshall, A. S. (1963), *The Chambered Tombs of Scotland*, Edinburgh: Edinburgh University Press.

Hertz, R. (1960), *Death and The Right Hand* (trans. Rodney and Claudia Needham), Aberdeen: Cohen and West.

Hingst, H. (1971), 'Ein befestigtes Dorf aus der Jungsteinzeit in Büdelsdorf, Kr. Rendsburg-Eckerförde', *Offa* 28, 90–93.

Hingst, H. (1985), 'Großsteingräber in Schleswig-Holstein', *Offa* 42, 57–112.

Hodder, I. and Shand, P. (1988), 'The Haddenham long barrow: an interim report', *Antiquity* 62, 349–53.

Hoika, J. (1986), 'Die Bedeutung des Oldenburger Grabens für Besiedlung und Verkehr im Neolithikum, *Offa* 43, 185–208.

Hoika, J. (1990), 'Megalithic Graves in the Funnel Beaker Culture of Schleswig-Holstein', *Przegląd Archeologiczny* 37, 53–119.

Hoika, J. (1999), 'Trichterbecherkultur – Megalithkultur? Überlegungen zum Bestattungsbrauchtum der Trichterbecherkultur in Schleswig-Holstein und Mecklenburg', in K. W. Beinhauer, G. Cooney, C. Guksch and S. Kus (eds), *Studien zur Megalithik: Forschungsstand und ethnoarchäologische Perspektiven*, Weissbach: Verlag Beier & Beran, 173–98.

Holsten, R. and Zahnow, G. (1920), 'Die steinzeitlichen Gräber des Kreises Pyritz', *Mannus* 1/2, 104–34.

Holten, L. (2000), 'Death, Danger, Destruction and Unintended Megaliths: an Essay on Human Classification and its Material and Social Consequences in the Neolithic of South Scandinavia', in A. Ritchie (ed.), *Neolithic Orkney in its European Context*, Cambridge: McDonald Institute for Archaeological Research, 287–97.

Jacob-Friesen, K. H. (1925), 'Die "Sieben Steinhäuser" im Kreise Fallingbostel', *Führer zu urgeschichtlichen Fundstätten Niedersachsens* 1, 3–24.

Jacobsson, B. (1986), 'The Skogsdala Dolmen. A Long Dolmen beneath a Bronze Age Burial Mound at Skogsdal, South Scania, Sweden', *Meddelanden från Lunds universitets historiska museum 1985–86*, 84–114.

Jager, S. W. (1985), 'A prehistoric route and ancient cart-tracks in the *Gemeente* of Anloo (Province Drenthe)', *Palaeohistoria* 27, 185–245.

Jankowska, D. (1999), 'Megalithik und kujawische Gräber', in K. W. Beinhauer, G. Cooney, C. Guksch and S. Kus (eds), *Studien zur Megalithik: Forschungsstand und ethnoarchäologische Perspektiven*, Weissbach: Verlag Beier & Beran, 215–26.

Johansen, B.-J. (2003), *Øm Jættestue. En stenaldergrav i Danmark*, Lejre: Little Creek Publishing.

Johansson, L. (1982), 'Bistoft LA 11. Siedlungs- und Wirtschaftsformen im frühen Neolithikum Norddeutschlands und Südskandinaviens', *Offa* 38 (1981) 91–129.

Jones, A. (1999), 'Local Colour: Megalithic Architecture and Colour Symbolism in Neolithic Arran', *Oxford Journal of Archaeology* 18, 339–50.

Jones, A. and MacGregor, G. (eds) (2002), *Colouring the Past. The Significance of Colour in Archaeological Research*, Oxford: Berg.

Jørgensen, E. (1977a), *Hagebrogård – Vroue – Koldkur. Neolithische Gräberfelder aus Nordwest-Jütland*, Arkæologiske Studier IV, Copenhagen: Akademisk Forlag.

Jørgensen, E. (1977b), 'Brændende Landgysser', *Skalk* 1977, 7–13.

Joussaume, R. (1997), 'Les longs tumulus du Centre-Ouest de la France', in R. R. Casal (ed.), *O Neolítico Atlántico e as Orixes do Megalitismo*, Acta do Coloquio Internacional (Santiago de Compostela, 1–6 de abril de 1996), Universidade de Santiago de Compostela, 279–97.

Joussaume, R. (1998), 'Les Tumulus de Champ-Châlon à Benon', in R. Joussaume (ed.) *Les premiers paysans du Golfe. Le Néolithique dans le Marais poitevin*, Chauray: Éditions Patrimoines et Médias, 58–9.

Joussaume, R. (2003), *Les Charpentiers de la pierre. Monuments mégalithiques dans le monde*, Paris: La Maison des Roches.

Joussaume, R. and Laporte, L. (2006), 'Monuments funéraires néolithiques dans l'ouest de la France', in R. Joussaume, L. Laporte and C. Scarre (eds) 2006, *Origine et développement du mégalithisme de l'ouest de l'Europe*, Colloque international du 26 au 30 octobre 2002, Musée des Tumulus de Bougon (Deux-Sèvres), Vols 1 and 2, Niort: Conseil Général des Deux-Sèvres, 319–43.

Joussaume, R., Laporte, L. and Scarre, C. (eds) (2006), *Origine et développement du mégalithisme de l'ouest de l'Europe*, Colloque international du 26 au 30 octobre 2002, Musée des Tumulus de Bougon (Deux-Sèvres), Vols 1 and 2, Niort: Conseil Général des Deux-Sèvres.

Kaelas, L. (1983), 'Megaliths of the Funnel Beaker Culture in Germany and Scandinavia', in C. Renfrew (ed.), *The Megalithic Monuments of Western Europe*, London: Thames and Hudson, 77–91.

Karsten, P. (1994), *Att kasta yxan i sjön. En studie över rituell tradition och förändring utifrån skånska neolitiska offerfynd*, Acta Archaeologica Ludensia, Series IN 8, No. 23, Stockholm: Almqvist & Wiksell International.

Kaul, F. (1988), 'Neolitiske gravanlæg på Onsved Mark, Horns Herred, Sjælland', *Aarbøger 1987*, 27–83.

Kaul, F. (1994), 'Ritualer med menneskeknogler i yngre stenalder', *Kuml 1991–92*, 7–49.

Kaul, F. (1997), 'Recent finds of miniature "megalithic" art from the island of Bornholm and from Scania', in A. Casal (ed.), *O Neolitico Atlántico e as Orixes do Megalitismo*, Acta do Coloquio Internacional (Santiago de Compostela, 1–6 de abril de 1996), Universidade de Santiago de Compostela, 161–72.

Kaul, F., Nielsen, F.O. and Nielsen, P.O. (2002), 'Vasagård og Rispebjerg. To indhegnede bopladser fra yngre stenalder på Bornholm', *Nationalmuseets Arbejdsmark 2002*, 119–38.

Keiller, A. and Piggott, S. (1938), 'Excavation of an untouched chamber in the Lanhill long barrow', *Proceedings of the Prehistoric Society* 4, 122–50.

208

Kersten, K. and La Baume, P. (1958), *Vorgeschichte der nordfriesischen Inseln*, Veröffent-lichungen das Landesamtes für Vor- und Frühgeschichte in Schleswig, Neumünster: Karl Wachholtz.

Kirsch, E. (1994), *Beiträge zur älteren Trichterbecherkultur in Brandenburg*, Potsdam: Brandenburgisches Landesmuseum für Ur- und Frühgeschichte.

Kjærum, P. (1955), 'Tempelhus fra Stenalder', *Kuml 1955*, 7–35.

Kjærum, P. (1957), 'Storstensgrave ved Tustrup', *Kuml 1957*, 9–23.

Kjærum, P. (1969), 'Jættestuen Jordhøj', *Kuml 1969*, 9–66.

Kjærum, P. (1977), 'En Langhøjs Tilblivelse', *Antikvariske Studier* 1977, 19–26.

Klassen, L. (1999), 'Prestigeøkser af sjældne alpine bjergarter: en glemt og overset fund-gruppe fra ældre stenalderens slutning i Danmark', *Kuml 1999*, 11–51.

Klassen, L. (2000), *Frühes Kupfer im Norden. Untersuchungen zu Chronologie, Herkunft und Bedeutung der Kupferfunde der Nordgruppe der Trichterbecherkultur*, Moesgård: Jysk Arkæologisk Selskab.

Klassen, L. (2004), *Jade und Kupfer. Untersuchungen zum Neolithisierungsprozess im west-lichen Ostseeraum unter besonderer Berücksichtigung der Kulturentwicklung Europas 5500–3500 BC*, Moesgård: Jysk Arkæologisk Selskab.

Knöll, H. (1959), *Die nordwestdeutsche Tiefstichkeramik und ihre Stellung im nord- und mitteleuropäischen Neolithikum*, Münster: Aschendorffsche Verlagsbuchhandlung.

Knöll, H. (1983), *Die Megalithgräber von Lengerich-Wechte (Kreis Steinfurt)*, Münster: Aschendorff.

Koch, E. (1998), *Neolithic Bog Pots from Zealand, Møn, Lolland and Falster*, Copenhagen: Det Kongelige Nordiske Oldskriftselskab.

Kopytkoff, I. (1971), 'Ancestors as Elders in Africa', *Africa* 41, 129–42.

Körner, G. and Laux, F. (1980), *Ein Königreich an der Luhe*, Lüneburg: Museumsverein für das Fürstentum Lüneburg.

Kossian, R. (2003), 'The Neolithic settlement site "Hunte 1" near lake Dümmer, in Diepholz District (Lower Saxony, Germany) – a survey', in A. Bauerochse and H. Haßmann (eds), *Peatlands: archaeological sites – archives of nature – nature conservation – wise use*, Proceedings of the Peatland Conference 2002 in Hannover, Germany, Rahden/Westf., Verlag Marie Leidorf, 79–88.

Kossian, R. (2005), *Nichtmegalithische Grabanlagen der Trichterbecherkultur in Deutsch-land und den Niederlanden*, Vols 1 and 2, Veröffentlichungen des Landesamtes für Denk-malpflege und Archäologie Sachsen-Anhalt, Halle: Landesmuseum für Vorgeschichte.

Kozak-Zychman, W. and Gauda-Pilarska, E. (1998), 'Charakterystyka antropologiczna szczątków kostnych z grobów ludności kultury pucharów lejkowatych i kultury ceramiki sznurowej w Malicach Kościelnych (Stan. 1), woj. Tarnobrzeskie', *Archeologia Polski Środkowowschodniej* 3, 56–60.

Krause, E. and Schoetensack, O. (1893), 'Die megalithischen Gräber (Steinkammergräber) Deutschlands. I. Altmark', *Zeitschrift für Ethnologie* 25, 105–70.

Kristensen, I. K. (1991), 'Storgård IV. An Early Neolithic Long Barrow near Fjelsø, North Jutland', *Journal of Danish Archaeology* 8 (1989), 72–87.

Kristiansen, K. (1984), 'Ideology and material culture: an archaeological perspective', in M. Spriggs (ed.), *Marxist Perspectives in Archaeology*, Cambridge: Cambridge University Press, 72–100.

Kristiansen, K. (1990), 'Ard marks under barrows: a response to Peter Rowley-Conwy', *Antiquity* 64, 322–7.

Kristiansen, K. and Larsson, T. B. (2005), *The Rise of Bronze Age Society. Travels, Transmis-sions and Transformations*, Cambridge: Cambridge University Press.

209

Kruk, J. and Milisauskas, S. (1982), 'Die Wagendarstellung auf einem Trichterbecher aus Bronocice in Polen', *Archäologisches Korrespondenzblatt* 12, 141–44.

La Cour, V. (1927), *Sjællands ældeste Bygder: en arkæologisk-topografisk Undersøgelse*, Copenhagen: Aschehoug.

Laporte, L., Joussaume, R. and Scarre, C. (2002), 'Le Tumulus C de Péré à Prissé-la-Charrière (Deux-Sèvres)', *Gallia Préhistoire* 44, 167–214.

Laporte L. and Le Roux, C.-T. (2004), *Bâtisseurs du Néolithique. Mégalithismes de la France de l'Ouest*, Paris: La Maison des Roches.

Laporte, L. and Tinévez, J.-Y. (2004), 'Neolithic Houses and Chambered Tombs of Western France', *Cambridge Archaeological Journal* 14, 217–34.

Larsson, L. (1988a), 'A Construction for Ceremonial Activities from the Late Mesolithic', *Meddelanden från Lunds universitets historiska museum 1987–1988*, 5–18.

Larsson, L. (ed.) (1988b), *The Skateholm Project. I. Man and Environment*, Societatis Humaniorum Litterarum Lundensis LXXIX, Lund: Almqvist & Wiksell International.

Larsson, L. (1992), 'Neolithic settlement in the Skateholm area, southern Scania', *Meddelanden från Lunds universitets historiska museum 1987–1988*, New Series 9, 5–44.

Larsson, L. (1995), 'Man and sea in southern Scandinavia during the Late Mesolithic. The role of cemeteries in the view of society', in A. Fischer (ed.) *Man and Sea in the Mesolithic. Coastal settlement above and below present sea level, Proceedings of the International Symposium, Kalundborg, Denmark 1993*, Oxbow Monograph 53, Oxford: Oxbow Books, 95–104.

Larsson, L. (2000), 'Axes and Fire – Contacts with the Gods', in D. Olausson and H. Vandkilde (eds), *Form, Function and Context. Material culture studies in Scandinavian archaeology*, Acta Archaeologica Lundensia series in 18, no. 31, Lund: Almqvist & Wiksell International, 93–103.

Larsson, L. (2001), 'The Sun from the Sea – Amber in the Mesolithic and Neolithic of Southern Scandinavia', in A. Butrimas (ed.), *Baltic Amber, Proceedings of the International Interdisciplinary Conference: Baltic Amber in Natural Sciences, Archaeology and Applied Arts*, Vilnius: Acta Academiae Artium Vilnensis 21, 65–75.

Larsson, L. (2004), 'The Mesolithic Period in Southern Scandinavia: with Special Reference to Burials and Cemeteries', in A. Saville (ed.), *Mesolithic Scotland and its Neighbours, The Early Holocene Prehistory of Scotland, its British and Irish Contexts, and some Northern European Perspectives*, Edinburgh: Society of Antiquaries of Scotland, 371–92.

Laux, F. (1979), 'Die Großsteingräber im nordöstlichen Niedersachsen', in H. Schirnig (ed.) *Großsteingräber in Niedersachsen*, Hildesheim: Verlagsbuchhandlung August Lax, 59–82.

Laux, F. (1980), 'Die Steingräber in der Lüneburger Heide', in G. Körner and F. Laux, *Ein Königreich an der Luhe*, Lüneburg: Museumsverein für das Fürstentum Lüneburg, 91–218.

Laux, F. (1984a), 'Bemerkungen zu jungsteinzeitlichen Grabanlagen im Aller-Tal', *Die Kunde* 34/35 (1983/84), 36–76.

Laux, F. (1984b), 'Die Zeit der großen Steingräber', *Führer zu archäologischen Denkmälern in Deutschland* 9, 34–46.

Laux, F. (1989), 'König Surbolds Grab bei Börger im Hümmling', *Nachrichten aus Niedersachsens Urgeschichte* 58, 117–27.

Laux, F. (1991), 'Überlegungen zu den Großsteingräbern in Niedersachsen und Westfalen', *Neue Ausgrabungen und Forschungen in Niedersachsen* 19, 21–99.

Laux, F. (1996), 'Großsteingräber zwischen Weser und Elbe', in W. Budesheim and H. Keiling (eds), *Zur jüngeren Steinzeit in Norddeutschland. Einblicke in das Leben der ersten Bauern*, Beiträge für Wissenschaft und Kultur 2, Neumünster: Wachholtz, 42–63.

Laux, F. (2003), 'Das Steingrab in der Fischbeker Heide', *Hammaburg* NF 14, 7–179.

Leclerc, J. and Tarrête, J. (2006), 'Du Bassin Parisien à la Suisse', in R. Joussaume, L. Laporte, and C. Scarre (eds), *Origine et développement du mégalithisme de l'ouest de l'Europe*, Colloque international du 26 au 30 octobre 2002, Musée des Tumulus de Bougon (Deux-Sèvres), Vols 1 and 2, Niort: Conseil Général des Deux-Sèvres, 381–406.

Lecornec, J. (1994), *Le Petit Mont, Arzon, Morbihan*, Documents archéologiques de l'Ouest, Rennes: Association pour la diffusion des recherches archéologiques dans l'Ouest de la France.

Lehmkuhl, U. (1991), 'Interpretationsmöglichkeiten neolithischer Bestattungssitten anhand von Tierknochenfunden aus Gräbern in Mecklenburg-Vorpommern', in F. Horst and H. Keiling (eds), *Bestattungswesen und Totenkult*, Berlin: Akademie-Verlag, 371–6.

Lepiksaar, J. (1971), 'Das Skelettmaterial von Carlshögen und Ramshög', in M. Strömberg, *Die Megalithgräber von Hagestad: Zur Problematik von Grabbauten und Grabriten*, Lund: CWK Gleerups Förlag, 328–93.

Le Roux, C.-T. (ed.) (2006), *Monuments mégalithiques à Locmariaquer (Morbihan). Le long tumulus d'Er Grah dans son environnement*, XXXVIIIe supplément à Gallia Préhistoire, Paris: CNRS Éditions.

L'Helgouac'h, J. (1983), 'Les idoles qu'on abat …', *Bulletin de la Société polymathique du Morbihan*, 110, 57–68

L'Helgouac'h, J. (1998), 'L'apparition du Néolithique et son développement jusqu'à la fin du IVe millénaire', in P.-R. Giot, J. L'Helgouac'h and J.-M Monnier, *Préhistoire de la Bretagne*, Rennes: Éditions Ouest-France, 233–427.

Liversage, D. (1981), 'Neolithic monuments at Lindebjerg, Northwest Zealand', *Acta Archaeologica* 51 (1980), 85–152.

Liversage, D. (1992), *Barkær. Long Barrows and Settlements*, Arkæologiske Studier IX, Copenhagen: Akademisk Forlag, Universitetsforlaget.

Madsen, A. P. (1896), *Gravhøje og Gravfund fra Stenalderen i Danmark: Det Østlige Danmark*, Copenhagen: Gyldendalske Boghandel.

Madsen, A. P. (1900), *Gravhøje og Gravfund fra Stenalderen i Danmark: Fyen og Jylland*, Copenhagen: Gyldendalske Boghandel.

Madsen, T. (1979), 'Earthen Long Barrows and Timber Structures: Aspects of the Early Neolithic Mortuary Practice in Denmark', *Proceedings of the Prehistoric Society* 45, 301–20.

Madsen, T. (1980), 'En tidligneolitisk langhøj ved Rude i Østjylland', *Kuml 1979*, 79–108.

Madsen, T. (1988), 'Causewayed Enclosures in South Scandinavia', in C. Burgess, P. Topping, C. Mordant and M. Maddison (eds), *Enclosures and Defences in the Neolithic of Western Europe*, Oxford: British Archaeological Reports, 301–36.

Malmer, M. P. (2002), *The Neolithic of South Sweden, TRB, GRK, and STR*, Stockholm: The Royal Swedish Academy of Letters, History and Antiquities.

Masset, C. (1997), *Les Dolmens. Sociétés néolithiques, Pratiques funéraires*, Paris: Éditions Errance.

Masters, L. (1983), 'Chambered Tombs and Non-Megalithic Barrows in Britain', in C. Renfrew (ed.), *The Megalithic Monuments of Western Europe*, London: Thames and Hudson, 97–112.

Metcalf, P. and Huntington, R. (1995), *Celebrations of Death. The Anthropology of Mortuary Ritual,* Cambridge: Cambridge University Press (2nd edn).

Metzler, A. (2003), 'Early Neolithic peatland sites around lake Dümmer', in A. Bauerochse and H. Haßmann (eds), *Peatlands: archaeological sites – archives of nature – nature conservation – wise use,* Proceedings of the Peatland Conference 2002 in Hannover, Germany, Rahden/Westf.: Verlag Marie Leidorf GmbH, 62–7.

Michaelsen, K. (1978), 'Die Ausgrabungen der beiden Hünenbetten von Kleinenkneten in Oldenburg 1934–39', *Oldenburger Jahrbuch* 75/76 (1975/6), 215–49.

Midgley, M. S. (1985), *The Origin and Function of the Earthen Long Barrows of Northern Europe*, Oxford: British Archaeological Reports.

Midgley, M. S. (1992), *TRB Culture. The First Farmers of the North European Plain*, Edinburgh: Edinburgh University Press.

Midgley, M. S. (1997a), 'The Earthen Long Barrows of Northern Europe: A Vision of the Neolithic World', *COSMOS (The Journal of Traditional Cosmology Society)* 11, 117–23.

Midgley, M. S. (1997b), 'The Earthen Long Barrow Phenomenon of Northern Europe and its Relation to the Passy-type Monuments of France', in C. Constantin, D. Mordant and D. Simonin (eds), *La Culture de Cerny. Nouvelle économie, nouvelle société au Néolithique,* Actes du Colloque International de Nemours 1994, Mémoires du Musée de Préhistoire d'Île-de-France no. 6, 679–85.

Midgley, M. S. (2000), 'The earthen long barrow phenomenon in Europe: Creation of monumental cemeteries', in I. Pavlů (ed.), *In Memoriam Jan Rulf,* Praha: Památky archeologické – Supplementum 13, 255–65.

Midgley, M. S. (2002), 'Early Neolithic farming communities in Northern Europe: Reconsideration of the TRB culture', *Archeologické rozhledy* 54, 208–22 (Festschrift for Marie Zápotocká).

Midgley, M. S. (2005), *The Monumental Cemeteries of Prehistoric Europe*, Stroud: Tempus.

Midgley, M. S. (2006), 'The megalithic tombs of the north European plain', in R. Joussaume, L. Laporte, and C. Scarre (eds) *Origine et développement du mégalithisme de l'ouest de l'Europe*, Colloque international du 26 au 30 octobre 2002, Musée des Tumulus de Bougon (Deux-Sèvres), Vols 1 and 2, Niort: Conseil Général des Deux-Sèvres, 63–87.

Mohen, J.-P. (2003), *Cultes et Rituels mégalithiques. Les sociétés néolithiques de l'Europe du nord*, Paris: La Maison des Roches.

Mohen, J.-P. and Scarre, C. (2002), *Les Tumulus de Bougon. Complexe mégalithique du Ve au IIIe millénaire*, Paris: Éditions Errance.

Montelius, O. (1905), 'Orienten och Europa', *Antikvarisk Tidskrift för Sverige* 13, 1–252.

Morgan, F. de M. (1959), 'The Excavation of a Long Barrow at Nutbane, Hants', *Proceedings of the Prehistoric Society* 25, 15–51.

Müller, J. (1990a), 'Die Arbeitsleistung für das Großsteingrab Kleinenkneten 1', in M. Fansa (ed.), *Experimentelle Archäologie in Deutschland, Archäologische Mitteilungen aus Nordwestdeutschland* 4, 210–19.

Müller, J. (1990b), 'Arbeitsleistung und gesellschaftliche Leistung bei Megalithgräbern. Das Fallbeispiel Orkney', *Acta Praehistorica et Archaeologica* 22, 9–35.

Müller, J. (2001), *Soziochronologische Studien zum Jung- und Spätneolithikum im Mittelelbe-Saale-Gebiet (4100–2700 v. Chr.)*, Rahden/Westf.: Verlag Marie Leidorf GmbH.

Müller, S. (1914), 'Sønderjyllands stenalder', *Aarbøger* 3, 169–322.

Nelson, H. (1988), *Zur inneren Gliederung und Verbreitung neolithischer Gruppen im südlichen Niederelbegebiet*, Oxford: British Archaeological Reports Int. Ser. 459.

Nielsen, N. (2003), 'Ormslev-dyssen – en dysse uden høj?', *Kuml 2003*, 125–56.

Nielsen, P. O. (1982), *Dysse og dolke i stenalderen*, Stenalderen 3, Copenhagen: Lademanns Danmarkshistorie.

Nielsen, P. O. (1984), 'Flint axes and megaliths – the time and context of the early dolmens in Denmark', in G. Burenhult (ed.), *The Archaeology of Carrowmore*, Theses and Papers in North-European Archaeology 14, Stockholm: Institute of Archaeology, University of Stockholm, 376–86.

Nielsen, P. O. (1999), 'Limensgård and Grødbygård. Settlements with houses from the Early, Middle and Late Neolithic on Bornholm', in C. Fabech and J. Ringtved (eds), *Settlement and Landscape, Proceedings of a conference in Århus, Denmark, May 4–7 1998*, Århus: Jutland Archaeological Society, 149–65.

Nielsen, P. O. (2004), 'Causewayed camps, palisade enclosures and central settlements of the Middle Neolithic in Denmark', *Journal of Nordic Archaeological Science* 14, 19–33.

Niesiołowska-Śreniowska, E. (1999), 'The early TRB "ploughmarks" from Sarnowo in central Poland: a new interpretation', *Oxford Journal of Archaeology* 18, 17–22.

Nilsson, S. (1868), *The Primitive Inhabitants of Scandinavia*, London: Longmans, Green.

Nordman, C. A. (1935), 'The Megalithic Culture of Northern Europe' (The Rhind Lectures 1932), *Finska Fornminnesföreningens Tidskrift* 39:3, 1–137.

Parker Pearson, M. and Ramilisonina (1998), 'Stonehenge for the ancestors: the stones pass on the message', *Antiquity* 72, 308–26.

Paulsen, H. (1990), 'Untersuchung und Restaurierung des Langbettes von Karlsminde, Gemeinde Waabs, Kreis Rendsburg-Eckernförde', *Archäologische Nachrichten aus Schleswig-Holstein* 1990, 18–60.

Péquart, M. and Péquart, S. J. (1954), *Hoëdic. Deuxième station-nécropole du Mésolithique côtier armoricain*, Anvers: De Sikkel.

Persson, P. and Sjögren, K.-G. (1996), 'Radiocarbon and the chronology of Scandinavian megalithic graves', *Journal of European Archaeology* 3 (1995), 59–87.

Persson, P. and Sjögren, K.-G. (2001), *Falbygdens gånggrifter, Del 1. Undersökningar 1985– 1998*, Göteborg: Göteborgs Universitet.

Petzsch, W. (1928), 'Die Steinzeit Rügens', *Mitteilungen aus der Sammlung vaterländischer Altertümer der Universität Greifswald* 3, 8–15.

Pieper, P. (2003), 'Peat bog corpses', in A. Bauerochse and H. Haßmann (eds), *Peatlands: archaeological sites – archives of nature – nature conservation – wise use,* Proceedings of the Peatland Conference 2002 in Hannover, Germany, Rahden/Westf., Verlag Marie Leidorf GmbH, 107–14.

Piera, S. (2003), 'Structures sociales et organisation des inhumations dans les tombes à couloir du Néolithique moyen: l'exemple de Fontenay-le-Marmion (Calvados)', in P. Chambon and J. Leclerc (eds), *Les pratiques funéraires néolithiques avant 3500 av. J.-C. en France et dans les régions limitrophes*, Mémoires de la Société préhistorique française 33, Presses de la Simarre, Joué-lès-Tours, 287–300.

Piggott, S. (1962), *The West Kennet Long Barrow*, London: HMSO.

Piggott, S. (1974), 'Excavation of the Dalladies Long Barrow, Fettercairn, Kincardineshire', *Proceedings of the Society of Antiquaries of Scotland* 104, 23–47.

Preuß, J. (1966), *Die Baalberger Gruppe in Mitteldeutschland*, Berlin: VEB Deutscher Verlag der Wissenschaften.

Price, N. (ed.) (2001), *The Archaeology of Shamanism*, London: Routledge.

Price, T. D. (ed.) (2000), *Europe's First Farmers*, Cambridge: Cambridge University Press.

Rech, M. (1979), *Studien zu Depotfunden der Trichterbecher- und Einzelgrabkultur des Nordens*, Offa-Bücher 39, Neumünster: Wachholtz.

Reilly, S. (2003), 'Processing the Dead in Neolithic Orkney', *Oxford Journal of Archaeology* 22, 133–54.

Renfrew, C. (1972), 'Monuments, mobilization and social organization in neolithic Wessex', in C. Renfrew (ed.), *The explanation of culture change: models in prehistory*, London: Duckworth, 539–58.

Renfrew, C. (1973), *Before Civilization: The radiocarbon revolution and European Prehistory*, London: Jonathan Cape.

Renfrew, C. (1976), 'Megaliths, territories and populations', in S. J. de Laet (ed.), *Acculturation and Continuity in Atlantic Europe*, Brugge: De Tempel, 198–220.

Renfrew, C. (1979), *Investigations in Orkney*, London: The Society of Antiquaries of London.

Renfrew, C. (1980), 'Toward a Definition of Context: the North German Megaliths', *Nachrichten aus Niedersachsens Urgeschichte* 49, 3–20.

Richards, C. (ed.) (2005), *Dwelling among the monuments: the Neolithic village of Barn-house, Maeshowe passage grave and surrounding monuments at Stenness, Orkney*, Cambridge: McDonald Institute for Archaeological Research.

Rønne, P. (1979), 'Høj over høj', *Skalk* 1979, 3–8.

Rosenberg, G. (1929), 'Nye Jættestuefund', *Aarbøger 1929*, 189–262.

Rowley-Conwy, P. (1987), 'The interpretation of ardmarks', *Antiquity* 61, 263–6.

Runcis, J. (2002), *Bärnstensbarnen. Bilder, berättelser och betraktelser*, Stockholm: Riksantikvarieämbetet, Skrifter No. 41.

Runcis, J. (2005), 'The Burial-Ground at Borgeby: Point of departure for a tentative Neolithic', in T. Artelius and F. Svanberg (eds), *Dealing with the Dead. Archaeological Perspectives on Prehistoric Scandinavian Burial Ritual*, Stockholm: Riksantikvarieämbetet (Swedish National Heritage Board), Skrifter No. 65, 19–43.

Sahlström, K. E. (1935), 'Väglederna inom den västgötska gånggriftsbygden', *Västergötlands Fornminnesförenings Tidskrift* 4, 5–31.

Saville, A. (1990), *Hazleton North: the excavation of a Neolithic long cairn of the Cotswold-Severn group*, London: Historic Buildings and Monuments Commission for England.

Saxe, A. (1970), 'Social Dimensions of Mortuary Practices', unpublished Ph.D. dissertation: University of Michigan.

Scarre, C. (2002a), 'Coast and cosmos. The Neolithic monuments of northern Brittany', in C. Scarre (ed.), *Monuments and Landscape in Atlantic Europe. Perception and Society during the Neolithic and Early Bronze Age*, London: Routledge, 84–102.

Scarre, C. (2002b), 'Epilogue: Colour and Materiality in Prehistoric Society', in A. Jones and G. MacGregor (eds), *Colouring the Past. The Significance of Colour in Archaeological Research*, Oxford: Berg, 227–42.

Scarre, C. (2003), 'Diverse Inspirations: Landscapes, longhouses and the neolithic monument forms of northern France', in G. Burenhult (ed.), *Stones and Bones. Formal disposal of the dead in Atlantic Europe during the Mesolithic-Neolithic interface 6000–3000 BC*, Oxford: Archaeopress, 39–52.

Scarre, C. (2005), *Monuments mégalithiques de Grande-Bretagne et d'Irlande*, Paris: Éditions Errance.

Scarre, C. (2006), 'Sourcing the stones: the deeper significance of megalithic architecture', unpublished paper delivered at the XV Congress of UISPP, Lisbon.

Scarre, C., Laporte, L. and Joussaume, R. (2003), 'Long Mounds and Megalithic Origins in Western France: Recent Excavations at Prissé-la-Charrière', *Proceedings of the Prehistoric Society* 69, 235–51.

Schirnig, H. (1979), 'Siedlungsräume der Trichterbecherkultur am Beispiel des Landkreises Uelzen', in H. Schirning (ed.) *Großsteingräber in Niedersachsen*, Hildesheim: Verlagsbuchhandlung August Lax, 223–7.

Schirnig, H. (1982), *Die Sieben Steinhäuser bei Fallingbostel*, Hildesheim: Verlag August Lax.

Schlicht, E. (1961), 'Von alten Verkehrswegen: Die Hünengräberstraße des Hümmlings', *Jahrbuch des Emsländischen Heimatvereins* 8, 74–85.

Schlicht, E. (1968), *Die Funde aus dem Megalithgrab 2 von Emmeln, Kreis Meppen*, Göttinger Schriften zur Vor- und Frühgeschichte Band 9, Neumünster: Karl Wachholtz Verlag.

Schlicht, E. (1973), 'Kupferschmuck aus Megalithgräbern Nordwestdeutschlands', *Nachrichten aus Niedersachsens Urgeschichte* 42, 13–52.

Schlicht, E. (1979), 'Die Großsteingräber im nordwestlichen Niedersachsen', in H. Schirnig (ed.), *Großsteingräber in Niedersachsen*, Hildesheim: Verlagsbuchhandlung August Lax, 43–58.

Schmatzler, E. and Bauerochse, A. (2003), 'History of mire conservation in Lower Saxony – inventory, protection and management', in A. Bauerochse and H. Haßmann (eds), *Peatlands: archaeological sites – archives of nature – nature conservation – wise use,* Proceedings of the Peatland Conference 2002 in Hannover, Germany, Rahden/Westf.: Verlag Marie Leidorf GmbH, 217–24.

Schnapp, A. (1996), *The Discovery of the Past. The Origins of Archaeology,* London: British Museum Press.

Schuldt, E. (1961), 'Abschließende Ausgrabungen auf dem jungsteinzeitlichen Flachgräberfeld von Ostorf 1961', *Jahrbuch für Bodendenkmalpflege in Mecklenburg* 1961, 131–78.

Schuldt, E. (1966a), 'Vier Großsteingräber von Serrahn, Kreis Güstrow', *Jahrbuch für Bodendenkmalpflege im Mecklenburg* 1965, 24–53.

Schuldt, E. (1966b), *Dolmen und Ganggräber an der Recknitz,* Schwerin: Museum für Ur- und Frühgeschichte.

Schuldt, E. (1967), *Riesensteingräber an der Warnow,* Schwerin: Museum für Ur- und Frühgeschichte.

Schuldt, E. (1968), *4000jährige Gräber im Everstorfer Forst,* Schwerin: Museum für Ur- und Frühgeschichte.

Schuldt, E. (1970), *Dolmenlandschaft an der Schwinge,* Schwerin: Museum für Ur- und Frühgeschichte.

Schuldt, E. (1971), *Steinzeitliche Grabmonumente der Insel Rügen,* Schwerin: Museum für Ur- und Frühgeschichte.

Schuldt, E. (1972), *Die mecklenburgischen Megalithgräber,* Berlin: VEB Deutscher Verlag der Wissenschaften.

Sellier, D. (1991), 'Analyse morphologique des marques de la météorisation des granites à partir de mégalithes morbihannais. L'exemple de l'alignement de Kerlescan à Carnac', *Revue Archéologique de l'Ouest* 8, 83–97.

Sellier, D. (1995), 'Éléments de reconstitution du paysage prémégalithique sur le site des alignements de Kerlescan (Carnac, Morbihan) à partir de critères géomorphologiques', *Revue Archéologique de l'Ouest* 12, 21–41.

Shanks, M. and Tilley, C. (1982), 'Ideology, Power and Ritual Communication: A Reinterpretation of Neolithic Mortuary Practices', in I. Hodder (ed.), *Symbolic and Structural Archaeology,* Cambridge: Cambridge University Press, 129–54.

Sherratt, A. (1987), 'Wool, Wheels and Ploughmarks: Local Developments or Outside Introductions in Neolithic Europe?', *Bulletin of the Institute of Archaeology (University of London)* 23, 1–15.

Sherratt, A. (1990), 'The genesis of megaliths: monumentality, ethnicity and social complexity in Neolithic north-west Europe', *World Archaeology* 22, 147–67.

Sherratt, A. (1991), 'Sacred and Profane Substances: the Ritual Use of Narcotics in Later Neolithic Europe', in P. Garwood, D. Jennings, R. Skeates and J. Toms (eds), *Sacred and Profane, Proceedings of a Conference on Archaeology, Ritual and Religion. Oxford 1989,* Oxford: Oxford University Committee for Archaeology, Monograph No. 32, 50–64.

Sherratt, A. (1995), 'Instruments of conversion: the role of megaliths in Mesolithic-Neolithic transition in north-west Europe', *Oxford Journal of Archaeology* 14, 245–60.

Simonin, D., Bach, S., Richard, G. and Vintrou, J. (1997), 'Les sépultures sous dalle de type Malesherbes et la nécropole d'Orville', in C. Constantin, D. Mordant and D. Simonin, (eds), *La culture de Cerny. Nouvelle économie, nouvelle société au Néolithique,* Actes du Colloque international de Nemours, 9–10–11 mai 1994, Mémoires du Musée de Préhistoire d'Île-de-France, no. 6, 341–79.

Sjögren, K.-G. (1986), 'Kinship, Labour and Land in Neolithic Southwest Sweden: Social Aspects of Megalithic Graves', *Journal of Anthropological Archaeology* 5, 229–65.

Sjögren, K.-G. (2003a), *"Mångfalldige uhrminnes grafvar ... ". Megalitgravar och samhälle i Västsverige*, Institutionen för arkeologi, Göteborg: Göteborgs universitet.

Sjögren, K.-G. (2003b), 'Megaliths, settlement and subsistence in Bohuslän, Sweden', in G. Burenhult (ed.), *Stones and Bones, Formal disposal of the dead in Atlantic Europe during the Mesolithic-Neolithic interface 6000–3000 BC*, Oxford: Archaeopress, 167–76.

Skaarup, J. (1985a), *Yngre Stenalder på øerne syd for Fyn*, Rudkøbing: Langelands Museum.

Skaarup, J. (1985b), *Stengade. Ein langeländischer Wohnplatz mit Hausresten aus der frühneolithischen Zeit*, Rudkøbing: Langelands Museum.

Sprockhoff, E. (1926), *Die Kulturen der jüngeren Steinzeit in der Mark Brandenburg*, Berlin and Leipzig: Walter de Gruyter.

Sprockhoff, E. (1938), *Die nordische Megalithkultur*, Berlin and Leipzig: Walter de Gruyter.

Sprockhoff, E. (1966), *Atlas der Megalithgräber Deutschlands, Teil 1: Schleswig-Holstein*, Bonn: Rudolf Habelt Verlag.

Sprockhoff, E. (1967), *Atlas der Megalithgräber Deutschlands, Teil 2: Mecklenburg, Brandenburg*, Bonn: Rudolf Habelt Verlag.

Sprockhoff, E. (1975), *Atlas der Megalithgräber Deutschlands, Teil 3: Niedersachsen, Westfalen*, Bonn: Rudolf Habelt Verlag.

Steinmann, C. (2001), *Social Backgrounds of the Megalithic Phenomenon in Northeast Germany*, Manuscript of the Philosophical Doctorate, Reading University.

Strassburg, J. (2000), *Shamanic Shadows. One Hundred Generations of Undead Subversion in Southern Scandinavia, 7,000–4,000 BC*, Stockholm Studies in Archaeology 20, Stockholm: Stockholm University

Strömberg, M. (1968), *Der Dolmen Trollasten*, Acta Archaeologica Lundensia Series 8, No. 7, Lund.

Strömberg, M. (1971), *Die Megalithgräber von Hagestad: Zur Problematik von Grabbauten und Grabriten*, Lund: CWK Gleerups Förlag.

Svensson, M. (2004), 'The second Neolithic concept, 3000–2300 BC', in M. Andersson, P. Karsten, B. Knarrström and M. Svensson (eds), *Stone Age Scania, Significant places dug and read by contract archaeology*, Malmö: Riksantikvarieämbetets Förlag, Skrifter no. 52, 191–248.

Taylor, T. (2002), *The Buried Soul. How Humans Invented Death*, London: Fourth Estate.

Tempel, W. D. (1978), 'Bericht über die Ausgrabung des Megalithgrabes I in Ostenwalde, Gemeinde Werlte, Kreis Aschendorf-Hümmling', *Neue Ausgrabungen und Forschungen in Niedersachsen* 12, 1–31.

Thorsen, S. (1981), '"Klokkehøj" ved Bøjden. Et sydvestfynsk dyssekammer med bevaret primærgrav', *Kuml 1980*, 105–46.

Thorvildsen, K. (1946), 'Grønhøj ved Horsens. En jættestue med offerplads', *Aarbøger 1946*, 73–94.

Thrane, H. (1982), 'Dyrkningsspor fra yngre stenalder i Danmark', in H. Thrane (ed.), *Om Yngre Stenalders Bebyggelseshistorie*, Odense: Skrifter fra Historisk Institut, 20–8.

Thrane, H. (1989), 'Danish Plough-Marks from the Neolithic and Bronze Age', *Journal of Danish Archaeology* 8, 111–25.

Tilley, C. (1993), 'Art, Architecture, Landscape [Neolithic Sweden]', in B. Bender (ed.), *Landscape Politics and Perspectives*, Oxford: Berg, 49–84.

Tilley, C. (1994), *A phenomenology of landscape*, Oxford: Berg.

Tilley, C. (1996), *An ethnography of the Neolithic, Early prehistoric societies in southern Scandinavia*, Cambridge: Cambridge University Press.

Tilley, C. (1998), 'Megaliths in Texts', in M. Edmonds and C. Richards (eds), *Understanding the Neolithic of North-Western Europe*, Glasgow: Cruithne Press, 141–60.

Tilley, C. (1999), *The Dolmens and Passage Graves of Sweden. An Introduction and Guide*, Institute of Archaeology, London: University College.

Tilley, C. (2004), *The Materiality of Stone. Explorations in Landscape Phenomenology*, Oxford: Berg.

Trigger, B. (1990), 'Monumental architecture: a thermodynamic explanation of symbolic behaviour', *World Archaeology* 22, 119–32.

Tunia, K. (2003), 'Drewniane "megality" nad Wisłą', *Zaginione Cywilizacje, Wiedza i Życie*, Numer Specjalny, 68–71.

Turner, V. (1967), *The Forest of Symbols. Aspects of Ndembu Ritual*, Ithaca: Cornell University Press.

Vaquero Lastres, J. (1999), *Les extrêmes distincts. La configuration de l'espace dans les sociétés ayant bâti des tertres funéraires dans le Nord-Ouest ibérique*, Oxford: British Archaeological Reports.

Verjux, C., Simonin, D. and Richard, G. (1998), 'Des sépultures mésolithiques aux tombes sous dalles du Néolithique moyen I en région Centre et sur ses marges', in J. Guilaine (ed.), *Sépultures d'Occident et genèses des mégalithismes (9000–3500 avant notre ère), Séminaire du Collège de France*, Paris: Éditions Errance, 59–70.

Vyner, B. E. (1984), 'The excavation of a Neolithic cairn at Street House, Loftus, Cleveland', *Proceedings of the Prehistoric Society* 50, 151–95.

Whaling, F. (1985), 'Yin Yang, Zoroastrian Dualism, and Gnosticism: Comparative Studies in Religious Dualism', in E. Lyle (ed.), *Duality*, Cosmos 1 (Edinburgh: The Yearbook of the Traditional Cosmology Society), 44–60.

Whittle, A. (2000), '"Very Like a Whale": Menhirs, Motifs and Myths in the Mesolithic-Neolithic Transition in Northwest Europe', *Cambridge Archaeological Journal* 10, 243–59.

Wierzbicka, A. (1990), 'The meaning of color terms: semantics, culture and cognition', *Cognitive Linguistics* 1, 99–150.

Woodburn, J. (1982), 'Social dimensions of death in four African hunting and gathering societies', in M. Bloch and J. Parry (eds), *Death and the Regeneration of Life*, Cambridge: Cambridge University Press, 187–210.

Wysocki, M. and Whittle, A. (2000), 'Diversity, lifestyles and rites: new biological and archaeological evidence from British Earlier Neolithic mortuary assemblages', *Antiquity* 74, 591–601.

Zich, B. (1993), 'Die Ausgrabungen chronisch gefährdeter Hügelgräber der Stein- und Bronzezeit in Flintbek, Kreis Rendsburg-Eckernförde. Ein Vorbericht', *Offa* 49/50 (1992/93), 15–31.

Zich, B. (n.d.a), 'Gradually extended Long Barrows and contemporaneous Vehicle Tracks from Flintbek, North Germany', unpublished manuscript.

Zich, B. (n.d.b), 'Neolithic vehicle tracks covered by long barrow LA 3 in Flintbek, North Germany', unpublished manuscript.

INDEX

References in italics indicate illustrations

accessible chambers 57; artefacts 135; capstones 56; construction 82; development 195–6; diversity 192; multiple burials 19; religious ideas 114; secondary use 135; size 58; votive deposits 58
aesthetics 56; axes 8; colours 155; megalithic construction 48; symbolism 32
agriculture 3; megalithic tombs 40–2; TRB culture 40
Ålborg 39; flint 8
Aldersro: disarticulated bones 127
amber: colours 160–1; grave goods 20, 136, 138, 166; jewellery 143–4, 161; as ornaments 21; raw materials 10; symbolism 144
ancestors: 109, 113; in chambers 74, 101, 196, 197; decapitation 116; honour of 124, 140; importance 147, 196–8; long barrows 194; offerings to 135, 141, 135, 154; protection of 97; transformation into 116, 196; travel 200; veneration of 146, 165, 175
ancestral rites: body and soul 147; burials 124; pottery 140; skulls 124
architecture: builders 26, 107; contrasts 161; landscape 32; megalithic tombs 192; passage graves 73; regional differences 193–4; sacred 73–4
arrowheads: flint 7; grave goods 21, 135, 142
axes 7, 37–8; causewayed enclosure 175; copper 144; grave goods 138, 142; polished flint 8; tree splitting 18; votive offerings 152

Bakkebølle: capstone 157; dolmens *67*

Barendorf: fragmentary remains 117; grave goods 117
Barkær: graves 18; imposing monuments 18; interpretation 13; long barrows 12, 165; timber façade 14; votive offerings 17
Barskamp: dolmens 62; river crossings 37; tomb clusters 38
Basedow: children 133; skeletons 117; skulls 124
Bigum: burnt flint 104; capstones 49
Birkehøj: construction 92; intermediary layers 95; mound construction *93*; post holes 99
Bjørnsholm: shell midden 14; timber façade 14
bodies: burials 16; public display 16
Bogø dolmen: grave goods 113, 135, *136*
bogs: ceremonies 198; complete bodies 109, 171; food offerings 170–1; reduced 35; skeletons 109, 171; votive deposits 148; votive offerings 9
bone: jewellery 143; raw materials 10
bones: breakage 20, 116, 117, 154; burnt 114, 126, 133, 134, 159; charred 20, 114, 133; disarticulated 109, 115, 117, 126; piles of 116, 117, 120, 121, 125, 127, 128, 131, 135, 187, 188; selection 109, 115, 135, 136, 187
Borgeby: amber 144; child cemetery 197; children 133
Bornholm: coastal megaliths 36; cornerstones 162; houses 5; navigational skills 38; transport 10
Bougon: multiple burials 190–1; secondary burials 191
boulders: construction 43; inclined 84; size 46; splitting 84, 162; twin stones 162–3
Brandsbjerg: seated burial 128

218

Brejninggård: long passages 63
Bundsø: ceremonial enclosures 5; human remains 174; skulls 124
burial(s): ceremonies 16, 26, 73,103; chambers 186; complete bodies 127, 128; customs 19, 189; decomposition 128; evidence 145; flat graves 2, 24; floors 101; fragmentary remains 145; gender 133; lack of 180; long barrows 2; within monuments 20; multiple 19, 58, 110, 113, 138; partial 113, 115, 116; practices 145; secondary 117, 127, 138, 189
burial chambers 24–5; construction 11, 17
burial practices: development 195; megalithic tombs 110; posthumous manipulation 20; religious ideas 198
burial rites: causewayed enclosure 176
burial structures: diversity 191
burnt flint: deposits 5, 18; floor constructions 103
Burtevitz: orthostats 84
Bygholm Nørremark: aggrandisement 14–15; arrowheads 21; graves 14; imposing monuments 18; long barrows 165; long mounds 17; multiple burials 19; timber palisades 14

Campemoor: trackways 6, 36, 38
capstones: bi-chambers 79; construction 58, 62, 74, 89; intermediary layers 95; keystones 95; passage graves 48, 49; placement 93–9; scaffolding 99; sealed chambers 109, 113; size 48, 75, 157; weight distribution 94
Carlshögen: children 133; compartments 129; flint 141–2; floor constructions 106; human remains 120; multiple burials 118; skulls 124
causewayed enclosure: burial rites 176; ceremonies 175, 198; human remains 174; locations 173; pottery 174; rituals 174; timber palisades 173; trade 176–7; use of timber 11, 166; votive offerings 8, 173
ceremonial enclosures: ceremonial activities 24; food offerings 141; rituals 108; Sarup 5; votive offerings 9
ceremonies 56; closed chambers 113; honouring the dead 58; megalithic tombs 148, 167; passage graves 73; pottery 175; skulls 124; use of bones 120; votive offerings 152
chambers: compartments 105; dilapidation

110; diversity 191–2; family burials 127, 188–9; niches 105; not covered 49; passages 99; plan 188; repeated use 109; shapes 181, 182; shelves 105; size 19, 46; stability 74–5; styles 62; timber 114, 187; vertical slabs 105
cists 17, 25, 71, 104, 115, 176, 181, 188; multiple burials 19
communication 10, 36, 38, 79, 175, 176, 198, 200
compartments: 101, 104, 105, 107, 117, 129, 137, 141; burnt flint 106; floor constructions 106
Condé-sur-Ifs: 188, 189; multiple burials 191
construction: accessible chambers 89; over burial pits 124; chambers 85; engineering 82–3; entrances 70; keystones 95, 98; megalithic tombs 43, 82, 161; methods 95; principles 48; raw materials 32; rituals 49; timber 99
copper: axes 144; grave goods 21, 145; raw materials 10; trinkets 143
Corded Ware 2, 5; repeated use 109; secondary use 118, 128; succeeded TRB culture 10; twin male burials 165
cornerstones: keystones 95; sequence 89
cosmology: 184, 195; Neolithic 27, 160, 165, 196; significance 28; TRB 154, 176
crafts 6; navigational skills 10; woodworking 10
crops: barley 42; einkorn 42; emmer 42
crushed flint: between capstones 92; dry chambers 92; floor 103, 104
cult houses 167–8

Dagstorp 4; houses 5; votive deposits 169
Dala: seated burial 110, 128
Damsbo Mark: children 133; multiple burials 127
Denghoog: drainage 93
depositions: flint 108; human remains 107; pottery 108; rituals 121; tools 108
disarticulated: bodies 115, 188; bones 109; burial 115, 116, 126; individuals 119, 126, 127; remains 120, 127
dolmens 15, 25, 26; ancestral lands 42; ard marks 42; British Isles 185; burnt bones 134; capstones 94, 156; children 133; closed 56; complete bodies 109; construction 43; covered 49; crushed flint 91; damage 28; distribution 29; entrance arrangements 59; grave goods 135, 137;

lack of 28; megalithic chambers 56; miniature 71; open 73, 114; pottery 3, 140; Rastorf 3; raw materials 157; shapes 57, 58; single burials 19, 110, 113; size 58; soil analyses 41; tomb dispersal 32; Vroue Hede 35

Drebenstedt 44–5

dry-stone walling 44, 51; guard stones 55; Sarup Gamle Skole 71; slabs 89; stability 89

duality 161–3, 166, 194; mirror-image 79, 162–3; *see also* twins

Emmeln: arrowheads 142; pottery 139
erratic *see* glacial erratic
Everstorfer Forst: accessible chambers *64*; burnt flint 104; dolmens *52*; façade *59*; fragmentary remains 117; kerbstones 51; moraine ridges 37; subterranean chambers 56

Fakkemose dolmen: posthumous manipulation 115; pottery 149
Fergusson, James: *Rude Stone Monuments* 23
Fischbek: pottery 149, 150, 151
Fjälkinge 32; pottery 149
flasks: collared 20, 135, 136, 139, 140, 141; lugged 111, 113, 117, 135, 137
flat graves: burials 2, 19, 22, 24, 109, 196; complete bodies 109; continuous use 133; customs 19; disarticulated bodies 115; grave goods 135, 136; pottery 139; skeletons 109
flint 158; crushed 43, 91; extraction and processing 8; funerary tradition 141; grave goods 141–2; mining 6–8; tools 20; votive offerings 17
flint axes: grave goods 21, 135
Flintbek: ard marks 40; arrowheads 21; burnt flint 148, 153; long barrows 12, 14; long mounds 17; plan *15*, stone kerb settings 14; wheel tracks *15*, 38; wooden coffins 17
floor(s) 101–7; burnt 103–6; constructions 101, 103–7; symbolism 101
Frälsegården: collapsed skeleton *131*; multiple burials 119; wild boar hides 143
Frederik VII (King of Denmark): capstones 94
Frejlev Skov: chamber shapes 77; skulls 120; twin stones 162
Frellesvig: grave goods 137; pottery 139, 150, 151

Friedrichsruhe: burnt flint 104; fragmentary remains 117, *118*; grave goods 135–6

Gaj: long barrows 13; wild boar tusks 21
garments: grave goods 134, 143
Gillhög: amber 144; burnt bones 134; children 133; passage graves 95; pottery 149, 150; votive offerings 152
glacial erratic boulders 51; construction 41; construction material 45, 46; megalithic tombs 11; raw materials 156, 194; splitting 18, 62
Globular Amphora: culture 2; repeated use 109; secondary use 118; succeeded TRB culture 10
gneiss: construction material 45; dry-stone walling 89; raw materials 92, 155
Gnewitz: distribution of tombs 37; floor constructions 106; graves 17; partitions *107*
Græse: long passages 77
granite: construction material 45, 53; dry-stone walling 89; floor constructions 101; grit 103; raw materials 92, 155
grave goods 20, 134–43; amber 136, 166; arrowheads 135, 142–3; axes 138; beliefs 147; boar's tusk 137; bone dagger 137; copper 21; defined 134; flasks 111, 117, 135, 136; flint 141; flint axes 21, 135; flint knife 111, 135; floors 101; garments 134; jewellery 21, 134, 147; open chambers 135; ornaments 21; pottery 137, 138; sacrifices 171–2; symbolism 135; tools 134, 135; votive offerings 135
Grøfte: disarticulated bones 113; grave goods 113, 135; human remains *114*; multiple burials 113; skeletal deposition 113; splitting boulders 162
Grønjægers Høj: boulders 157; capstones 113; kerbstones 51, 156; long dolmen *55*; splitting boulders 162; twin passage graves 163, *164*
Grønnehøj: casing stones 99; kerbstones 51; passage graves *52*
Groß Labenz: splitting boulders 162
Groß Upahl 127
Großer Karlstein: chamber sizes 75; megalithic chambers *46*
Grovlegård: capstones 63; splitting boulders 162
guard stones (*Wächtersteine*) 55, *58*, 156
Gundsølille: burnt bones 134; burnt flint 104;

construction 101; multiple burials 119; raised platforms 50

Haaßel: dolmens 62; subterranean chambers 56
Haga: chambers 62; dolmens *70*
Hagebrogård: pottery 150; votive offerings 153
Halskov Vænge: glacial erratic boulders *47*
Heidenopfertisch: capstones 75, *76*
Hindby Mosse: votive deposits 169; votive offerings 153
Hjelm: rectangular chambers *78*
Hjelmar's Cairn: multiple burials 118; niches 105, *130*; platforms 50
Hjortegårdene: burnt bones 134; disarticulated bones *116*; orthostats 84
Hofterup: dolmens *67*
Holy Cross Mountains: flint 8; raw materials 21
Hulbæk: axes 142
Hulbjerg: burnt flint 104; compartments 105; complete bodies 127–8; pottery 139, 150
human remains: bone fragmentation 109; burnt bones 159; ceremonies 186; charred 20, 126, 133; complete bodies 109; decomposition 109, 129–30; depositions 107, 113, 145; disarticulated 109; disarticulated bones 113, 120, 131; fragmentary 114, 117, 188; gender 188–9; inhumations 187; manipulation 20; megalithic tombs 108; passage graves 117; posthumous manipulation 115; preservation 19, 108, 109–10, 146, 174; sacrifices 171–2; secondary burials 181, 189, 196; skeletal deposition 109, 113

ideological spheres 10; transformations 2
Issendorf: food offerings 140; pottery 151

jewellery 6; amber 143; bone 143; examples *7*; grave goods 20, 134, 143; jet 143; raw materials 10; slate 143
Jordehøj: ard marks 40; burnt flint 153; drainage 92, 93; grazing lands 42; kerbstones 51; orthostats 84; passage graves *91*; twin stones 162
Jordhøj: burnt flint 153; drainage 92–3; niches 105; votive offerings 150, 151, 153

Kalundborg: burnt flint 103; excavation 91
Karleby: passage graves *84*

Karlstein: glacial erratic boulders *47*
Katelbogen: burnt flint 104; charcoal 104; fragmentary remains 119
Kellerød 56; grave goods 111, 135; plan *112*; single burials 111
kerbstones: colours 98, 156
keystones: colours 159; construction 98; intermediary layers 98
Kinderballe: burnt flint 104; human remains 120; multiple burials 119; plan *123*
Kläden *60*
Kleinenkneten: food offerings 140; fragmentary remains 119; grave goods 137; orthostats 99; passage graves 44–5; twin stones 162
Klekkendehøj: ard marks 40–1; burnt flint 104; capstones 49; cornerstones 99; double passage grave 40–1; drainage 93; orthostats 84, 95; soil analyses 42; stone packing 50; twin passage grave *80*
Klokkehøj: bone dagger 137; children 133; decapitation 121; disarticulated bones 115–16; floor constructions 103; multiple burials 137
Knudshoved Odde: chamber shapes 77; dry-stone walling *90*; passage graves *87*; passages *102*; twin stones 162
Konens Høj: chamber type 17, 18; copper 21
Kong Askers Høj: chamber shapes 79; passages *102*
Kong Svends Høj: ard marks 41, 42; burnt flint 104, 153; chamber shapes 77, *79*; fragmentary remains 119; guard stones 55; intermediary layers 95; keystones 95; pottery 150, 151; raw materials 155; twin stones 163; waterproofing 93
König Surbold: chamber sizes 75; plan *75*
Korshøj: long passages 100; orthostats 84
Kragnæs: pottery 139, 150; votive offerings 153
Kyndeløse: burnt bones 134; skulls 120

La Hoguette: skeletons *190*
Lancken Granitz: disarticulated bones 117; entrance arrangements *71*; extended dolmens 70; floor partitioning *106*
Landbogården: plan *132*; seated burial 131
Leśniczówka: copper 21; long barrows 13
Liepen: burnt flint 104, 106, 158; disarticulated bones 126; flint 142; fragmentary remains 117; human remains *126*

limestone: compartments 106; construction material 46; floor constructions 101

Lindebjerg 4; beakers 20; copper axes 144; long barrows 14; long mounds 17; timber façade 14

Lindgren, Anders 105, 118

linear arrangements: cemeteries 166; megalithic tombs 39

Lisch, Friedrich: colours 155; seated burial 129

long barrows 1; additional burials 14; ancestral lands 42; burials 2; cemeteries 12; children 133; commemorative sites 16; construction 14–16; cultivated fields 40; Danubian tradition 192; development 179; dimensions 14; disarticulated bones 187; extensions 16; funerary tradition 11; grave goods 135; human remains 114; internal divisions 16; location 12, 198; monuments 2; multiple burials 19, 110; raw materials 11; shapes 14; single burials 110; soil analyses 41; stone chambers 12; stone kerb settings 14; TRB culture 108; votive deposits 113, 140

long mounds 11–14; graves 22; houses 4

Lundehøj: drainage 92; intermediary layers 95

Luttra 26; capstones 94

Maglehøj: burnt flint 104; intermediary layers 97; packing materials 160

Malice Kościelne: multiple burials 19; wild boar tusks 21

Mankmoos 57; burnt flint 104; guard stones 55; subterranean chambers 56

Mehringen: burnt flint 153; pottery 148

Mesolithic 4; burial tradition 110; menhirs 184

Mönchgut: grave goods 138; multiple burials 119

monumental burial structures 11, 42; diversity 178; TRB culture 21

monuments 1; bi-chambers 98; emergence 11; exteriors 26; imposing 18; long barrows 2; megalithic tombs 108

Mosegården 4; long barrows 14; long mounds 17; timber palisades 14

mounds 25, 26; boulders 51; decay 49–50; destruction of tombs 49; extensions 14; raised 50; surfaces 49

multiple burials 19, 58, 110, 138

Munkwolstrup 57; accessible chambers 65; chamber floor 103; guard stones 55; reconstruction 62

Mürow: accessible chambers 64

Mutter Gribs Hule: burnt flint 104; construction 101; niches 105

Naschendorf 52, 60, 118; accessible chambers 64; chamber shapes 77; dolmens 59; façades 55; fragmentary remains 117; grave goods 136; plan 59; pottery 139, 149

navigational skills 38; travel 10

Nebel: disarticulated bones 121; skulls 120

Neolithic: beliefs 147; cosmology 27, 160, 165, 196; disc wheels 15; funerary tradition 24; menhirs 184; mounds 4; social practices 27

Neu Gaarz: axes 142; partitions 106; post holes 99

niches: chambers 105; family burials 129; seated burial 128

Nissehøj: intermediary layers 96; pottery 154; twin stones 162; votive offerings 124

Nobbin: construction 70; guard stones 55, 58; kerbstones 156

Noordlaren: post holes 100

Oldendorf: disarticulated bones 119; floor constructions 101; grave goods 137, 138; pottery 139; skulls 120; votive deposits 141

Olshøj: capstones 94; twin stones 162

Ølstykke: boulders 84; charcoal 103; crushed flint 103; grave goods 111, 135; plan 112; single burials 111

Onskulle: compartments 105; complete bodies 118; passage graves 110, 111; seated burial 128

Onsved Mark: long barrows 12; pottery 153; votive offerings 17, 149

Ormshøj: burning 42; burnt bones 134; burnt flint 104; casing stones 99; compartments 105; pottery 150

orthostats 88–9; bi-chambers 79; carvings 38; construction 58, 62, 74; flint 142; Græse 77; long passages 62; passages 99; placement 62; Poppostein 62; post holes 99; Sarup Gamle Skole 71; sequence 89; stability 84, 88–9; symbolism 89; twin passage graves 163

Ostenwalde: cremation 133; pottery 140

Ostorf: amber 144; flint 142; posthumous manipulation 115

oxen 4, 45

Pærgaard: burnt bones 134
palisade: timber 5, 6, 14
partial burial: multiple burials 116
passage graves 25, 26, 42, 99–101; ancestral
   lands 42; ard marks 42; burnt bones 134;
   burnt flint 104; capstones *48*, 94; children
   133; closed 101; complete bodies 109, 128,
   188–9; construction 43; covered 49;
   crushed flint 91; development 193;
   disarticulated bones 124; double passage
   35; food offerings 140; fragmentary
   remains 115; grave goods 137; guard
   stones 55; Ireland 185; Karleby *34*;
   menhirs 182; packing materials 159; partial
   human remains 117; passage length 81;
   preservation 119; raw materials 73;
   regional trait 28; regional variations 73–81;
   restoration 40, 50; Sarup Gamle Skole 71;
   secondary burials 181; shapes 73; short
   passages 62; soil analyses 41; tomb
   clusters 35; tomb dispersal 32; twin stones
   162; votive deposits 58; Vroue Hede 35
passages: construction 70, 101; depositions
   101; dry-stone walling 101; orthostats 99
pegmatite: construction material 53; raw
   materials 155
Pitted Ware 2; succeeded TRB culture 10
Poggendorf: orthostats 84
Poppostein: accessible chambers *65*;
   boulders 84; dolmens 62
porphyry: construction material 53; dry-stone
   walling 89; raw materials 155
Poskær Stenhus: boulders 84; capstones 63;
   dolmens *50*; kerbstones 51; polygonal
   dolmen 50; splitting boulders 162
post holes 5; construction 99; timber
   palisades 180
pottery 3, 6; burnt 134; clearances 140;
   decorated 9; examples *7*; food offerings
   140; grave goods 20, 137, 138;
   manufacture 6, 9; passage graves 3;
   placement 150–1; symbolism 154; TRB
   culture 134; votive deposits 168; votive
   offerings 139–40, 148–9
prehistoric routes 38, 39
Prissé-la-Charrière: chambers 181; long
   mounds *182*
Pyrzyce: linear arrangements 39; number of
   tombs 31

quartzite: compartments 106; raw
   materials 92, 157

Rævehøj: intermediary layers *97*; multiple
   burials 118, 119; skulls 120
Ramshög: children 133; disarticulated bones
   124; displaying bodies 146; flint 142;
   human remains 120, 129; multiple burials
   118
Rastorf: dolmens 3
raw materials 8, 21, 158; analysis 48;
   architecture 192; arkose 89; clay 92, 106;
   cobbles 91; colours 155; construction 43;
   earth 92; Falbygden plateau 80; flint 91,
   158; floor constructions 101; gneiss 89, 92,
   155; granite 89, 92, 101, 155; limestone
   101, 106; loam 92; long barrows 11;
   megalithic tombs 32; pegmatite 155;
   porphyry 89, 155; quartz 99; quartzite 92,
   106, 157; sandstone 89, 101, 156; shale 89;
   slate 89; stones 91; symbolism 27, 32, 92,
   155; timber 99; tufa 106
Regnershøj: burnt flint 104; orthostats 84
relationships: agriculture and the dead 42
Rispebjerg: causewayed enclosure 173
rituals 1, 5, 56; burials 147–8; burnt flint
   floors 104; cannibalism 20; charred bones
   133; coastal megaliths 43; cult houses 175;
   decomposition 147; depositions 121;
   development 195; dressing the dead 147;
   fire 152; funerary 9, 20; grave goods 134;
   human remains 120; jaw bones 124;
   meanings 27; opium 141; outside
   chambers 108; pottery 9; *Prachtbecher* 9;
   secondary burials 146, 181; votive
   offerings 17, 198
Röra: orthostats *86*
Rude: cists 17; copper 21; multiple burials
   19; votive offerings 17

sandstone: construction material 46;
   dry-stone walling 89; floor constructions
   101; raw materials 156
Sarnowo: arrowheads 21; excavation 4;
   human remains 114; long barrows 13;
   multiple burials 19; posthumous
   manipulation 20; wild boar tusks 21
Sarup: ard marks 42; causewayed enclosure
   173; ceremonial battleaxes 10; ceremonial
   enclosures 5; children 133; food offerings
   140; pottery 141, 175; timber palisades 18;
   tomb clusters 34–5; uncovered tombs 158
Sarup Gamle Skole: disarticulated bones
   127; enclosure 71; human remains 174;
   pottery 150; uncovered tombs 158

Sarup Gamle Skole II: passage graves 42
Sarup Gamle Skole X: raised platforms 50
Rastorf 3, 31
settlements 4, 34, 39; architecture 62;
    contexts 27; dry plains 35; fragmentary
    remains 146; long barrows 13; rituals 108,
    114, 169
shale: dry-stone walling 89
shelves: chambers 105
Sieben Steinhäuser: capstones 75; human
    remains *125*; multiple burials 119; partial
    burial 125; passage grave D *77*; twin stones
    162
single burials 19, 56
Skateholm: cult houses 168; jewellery 143;
    long barrows 13
skeletons: analysis 118, 133; preserved 9;
    Scandinavian bogs 9; secondary use 117
Skibshøj: fragmentary remains 114; graves
    17; human remains 20; long mounds 17;
    multiple burials 19
skulls: ancestral rites 124; fragmentary
    remains 120–1
slate: construction material 46; dry-stone
    walling 89; jewellery 143
Słonowice: copper 21; long barrows 12;
    single burials 20
Snæbum: burnt flint *82*, 104
social: change 10; practices 27; resources 8;
    spheres 2
Soderstorf: capstones *48*
Søndermø: pottery 152
Sparresminde: boulders *88*; chamber shapes
    78; dry-stone walling *90*; orthostats 88
Spejder Stenen: glacial erratic boulders 46, *47*
Sprove: orthostats *86*
Stengade: long barrows 13, 14; mineral crust
    20; ochre 20
Stöckheim: capstones 75, *76*
Stokkebjerg Skov: long dolmen *61*; splitting
    boulders 162
stone architecture: use of timber 11
stone-built structures: megalithic tombs 24
stone chambers: long barrows 12
stone kerb settings 15, 26, 43, 44, 51–6; long
    barrows 14
stone-packing graves: Vroue Hede 35
Storegård: amber 144; votive offerings 17
Strandby Skovgrave: disarticulated bones
    115; pottery 149
Suldrup: bi-chambers *83*
symbolism: architecture 192; builders 26,

107; burnt flint 105, 159; colours 159;
    construction 73; dualism 166; ethnographic
    evidence 39; floor constructions 101;
    funerary tradition 21–2; grave goods 135;
    links 140; long barrows 12; megalithic
    construction 48; megalithic tombs 27, 34;
    mortality 22; pottery 154; raw materials 32,
    92, 155; ritual ploughing 42; significance
    28; size 58; splitting boulders 62, 162

Table des Marchands: passage graves *184*
Tannenhausen: excavation 99; post holes *100*
terminology 24; interpretation 26
Thuine: kerbstones 51; orthostats 74, 99;
    passage graves *53*
timber: causewayed enclosure 166; chambers
    187; façades 185; stone architecture 11
timber palisades: causewayed enclosure 173;
    post holes 180
Tinaarloo: post holes *100*
Toftebjerg *66*
tomb dispersal 32; linear arrangements 35
tombs: orientation 33–4; placement 28
tool manufacture 6; expertise 8
trackways 175; Campemoor 6
trade: causewayed enclosure 176–7;
    trackways 200
travel: traditional societies 40; by water 10,
    36, 38
TRB culture: ceramics 161; ceremonies 120;
    chronology 2–3; demise 10; distribution
    1–2, *3*; houses 4; megalithic tombs 108;
    religious ideas 147, 148; sacrifices 171–2
Trekroner: children 133; partial multiple
    burials 116–17; preservation 117
Troelstrup 19; long mounds 17; timber
    palisades 14; timber passages 114; wooden
    coffins 17
Troldstuerne: burnt bones 134; burnt flint
    104; intermediary layers *98*; multiple
    burials 119; passage graves *87*; twin
    passage graves 163, *164*; twin stones 162
Trollasten: burnt bones 134; pottery 154;
    votive offerings 152
Tustrup: ard marks 42; burnt flint 104; cult
    house *69*; cult houses 167–8; lost capstones
    62; NW dolmen *69*; pottery 150, 152;
    reconstruction 158; SE dolmen *68*
twin passage graves: Denmark 163;
    distribution *81*; symbolism 165
twins: burials 166; concept of 165; Divine
    165, 167; ethnography 166

Ubby Dysselod: boulders *88*; casing stones 99; orthostats 84; twin passage graves 163, *164*; twin stones 162

Uggerslev: human remains *122*; multiple burials 118, 119; skulls 120

Utersum *72*; capstones 71; orthostats 70; subterranean chambers 71

Vasagård 5; causewayed enclosure 173

Västra Hoby: pottery 149, 154; votive offerings 152

Vedsted: burnt flint 104, 153; capstones 48; kerbstones 51; long passages 62; pottery 150

Visbeker Braut: façades *54*; kerbstones 51

Visbeker Bräutigam: façades *54*; kerbstones 51

votive deposits 58; bogs 148; ceramics 168; cult houses 168; megalithic tombs 148; over time 170; sealed chambers 153

votive offerings 8; axes 142; causewayed enclosure 8, 176; ceremonies 167; charred bones 133; Denmark 17; flint 152;

megalithic tombs 8, 139; regional differences 170; timber posts 185; tools 148, 152; waterlogged areas 8, 169

Vroue Hede: linear arrangements 166; pottery 150, 153; research 41; tomb dispersal 35

waterlogged areas: pottery 169; reduced 35; sacred areas 169; trackways 175; votive offerings 8, 169, 175

Wechte: fragmentary remains 119; grave goods 119; pottery 139

wheel tracks: Flintbek 15, *15*, 38

Wietrzychowice: graves 17; multiple burials 19

wild animals: bones 4; wild boar tusks 21

Wilsen: extended dolmen 49; raised platforms 51

wooden coffins 17, 18

woodworking: canoes 10; houses 10; skills 18

Zagaj Stradowski 13

Related titles from Routledge

The Atlantic Iron Age
Settlement and Identity in the First Millennium BC

Jon Henderson

It may be surprising to learn that this book is the first ever survey of the Atlantic Iron Age: this tradition is cited in archaeology frequently enough to seem firmly established, yet has never been clearly defined. With this book, Jon Henderson provides an important and much-needed exploration of the archaeology of western areas of Britain, Ireland, France and Spain to consider how far Atlantic Iron Age communities were in contact with each other.

By examining the evidence for settlement and maritime trade, as well as aspects of the material culture of each area, Henderson identifies distinct Atlantic social identities through time. He also pinpoints *areas* of similarity: the possibility of cultural 'cross-pollination' caused by maritime links and to what extent these contacts influenced and altered the distinctive character of local communities. A major theme running through the book is the role of the Atlantic seaboard itself and what impact this unique environment had on the ways Atlantic communities perceived themselves and their place in the world.

As a history of these communities unfolds, a general archaeological Atlantic identity breaks down into a range of regional identities which compare interestingly with each other and with traditional models of Celtic identity.

Bringing together the Iron Age settlement evidence for the Atlantic regions in one place for the first time, this excellent and original book is certain to establish itself as the definitive study of the Atlantic Iron Age.

Hb: 978–0–415–43642–7
Eb: 978–0–203–93846–1

Available at all good bookshops
For ordering and further information please visit:
www.routledge.com